Blessings
Shirley Woods

Onesimus

Shirley F. Woods

Wipf and Stock Publishers
Eugene, Oregon

Onesimus

By Shirley F. Woods
Copyright ©December 16, 2002Shirley F. Woods

ISBN 1-59244-086-X
Printed by $\dfrac{\text{Wipf and Stock Publishers}}{\text{199 W. 8th Ave, Suite 3, Eugene; Oregon 97401}}$

Biblical quotations are from various translations, usually modified by the author.

Contents

Acknowledgements

Many people have contributed to this book, Susan Geissler-O'Neil, Meg Brogan, Ed Brush, and William E. Swing notable among them. Bishop Swing provided support and encouragement over the course of more than two decades and the larger community within which this book came to life. Susan provided friendship and invaluable excitement in pulling the novel together. Meg Brogan was a companion and fellow pilgrim on the way. Ed Brush, fellow English teacher, provided a world of literature that is unimaginable without him.

Biblical quotations are from various translations, usually modified, reordered, or reworked by the author. This book is a work of fiction, not academic scholarship, and it has been typeset as fiction, largely without citation of biblical quotations.

Some of the dialogue from classical texts is from sources in the bibliography, some of it is entirely fictional.

Some of the Scripture quotations contained herein are from the New Revised Standard Version Bible, copyright ©1989 by the Division of Christian Education of the National Council of Churches of Christ in the U.S.A., and are used by permission. All rights reserved.

Some of the Scripture quotations contained herein are from the Revised Standard Version of the Bible, ©1971, by the Division of Christian Education of the National Council of Churches of Christ in the U.S.A., and are used by permission. All rights reserved.

A few of the Scripture quotations contained herein are from Anchor Bible translations (Colossians, Ephesians, 1 Corinthians, Philemon); ©1994, 1974, 1976, 2000 Doubleday, a division of Bantam Doubleday

Dell Publishing Group, Inc. All rights reserved.

This book was typeset by Andrew Porter in Times Roman with TEX and LATEX macros, on a Debian GNU Linux box.

Tongues of Mortals

> *To Apphia our sister, to Archippus our fellow sol-*
> *dier, and to the church in your house: Grace to you and*
> *peace from God our Father and the Lord Jesus Christ.*
> (Philemon 2,3)

These words, you will find, begin a brief letter appended to a collection of writings attributed to that great Apostle to the Gentiles, Paul of Tarsus. This collection is a little-known addition attesting to the teachings and faith of the followers of Jesus of Nazareth and is deserving of deep study by those who are called Christians. The letters were assembled by one whom I affectionately call "Uncle," for my father called him "Brother." He was indeed highly respected in his time as the Bishop of Ephesus. I tell the story now as I have heard it from the 'tongues of mortals,' for I am the only one left to tell it; herein I have pieced it together as it was variously told to me. I am now as old the bishop was when he went to meet the martyr Ignatius. When I leave this earthly tent, there will be none left to remember.

The story of the dinner party was told me by Apphia. She was my grandmother, and I remember her as a woman small and spare. She was brown as a leaf which an autumn breeze blows down, but she had control over her whole house. She had a tongue as sharp as a flesher's blade. Usually she kept it sheathed within her mouth, but woe to those nearby, when it escaped.

1

The Dinner Party

Archippus, citizen of Colossae, was seeking out his sister Apphia in the gynaeceum. He passed quietly and almost unnoticed through the work room where the women were spinning and weaving and tapped gently on the door of her private apartment. She was dressed, surprisingly enough for usually she was a late sleeper. "I have all of the plans in place," he burst out without further greeting.

Apphia, with her back to him, did not bother to turn but kept on patting her hair and examining her face in a mirror. There was a smile of superiority on her lips, "I still say that you should have some flute girls in."

Archippus fell into a chair and sighed, for it seemed so difficult to get the point through to his sister. "I have it well planned. It is very important to impress the new Roman prefect. Our whole future depends on it. The whole future of Colossae depends on it."

"The whole future of Colossae depends upon a couple of boorish soldiers? Oh come now. What do the Romans know of Colossae? What do they care about a village built of mud huts in the middle of Phrygia?"

Archippus felt the sting. "That's exactly the point; the prefect is not your regular soldier. He's a civilian who is earning his stripes to become procurator. That's why I am expecting so much from him. Colossae is well known. It is not just another mud village. It has a reputation in history. Alexander marched his army from the sea and on the second day he stopped at Colossae. He was on his way to Issus." Archippus began to review the history of his city when his sister stamped her foot.

"In the name of the Goddess, stop. What do the Romans care about Alexander and Xerxes? And what does it matter? Is it an earth shaking event when a couple of Roman soldiers get involved in a drinking match in a provincial town?"

Ignoring her retort, Archippus continued, "We are known, dear sister, in Rome. The prefect has with him a letter from the Emperor Claudius himself. In that letter the city is congratulated for its amenities, its wealth and its civic accomplishments. He will present that letter—"

"We are known, dear brother, in Rome, as indolent, beer swilling boors, who sell their own children into slavery rather than put in an honest day's labor."

Rather than pursue this argument which had already suffered much appraisal by both parties, Archippus began to muse to himself. "It is a demon; clearly it is a demon who persists in tormenting me. Every time I make my plans the demon sets itself against me, pouring discouragement from the mouths of everyone. Yes, it is the demon; the one who haunts this house, Apphia. We must take steps for further fumigation, and I have some new charms brought to me only three days ago by a wise merchant from Egypt."

Apphia slammed down her mirror on the dressing table. "I'm tired of all your demons; According to you it was a demon who pushed my dear husband into the river and drowned him there. Yet I have the a very good witness who says that he stooped down to drink and two slaves pushed him in and held him down until he drowned."

"Apphia, we've been through that. We tortured the slaves to make them confess until they were so broken that they were of no use to us again. One of them actually saw the black face of the demon in the water."

But Apphia broke into tears as she thought of the past. "Here I was, a widow, and only sixteen years old, carrying my first child. How could I have lived if I had not had my dear, dear Philemon. And you with your stupid incense almost suffocated the poor babe with all that foul smoke."

"But we cast out the demon, dear Apphia; and we gave him a good name so that the demon would not recognize him, 'Lovey'; and 'Eupator,' 'fortunate in his father.' By calling him 'fortunate in his father,' they could not know the baby was so unfortunate in his father. You must admit the ploy has worked. Philemon is a lovely child and spreads happiness wherever he goes. Trust me, Apphia; for I am your brother and older than you. You were left a widow at sixteen with no one else to look after your welfare."

Apphia sighed. "Yes, dear brother, it was fortunate for you. You came by chance to head a household you had no part in making. You became the warden of farms and vineyards, the master of slaves and maidservants, and the head of the house. And now I am approaching an age when I am no longer attractive to men. I grow old in my loneliness, forever a widow, nevermore a wife." She burst out crying.

Archippus rose quietly and left her to her bitterness. "I must exert more forcefulness in this house." Archippus was now a stately man in his mid-forties who generally walked with the assurance of a well-born Ionian Greek and spoke with the authority of a successful and scholarly gentleman. Somehow his sister Apphia, fifteen years younger than he, could always get the better of him, no matter what the subject under discussion. Here he was, entering upon an important political alliance for the family and his city. He had laid out his plans with the utmost care to show the polish and civility of the community; but his sister could only suggest "flute girls."

The next afternoon one could have seen two Roman gentlemen struggling up the cobbled street.

"I must say, Porcine, this miserable lane is in no way to be confused with a street. This place was palmed off on me as a city, but cities have streets, and I haven't seen a proper street since we disembarked in Asia."

"Well, sir, I'm here to tell you that this is as good as it gets. I've spent the last fourteen years in these parts; you'll find no paved strata here. In spite of its name, the place is not "colossal." When I left the City my old commander said, 'Romans are rightly contemptuous of the Phrygian wilderness. Their cities are mere country towns inhabited by well-to-do farmers; wealthy enough to claim immortality by paying to have their epitaphs engraved on their tombs.' I agree, The place is just one big cemetery. You have been invited, sir, as the new Praefectus Castrorum, to a dinner at the house of a Phrygian gentleman. And I am accompanying you as your military guard of honor, as befits a man of your superior estate. You may expect the gentry at the party to be impressed by your noble bearing, so smile and bear yourself nobly as a Roman governor should."

"Thank you for reminding me, my good Metellus, I shall endeavor to represent myself as one of Rome's best. What do you anticipate?"

"Well, noble Rufinus, you will meet your host, a certain Archippus. He is a native of the place but was educated in the Greek style. He is well mannered, a little stern, perhaps. I find him humorless. Somehow he came into his present estate through the death of his sister's husband. She was a young widow and needed a proper guardian. I must say he has made his fortune from her misfortune."

"And will we meet the lady, a rich widow, I take it?"

"Probably not, Phrygian ladies do not attend male dinner parties. But there might be a flute girl or two. Phrygian flute girls are appreciated even in The City." The centurian winked and smiled to himself.

Quintus Rufinus shook his head, "Yes, but Phrygian flute girls do not come with dowries, as may be expected from rich widows; and your poor Quintus has been exiled to this vile corner of the world to repair his fortunes. You understand, Porcinus, that this may be my very last chance."

Marcus Porcinus Metellus was silent. This was not the first Roman prefect, down on his luck, that he had escorted around the byways of the Lycus Valley. As for himself he was already savoring the thought of a country meal of roasted pig and fresh vegetables. There would be a good country wine, and, of course, the flute girls. He kicked aside a barking dog who seemed to take a dislike to his gentleman and said, "There's the house, up that little knoll."

Inside the house, in back of the peristyle in the triclinium, Archippus was making a quick once over of his arrangements. "Stamnion, run back and see if the pig is done. Roast pig should be almost white in the flesh, with the fat dripping down its sides and some of it crackling at the top, dressed with rosemary and our secret recipe of herbs. And while you are at it, see to it that the wine jars are open to let the wine breathe a little. Oh, we must impress our guests that we are quite as civilized as they are." Stamnion took off without a further word; he did not care to listen to his master's speech on refinement again.

"Asterion, have our fellow townsmen arrived? I do hope they have arrived. They must be here before our honored guests."

Asterion reported, "They have been standing in the peristyle for the past hour, sir. I do think you should give them leave to sit down."

Archippus shrugged; he did not intend that the townsmen of Colossae should be found lounging about when the gentlemen from Rome came in. Archippus turned to the remaining slave, a boy of about 10 years. "Now Onesimus, I want you to stand by me and do my bidding. You will take wine to the guests and stand by with a damp napkin to wipe any grease from their hands and lips—and oh, yes, the rose water. Where did I put the rose water?"

"I have it with me, my lord, just as you have told me." They had gone through with this little drama every hour for the past two days.

Just then the doorkeeper came in to report that two Romans could be seen nearing the top of the hill. Archippus clapped his hands for the serving men to be at the ready, and went into the peristyle to alert his Phrygian guests. "Look smart, now," he was commanding no one in particular and soon enough the Romans were ushered into the peristyle.

They found a familiar scene; the peristyle surrounded on three sides with decorative columns, a pool to one side with running water into it making a miniature water-fall. Plants producing greenery and flowers were tastefully placed about in ceramic pots. On the back side there was a slightly raised dais where Archippus stood flanked by three gentlemen of Colossae.

The play which had been well rehearsed proceeded. Archippus made a pretty speech of greeting and introduced the other members of his party:

> Krasos, a Colossian gentleman of Greek ancestry;
> Hierax, descendant of an old Phrygian family;
> Euporos, a moneyed gentleman of Colossae.

Gravely, the Roman Centurion made his reply: "Sirs, it is my honor to introduce to you Quintus Rufinus Urbanus, newly appointed Praefectus Castrorum, by order of the Emperor. A man of a noble family who comes to you with a message from Claudius Imperator himself."

Rufinus stood straight about to speak, but the centurion continued, "You all know me, of course. I, Marcus Porcinus Metellus, am a Roman Army man of seventeen years experience, fourteen of those years have been spent in this delightful outpost of Rome's majesty. We are old friends, are we not?" and he chuckled as if to acknowledge old drinking companions. At this point he produced a scroll, saluted the new Prefect to whom he gave the scroll. Rufinus gravely acknowledged the salute, unrolled the scroll and read a congratulatory message from the Emperor Claudius. It was inscribed in a fair hand with liberal flourishes by one of the better calligraphers of the princeps. Having read the proclamation, he presented the scroll to Archippus who was beside himself with delight. And so the party was ushered into the triclinium.

The tables had been set for six, surrounded by three couches. This meant two men to a couch, "a more comfortable arrangement than the usual three," explained Archippus, who had Rufinus settled next to him on his right. Krasos was seated on the right hand side sharing his couch with the Centurion, for Krasos spoke the Greek language well and even knew a few phrases of schoolboy Latin. Hierax was on the left side with Euporos. Hierax had impeccable credentials as a member of an old Phrygian family. He had been educated in Ephesus and so had some fluency in Greek. Euporos by his side, had once been in the wool trade, but having established his fortune he now lived as a gentleman. As a merchant he had traveled.

Archippus stood for a moment and poured a little wine into a silver bowl as he offered a brief prayer to the local gods. With that, dinner was served. It started with the usual eggs which had been dyed bright red, being cooked in water with onion skins. Then there were small salads with ceci in garlic sauce arranged nicely on greens, and a dish of cucumbers and leeks in vinegar. Everyone expressed amazement at the cucumbers so early in the season while Archippus smiled and explained that they were grown in his own greenhouses.

Krasos quoted a bit of poetry. He had been rehearsing all morning for his part in the drama.

> *And Kronos established three seasons,*
> *summer, winter and autumn, third*
> *and a fourth, spring,*
> *when everything blooms*
> *but who can live on flowers?*

"The poet Alcman wrote that in old times," he said citing the school books. "But is our good fortune to dine with Archippus who produces lettuce out of season."

Quick to respond, Hierax produced a bit of satire with which he tweaked his learned Greek neighbor. "We do not live on bread alone. The fate of the gourmand is food for comment; our Ephesian poet Hipponax sings their fate."

> *O to spend whole days at ease at table*
> *Swilling down tunafish and cheese in a steady stream*
> *for all the world like a eunuch from Lampasacus.*
> *Alas, I ate up the family fortune.*
> *Now I have to dig rocks on the mountainside*
> *and munch medium-sized figs with barley loaves.*

Not to be outdone, Euporos responded with his offering.

> *Nothing destroys a good man quicker than poverty:*
> *   not malarial fever, Kyrnos, nor old age.*
> *Better to hurl oneself into the abysmal sea*
> *   or over a blunt cliff–than be a victim*
> *of poverty. The poor man can do or say nothing*
> *   worthwhile. Even his mouth is gagged.*

"Theognis said it, and may we bless the gods that we are not such victims."

The three locals seemed to breathe with relief at the presentations of their contributions. The fish was being served with little cups of steaming broth flavored with herbs. Archippus was pleased and noted to himself that not one of the boys had lost his footing or slipped his hand from the soup bowl.

Porcinus growled to his couch mate, "Enough of these lessons. Where are the flute girls?" Krasos stared him down; he knew the centurion to be somewhat of a lout, but what does one expect from a soldier?

At this point the roasted pig was brought in, dripping in its succulence, with a crown of rosemary on its head and a red apple in its mouth. The diners applauded the chef's masterpiece while the bearers carved it into large sized servings to be set before the trenchermen.

Onesimus, Asterion and Stamnion stood each one behind his couch with steaming napkins so that any dripping could be wiped up daintily before it stained the wearers' clothing. This flustered the Roman Rufinus and the soldier Porcinus could hardly restrain himself from laughter.

The prefect tried to make conversation by comparing this meal to a Roman dinner party which had been ridiculed recently by a satirist. *"The banquet complete with full orchestra, singing and dancing slave waiters, rich, pretentious food and expensive wines, not to mention performances of various kinds designed to allow the host to show off his wit or his capacity for literary allusions dragged on through one tasteless exhibition after another until the host had to answer the call of nature and the guests got a chance to talk."*

"That was written by one of our Roman writers," explained Rufinus as he looked straight at Marcus the Centurion. Both of them smirked a little as their eyes said, "One down for our side."

The boys began to refill the silver goblets with a sweet wine while the tables were taken away and new servings of sugared fruits and sweet cakes appeared.

Now Archippus stood up and spoke. "My dear friends, we at Colossae are simple folk. Some of us prefer to live here rather than with our workers in the fields and vineyards. Yet, at heart we remain in the countryside. We cannot emulate the wealth and the wonders of the great city of Rome, or even of the sophistication of the cities of the coastlands. But we enjoy our rustic pleasures and wish to share our way of life with our guests with the hope that they will understand something of our society.

"I am reminded of such a party in Athens, how the great Plato described it. *Early in the evening after the company has been fed and the serious drinking has begun, Eryximachus proposed that instead of drinking heavily and listening to the flute-girl, they should send her away to entertain the women, drink lightly and entertain one another with speeches. The subject agreed on for the speeches is Eros, passionate love.*

"Now I propose that we select a subject to discuss and entertain each other with such edifying conversation."

The Colossians nodded in assent; after all, they had come prepared with conversational pieces with which to edify and show off their attainments to the foreign guests.

The Romans restrained themselves from showing panic. Metellus who had been subjected to such treatment before waved his hand to Urbanus that the ball was in his court.

The prefect cleared his throat and began thoughtfully, "The social context of the symposium was clearly a man's world; the very songs we have heard were composed for symposia of men in which scurrilous songs were of the essence. We Romans are quite at home with this. The symposium was one of those institutions which, like the gymnasium, were central to the culture of the learned Greeks of ancient times. The symposium was a drinking party. The celebrants were male (the only females present were flute-girls and other ladies of the night). And so I say, in order to be authentic, it is time to pour the wine and bring in the flute girls and all those other luscious ladies who are now enjoying themselves with the music and the acrobatics of the entertainers. Let the party begin." He raised his goblet and waved it around so that the boy had quite some difficulty in refilling it.

Metellus winced. He had not gotten through to his superior that Colossae was not Rome. He stuttered, "Gentlemen, the prefect is a little tipsy in his cups, and he forgets that in the colonies the ladies are not so free with their presence as in Rome."

Before he could be restrained, Rufinus continued, "It is clear that Plato's Symposium supposes, being Greek, that such parties were a breeding ground for love attachments with boys. I have noticed that our servers are very pretty youths and I am not opposed to that. Come now, let the party begin," and he pulled Onesimus by the tunic onto the couch. "Come on, Archipor; I see that you are our host's pretty boy. It's time for him to share."

The boy looked to his master for some sign that would tell him what he was to do, but Archippus stood up frozen and then cried, "No, sir! No! No such lechery starts in my house! I won't have it!"

Rufinus paid no attention, but continued, "Come on, Archipor, it's your turn to sing us a song." Now the boy was pleading with his eyes on his owner.

"Sing for him," Archippus commanded.

Onesimus, who had never sung before company, swallowed and started a song,

> *What is wisdom? What gift of the gods*
> *is held in honor like this;*
> *to hold your hand victorious*
> *over the heads of those you hate?*
> *Honor is precious forever.*

Metellus started up, "Honor—honor indeed. What kind of a song is that? What does a slave know of honor?"

Archippus was astonished, "Where did you learn a song like that, boy?"

"Philemon learned it in school," replied the boy.

Archippus seemed to understand, but he pretended not to notice when the prefect pulled the slave to him and began to fondle him.

"Love—Eros—Amor, that's what it's all about. Lets all make speeches about love; that's what a symposium is for. Pour me another drink."

This time Archippus poured the drinks. The centurion rushed over and tried to quiet his commander. Rufinus pushed him away and stood tottering on his feet and sang his song.

>*Who cares for reputation*
>*If he keeps his cash?*

"There'sh my part, gennamen. Now lets have the slaves entertain us with speeches and stories. Why should we ennertain them? You, boy, you go first." and he pointed to Asterion.

Asterion, somewhat older than Onesimus, took the challenge and cleared his throat. "A slave is not a thing; he is a human being. He has the moral duty of being a good slave, serving with loyalty and devotion. Still he does not belong to himself. He is a possession. If an ox or a horse or a slave dies, no one mourns." Sweating profusely at his temerity, Asterion stopped.

At a glance from Archippus, Stamnion carried on. "At any moment death may catch you unawares: you may fall victim to shipwreck or bandits, and leaving aside higher powers, the least of your slaves holds over you the power of life and death."

This show of thought from slaves, uneducated slaves at that, was irritating to Euporos who stood up and shouted, "A slave is inferior by nature. This inferiority goes hand in hand with legal inferiority. . . . The barrier between humans and subhumans is impregnable. It is indecent to say that a slave has been born free and sold himself into slavery. It is equally indecent even to think that a free man might sell himself that way. . . . slavery is a reality of nature that cannot be denied. It is not a charity to free a slave. One merely frees a slave because it is good business. To be a good master is to take good care of one's property. Slaves have neither property nor wives nor children. Their lovemaking and childbearing are like the breeding of livestock."

After this there was so much shouting going on that no one was paying any attention who was slave or free, or who was Roman, Greek or Phrygian. Archippus regained his composure and spoke with learning, "Slavery is an individual misfortune, a misfortune that might befall any one of us, for we are all men, subject to the same tricks of fate as these unfortunates. In wartime even the noblest of men may be reduced to slavery. It is Fortune that determines each man's fate. What then is the good man's duty? To do whatever he has to do whatever fate has placed him, be he king, citizen or slave."

By now Rufinus had fallen asleep. Onesimus freed himself from his embrace, stood up and smoothed his tunic.

Krasos showed his superior learning and remembered, "Freedom, according to Aristotle, is 'doing whatever one wants—to live precisely as you wish—since no one desires what is bad, the only one who is truly free is the one who wants to do what is good. But true liberty belongs to the gods alone."

The dinner guests stood up and bade Archippus farewell. Archippus called the porter to help Metellus with his drunken burden. The slaves were left to clean up the mess.

On the other side of the house where the cubicles are small and ill lighted, the three serving boys talked it over.

"I thought the old man would split a gut when the captain began to yell for the flute girls. You know how he is about having the ladies at his dinner parties."

Asterion began imitating Archippus with mincing steps and sweet toned words. Onesimus looked up inquisitively, for he had not quite understood the meaning of all that had happened the night before. Onesimus was the youngest of the three, barely ten years old. This had been the first dinner that he had been allowed to serve. Asterion was possibly nineteen, but who knows the age of a slave?

"Well, first off, it was when the captain asked you to sing. He figured that if there wasn't any flute girl, you must be the flute girl, being so young and smooth cheeked, y'know. Well, hey, where did you learn that song?"

Onesimus blushed, "I had to learn it for Philemon at the school. The young gentlemen have to know how to recite properly. It's part of their education."

Stamnion looked up, "If Philemon was supposed to learn it, why did you learn it?"

Onesimus hung his head, "Well, Philemon just plays all the time and never learns anything, so the schoolmaster beats him. Only, of course, the schoolmaster doesn't beat him, he beats me because I have to take Philemon's beating."

The other slaves looked on sympathetically. The situation was known to them. "Well," continued Onesimus, "I found out that if I answer for Philemon, the master just looks at him and says, 'very good, young sir,' and I don't get beat. Of course, Philemon might beat me on the way home from school, but he doesn't very often."

"It don't make much sense," opined Stamnion.

"Look, Jug Ears, does anything in the world make sense?" asked Asterion.

"There's a lot of things I don't understand about the Roman gentleman," ventured Onesimus. "Why did he call me *Archipor?*"

"That's Latin," explained Asterion. "It means 'Archie's Boy.' " The Roman's call their slaves by names like that. We're given Greek names, only they aren't really Greek names; they're names like you might give to a dog or a cow. *Stamnion*, that means Jug ears; *Asterion*, that's a star; I think it's because of my birthmark; and you're *Onesimus*, Useful. Really, I think Useless would be a better name."

Onesimus picked up a sandal and threw it at the older boy who ducked laughing. "Archipor, Archipor—by that he meant you were the Old Man's special pet. That's why he pulled you down, to pet you."

Onesimus blushed and became tearful. "I don't understand you." Both of the older boys laughed. Onesimus wasn't for real.

This Archippus was a philosopher of the ancient school. His studies had brought him to the understanding of all mysteries and he boasted of much knowledge, but in spite of that there was not much love for him as perhaps you have already sensed. He was accustomed to go to his private place, an aerie which he had constructed for his meditating, away from domestic interference, and overlooking the whole valley.

The Aerie

Archippus left the house alone and walked along a customary path until he reached a viewpoint which opened up the entire valley below. This was his favorite place. There he was likely to spend a whole morning in contemplation. Sometimes he would take with him a scroll with a bit of poetry to memorize. It was a habit he had formed in his youth while he was away at school, that very fine school on the Island of Rhodes. On this morning he was thinking of how he had returned to Phrygia because he had learned that his father had died leaving him a small piece of property. His only living relative, a sister, had married a farmboy, son of a small landowner from Colossae. Upon her father's death, his sister's husband was laying claim to the father's small estate as part of his wife's dowry. Quickly Archippus consulted a scribe, practiced in the law, who listened to his plight and commented that Black Fortune had certainly sent upon him a special demon for his torment.

Archippus took the word of the lawyer seriously and sought out a magician who had a reputation for bringing about success in legal matters. The magician worked out a special curse which he had learned from the Egyptians. The two of them went with a black rooster to a small temple built next to an evil smelling spring that spewed hot water from the ground. There they sacrificed the rooster. The snivelling caretaker of a priest took the parchment on which the curse was written and tacked it on the wall for all to read. The fees for all of this just about bankrupted the already poor student, but when destiny dogs you with misfortune, it is best to risk what little there is left on hope.

At home, that decaying house which he had inherited from his father, he found a long time friend bearing a letter. There was no regular post in those days; one had to rely upon such private messengers as could be found. Archippus broke the seals and frowned while reading.

"Bad news?" the friend was solicitous.

By this time Archippus was shaking. He could hardly speak.

"My sister's husband is dead, murdered by his slaves," she says.

"We have not shaken off the evil demon."

The friend spoke cautiously, "Ah, your sister's husband. Was he rich?"

Archippus knew little of his sister's husband other than that he owned a tilled farm in the valley near Colossae. The two sat down and considered who might be the heirs; for he was the very one who was claiming the estate as his dower right. This news changed the whole picture. Now there was no husband to make this claim. Surely the widow might have some rights; and an unborn babe, if it should be a boy ... " It might be wise to consult someone familiar with the law.

"It was supposed to be a very potent charm; perhaps it is working. Still I would not want to be blamed for my brother-in-law's death," Archippus paused. "Perhaps I should go to console my sister."

When Archippus arrived at the dead man's small cottage in a cluster of rustic dwellings set off from the fields he found a shambles. The terrified widow, a girl of only sixteen years, was large with child. The villagers were pillaging the house of its belongings all the while shouting "Death to the slaves." The two accused slaves were already almost dead, and now the fire torture was being applied to their feet. Archippus called out in a loud command, "Begone."

When they saw the commanding figure of a gentleman, the loutish peasants fled with such loot as they already held.

The girl looked up and cried out, "Brother, is that you?" Archippus knew then that his fortunes had changed.

Apphia's husband proved to have no heirs other than his wife, for his child was yet unborn. As the brother of the widow, Archippus quickly became her guardian for Phrygian women do not rule in their own right. The two slaves still protesting their innocence gladly acknowledged that their master had been drawn to the river by demonic forces as this new savior suggested. Archippus made a special trip to the spot. There in the bottom of the Lycus glittered specks of golden sand. It has been said that this was one of the places where in ancient times Phrygian King Midas bathed hoping to rid himself of the golden curse. Archippus shivered as he felt a cold wind off the mountain Miti, for so it is called since Midas is still known to haunt it. Close by at river bend the Lycus leaves its course and plunges into the dark netherworld from which it emerges again a dozen stadia away. Archippus could almost see the beckoning hands from that underworld which would lead him to a similar fate.

The brother returned and consoled his sister by saying that indeed her husband had been entranced by the face of a golden demon who had lured him to the river and whose devilish hands had pulled him to his death. He took the girl with the offering of a dove to the goddess to protect her from such demons and give her safe delivery. How otherwise can anyone act when very nature proves false?

These memories besieged the mind of Archippus as he looked across the fertile valley. Gone were the impoverished shanties that he had visited when he first found his sister there. The haphazard fields of scattered barley and spelt had been replaced by irrigated vineyards in straight rows. An orchard of olive trees separated the vineyard from a field of wheat, already red-spiked and waving in the wind. Beyond were fig trees heavy with unripe fruits. He could see the figures of the field slaves who were examining the fruit, for figs demand a special treatment. Along the fertile rows the poppies were in bud, soon to flower and produce their sweet sleep inducing seed. And closer yet, where the plain begins to meet the hillside were the gardens which produced the melons and the onions, the bitter herbs and the beans, so precious and so tender. These need special care and watchfulness. All of this was the work of Archippus, and of his field slaves. The slaves provided the labor; the farmer provided the mind that planned the harvest. Archipppus understood this well, and he often reminded his sister of her good fortune in that she had a philosopher for a brother rather than a know-nothing Phrygian peasant for a husband.

"One would think," mused her brother, "that she would show more gratitude. Philosophy can serve the prudent man well. If one recognizes the work of the Demiurge and his angels, one can turn a bad fate into prosperity."

When Archippus walked along the Lycus, he too saw the golden face of the River god as it glittered in the sands. He too reached down and scooped up a handful of that sand and studied the shining flakes that shone so enticingly in the sun.

"Fool's gold," he said; but then he applied the logic of philosophy. "All that glitters is not gold. But the syllogism has not been drained of all its meaning. All is not gold; but some is gold. The secret is to separate the *some* from the *all.*"

Archippus was cautious in his mining. He had no wish to raise false hopes and wild suspicions. Day by day he found the flakes of real gold and small nuggets in the river bottom. It was not long before he could buy the fields from their idle owners who were eager to change the land which brought them only labor for minted gold pieces which, like the demons who occupy them, lead them from greed to poverty. Too late they learn that the fields are gone, the gold is gone and starvation is only stayed by selling their children into slavery.

Archippus noted that the shadow of Mt. Miti to the East had withdrawn from his now sun drenched fields, and now the shadow from Mt. Cadmus in the west was lengthening down to the river. The cool western breeze fanned his hair and beard, and the slave boy Onesimus came down the path seeking him.

"You've come to draw me from my morning meditation, have you? Tell me, boy, do you know your letters?"

Onesimus' performance of the previous day had given Archippus cause for consideration.

"You mean the alpha to omega? Yes, sir I can recite them and I can draw them on the wax tablet."

"Then you should turn to good old Cadmus behind you and thank him for his gift," smiled the philosopher.

"Yessir, I know it was Cadmus brought the gift of letters from our Eastern land to Western Thebes. But he only brought them 13 letters. I do not know where the other letters came from," pondered the boy.

"You know that too?" said the master in astonishment. Onesimus paused and considered his words. "Philemon knows it, sir; I only carry his burdens." Archippus was silent, but patted Onesimus on the head.

The house which Archippus was approaching was not the same structure to which the returning student had come a dozen years past. In those days the house stood as it had for centuries with minimal remodeling, built in the old Greek style. A central doorway had opened to the street; to its left the porter's lodge furnished with wooden benches for those who might be waiting there, and to the right a minimal stable for donkeys or mules.

A narrow hallway once led from the door to the courtyard, which contained no pools or flowering greenery. On one side there had been a hearth, with an open cistern close by. Rough benches provided seating for residents who shared the space with chickens and perhaps a dog or two. Around the courtyard were built small chambers which connected with each other by inside doors. At the very back were two larger rooms. One was called the *andron* where men gathered for talk and entertainment, and the other, the *gynaeceum* in which the women gossiped and did their work. Time was when the house was considered spacious. The father of Archippus and Apphia had inherited it from his grandfather. Indeed the house and land had belonged to the same family from old times when the Ionians had first conquered the Phrygians. Somewhere in the Catalogue of the Iliad you will find the name of our ancestor, it is said. Archippus and Apphia spoke in the Greek tongue, though they knew Phrygian well enough, but chose to use it only in front of their slaves.

When the widowed Apphia and her brother returned to the house, it was in sad condition. The thatch above the andron had fallen in and the weather and water had undermined the entire back wall. The cistern was filled with trash and the private rooms had long provided space for mice and even larger animals. Because of its unlivable condition, Apphia's young husband had chosen to live in the village of the Phrygian farmers. Now that possibility seemed untenable, and so one morning Archippus ordered that their their few belongings loaded on a cart and moved back into the old ruin. They had not so much as a donkey to pull the cart but pulled and pushed it themselves up the road that had once been cobbled. This part of the city had long since fallen into disrepair and was more or less abandonned.

With them came Phryx, an old serving man who had been many
years with the murdered man's family. Now he had no place to go
except with the poor man's widow. Had he been younger he might
well have disappeared into the town or sought his fortune on the road,
but as it was he had no mind for taking charge of his own life.

With Apphia came her maid servant, Sambatis, a skinny wench
of no more than 14 years whose father had sold her to a farmer in a
neighboring village. Apphia's father-in-law had bought her and given
her as a gift to his son's bride. Sambatis had no sandals for her feet and
only one thin garment to cover her nakedness. Her dark hair hung to
her shoulders in snarls; her skin was dark and rough from working out-
of-doors both at planting time and harvest. Sambatis did not respond to
Greek; the old language was all she knew. Apphia who desired, if not
a lady's maid, at least a house servant, had found Sambatis difficult to
educate. Sambatis for her part took the blows from Apphia's hairbrush
stolidly and found no reason to complain as long as there was food for
her to eat. When they reached the old house the four of them set about
to clean it out and make it livable.

The second night of their occupancy, Archippus and Apphia sat at a
table where Archippus produced a tablet with a plan for the house that
he proposed to build. Apphia looked on in astonishment and chaffed
her brother as a dreamer.

"Where, dear brother, can we find the money to take on such a
project? We do not have two leptas to share between us; Certainly we
do not have the skills to build a house, and our slaves are uselessness
itself."

She laughed as she pointed at Phryx and Sambatis each curled in
a corner like a sleeping dog, snoring at their rest.

Archippus patted her hand. "Do not worry, little sister. I have
learned a thing or two at Rhodes; and I have a charm with me with
which I shall control the demon of the river."

He continued, "This rude courtyard will become the forward peristyle with columns here at the end of the entrance hall which will frame

the beauty of our outdoor garden. We will do away with the stable and enlarge the space so we can rent it out as a shop. We will make the hallway from the door wider so that more than one visitor at a time can enter, and the porter's lodge will be enlarged to enhance our prestige. You will see that an education at Rhodes is not for wastrels, nor merely set up for a rich man's pleasure."

It may have just been talk to lift up their spirits, but he was earnest in believing it. Archippus had no intention of taking up trowel and mortar to start building his house himself. He had been brought up, after all, as a member of the gentility; this did not mean that he was wealthy; many gentlemen down on their luck find ways of eking out their sustenance without resorting to the labor of hands. At this point in his life Archipppus had not truly experienced the poverty that comes from having no means; with a certain bravado he pointed to his higher education and introduction to philosophy as being sufficient to sustain his needs and help him to find a way out of his predicament. He had tried the magic arts and seemed to have some proof that "there was something in it."

However, he was the first to admit that in his experience pure magic was an insufficient inducement to use as a way of life. Philosophy counseled against it, though philosophers were not totally inoculated against its infection. It would seem that his discovery of gold was pure chance; chance, fate, is an acceptable explanation for the differing circumstances of almost anyone, rich man, poor man or even slave. Still it was more than mere good fortune that he was able to separate the glittering mica from the true metal. In the school he had been taught that the mica floats away with the stream while the real nugget drops heavily to the bottom. Native intelligence taught him that heavy nuggets collect in certain cul-de-sacs being washed along with the flow of the river. Native intelligence also told him that it would be fool-hardy to advertise his luck or even to be seen with a trove of golden nuggets in his possession. He therefore took care of how he displayed what fortune had seen fit to reveal to him. After a trip to visit a friend in Ephesus he returned with sufficient minted gold pieces to buy a field, just as one day he returned with a golden lavaliere as a present for his sister.

A gentleman, of course, will own land. To be a farmer does not mean that one works the land himself. It is not difficult to find many who are willing to stoop to the task of digging in the ground and cultivating the vines and trees for crusts enough of bread to feed themselves and the sour wine to lull them from their pain to sleep. The wit to know the difference between the labor of the arm and the labor of the brain is what Archippus attributed to philosophy. Not all who take up the study of philosophy understand this; there are many who do not know the art of cudgelling the brain.

The poets sing of the joys of the simple life, and celebrate rustic happiness. Pan plays his pipes as he lolls in the shade while Phyllis and Sylvio romp among the violets and the lilies. Archippus was infinitely more sophisticated than that. He intended to enjoy the pleasures of the good life and he worked to achieve that life quietly without outwardshow of labor.

He early deduced that he must keep his sister contented. At the first this was not difficult to do. She was young and unsophisticated and therefore had no great expectations. Her marriage had not brought her any great satisfaction. Her father had fallen into his misfortunes before he died and was only able to provide a small dower, a field and a moldering house in town. Her young husband was too inexperienced to be able to turn his own negligible patrimony into more than bare existence. Their own physical labor was all they had to cultivate a farm and besides that they had small knowledge of agriculture. His short life was not long enough to expand his experience.

The young Apphia was pregnant, and that was enough to put her into a state of terror. Her mother had died long ago; her only serving girl was more ignorant than herself. Archippus procured a midwife from the village who managed the affair successfully, and Apphia found herself the mother of a healthy baby boy. Archippus suggested that Philemon was an auspicious name with good Greek precedence, and he took the precaution to add "Eupator," not because it would keep away bad influences, but because it was by now perfectly obvious that the infant was born under a lucky sign. Apphia was so taken by her possession of her new treasure that she could hardly give the child over to his nurse for occasional respite. Archippus had found an experienced nurse in the town, not wanting to entrust the family future to the mercies of a peasant woman.

Archippus found artisans in Colossae who worked for wages to remodel and reconstruct their house. It did not go unnoticed that a wealthy young widow was living in their city; with no one but a brother to tend to her affairs. As for the child, it is well known that a child faces many hazards in the first half dozen years of life. Archippus soon found that the city was filled with fathers who were seeking alliances for their unmarried sons; and there were older widowers who industriously pursued the occupation of fortune hunting, offering themselves solicitously as a help meet for an unfortunate lady who had no husband. Archippus was kept busy fending off these flies who seemed to swarm from nowhere.

Likewise, Archippus found himself in the position of having to make a choice concerning his own future; for if there were fathers with unmarried sons, there were also mothers with unmarried daughters who constantly titillated him with reports of the veiled beauties who pined away behind closed lattices waiting for a husband to come and claim them. But well he understood that it was through Apphia that he had took the right to dominate the property, until the true heir came of age. While he fended off Apphia's suitors, he became less interested in finding a wife of his own who might bring his whole sand castle crashing down around him.

Apphia's heart was set upon the child Philemon, and little else occupied her mind. All of her needs were cared for; she had no need to prepare a meal for meals were prepared for her; she had no interest in spinning and weaving the wool, for merely watching the spinning and examining the finished textile requires not much effort and without effort there is very little to be interested in. A gardener brought in fresh roses every day; a seamstress consulted with her on the draping of a new gown; Archippus himself brought her jewels from the seaport cities which she never visited. And so Apphia began to grow vain, hard to please and vacuous.

Archippus kept his mind occupied with many things compared to which Apphia's problems were negligible. He was an architect and even a structural engineer; he paid enough attention to his farming operations that he was an agriculturist to be admired; he was judge and jury for his slaves and workmen; he began to be involved in the business of trade and shipping in the coastal cities and found himself engaged in banking, but he also had leisure enough to survey his holdings from a distance. For the nonce, there was no time for women.

I have told you something of Archippus and Apphia. He had died in the earthquake before I was born; but her I remember as a child remembers an ancient ancestor to whom he is occasionally brought to honor with his respect.

Of Sambatis, I can say little, for I can only piece together the fragments of her story that fell from the lips of those who did not love her. "Those who have not love, are nothing."

Sambatis

Her first memory was an angry face looking into hers and screaming, and then a blow that threw her to the ground. She struggled to get up and bit her lips to prevent making any sound. Already she had learned that any noise from her would bring another blow. That was the meaning of life for Sambatis; that and the ever present pain of hunger from her stomach. The blow had come about when she put her fingers in a bowl of gruel. Quietly she licked them clean of whatever stuck to them. The others came in an put their spoons in the bowl, but she remained quiet in the background. She did not have the energy to try to get her share. Sambatis knew that she was the smallest and least important person in the family, except perhaps the new infant at her mother's breast. It was not long before the babe was given to her to watch. When the child cried to loud or tried to crawl away, she hit it in the mouth.

By the time the baby was able to walk alone, Sambatis was given a clay bowl and sent out with the reapers. Her task was to pick up seeds which had fallen unnoticed to the ground. When the bowl was full she would bring it to her mother. If she did not fill it, she would get another beating. She did not mind the fields so much; she even enjoyed the oozy mud squeezing between her toes. She had no sandals; in fact she had no clothes at all. The hot sun beat down upon her scorched hide and turned it even darker; if it rained, she had her only bath. In winter's cold she huddled close to her brothers and sisters to keep warm. Sometimes there would be an excursion to the river and she would splash about in delight as the cool water swept over her body and soothe her flea-bitten skin while it washed the lice out of her hair. Her brothers would examine her to see if she had got them all. The naked have no secrets to keep.

One day her father took her by the hand and walked her along the river bank. She knew that something was about to happen for her mother had tied a leather string around her neck. Hanging down from the string was a small blue bead; it was a charm to bring her good fortune. Around the river bend there was a man with two other children in tow. Sambatis' father and the man haggled a bit. After the man gave her father some coins, she saw her father no more. The man took the three children to the village market and one by one they were sold. Sambatis took little interest in the dealing. Finally two men came up and looked at her, and after a bit of dickering over the price, she was given to these two who brought along a wagonload of wares. Together they walked along the river. At length, they unceremoniously dumped her among some thatched huts. The slaves who were already there stood and watched without emotion. Sambatis was given a wooden bowl and a wooden spoon. She was shown the cookpot where she could fill the bowl. Whatever it was, she ate it with relish. This was not going to be so bad, she thought. Early the next morning she was given a bag to fill, and sent out with the reapers. She did not question the fate which changed her from a beggar's daughter into a slave.

In her growing up she did not learn much; indeed there was little to learn. She snatched at such enjoyment as came her way, a refrain from a song, laughter at some one else's predicament, picking lice from someone's hair, splashing in the river.

The master came down to examine the work and to look over his slaves. He did this occasionally, sometimes picking out a sickly one to be removed from the work force. What happened to them one could only guess. But on this day he chose out Sambatis, not because she was ailing, but because she was not as skinny as the other girls and her skin was not broken with running sores. When she smiled, she showed a complete set of teeth. The master took her to his house and showed her to his son. Sambatis recognized him as the younger man who had been with the master when she was purchased. The son stroked her skin and pinched her. He laughed when she yelped. The young man gave her over to a female house slave who put a garment on her and helped her comb her hair, after which she was given the wooden comb to keep. A dress and a comb, these were the first "things" she had ever had. The old woman chattered a bit and told her that she had been chosen as a hand maiden for the young man's bride. She tried to give her some instruction as to her demeanor, but Sambatis was not used to conversation and did not understand all that she was told.

The day of the wedding came; there was merriment and there was food and more excitement than Sambatis had ever seen, with laughter and music and dancing. Sambatis watched wide eyed as she ate; no one kept her from the tables. The bridal party arrived on camels. The bride was helped off her camel and seated on a throne next to the throne of the young man, the groom. The bride sat stiffly, she was veiled and wrapped in shawls of many colors. Gold coins jangled on her forehead, matching the bracelets on her wrists. She did not eat, but sipped a bit of sweetened liquid from a cup. Sambatis had never seen anything quite so grand. The next day, or maybe it was the day after that, Sambatis was given to the bride who was no longer veiled. Sambatis saw a girl, not much older than herself and considerably more frightened.

Sambatis had never before lived in a house. To be a house slave was much different from being a field slave. One could easily see that it took some training, but the old woman was not there for she remained in the master's house and the bride and groom went to a small place of their own at the edge of the village. Besides Sambatis there was only one slave there, Phryx. He had been the old master's doorkeeper but was getting old and hard of hearing. Here he was expected to do some cooking and help out wherever help was needed. Sambatis was instructed that she must stay by her mistress and do her bidding.

Apphia, the bride, had had no experience with housekeeping though she had been instructed in the womanly arts of spinning and weaving. In this house there seemed to be no spinning and weaving to be done, at least there were no implements for doing it, and no room to put them in had they been available. Apphia had little to do with meal preparation, only to assent to it and then eat what had been prepared. Sambatis was there to do her bidding, but Apphia did not have much knowledge of what to bid her servant to do. If Sambatis was a slow learner, then Apphia was a poor teacher.

In frustration Apphia would strike at Sambatis with whatever was at hand. Sambatis stood stolidly and unemotionally until Phryx took her aside and told her it would be better if she would shed some tears. After that Sambatis wept openly over her misdeeds, and this seemed to give Apphia some satisfaction. Apphia complained to her husband that she had never known anyone so stupid. The young man shrugged; what could he do? But eventually Apphia and Sambatis came to some sort of understanding and began to play a bit with each other and giggle over their own common jokes.

Sambatis was probably the first one to notice Apphia's pregnancy, for she had watched other women who were with child. She was not unaware of how that came about for slaves understand instinctively about physical matters. It was scarcely half a year since the wedding when the black day came. A slave came running in with the news that the master had fallen into the river and had drowned. Others came, carrying the whitened dead body. From then on there was chaos. Who could remember or interpret all that happened? But on that worst last day the whole village seemed to descend upon the two frightened women, who remained alone in the house, for the villagers carried off Phryx and another male slave who was with him, to torture for their evidence. Then without warning the village women began to plunder the house of all of its furnishings. Who knows what would have happened had not Archippus shown himself at that very moment?

It was Archippus who now was master and he was such a man as Sambatis had not seen before. He was washed and combed and shaved and dressed every day in clean white linen which somehow stayed white the while the very walls of his house were crumbling down around him. He kept Phryx around to watch the house and keep away the thieves, but he had two other slaves to cook and run errands at his bidding. First off, new walls were put up in a chamber for Apphia with a coat of whitewash to make them gleam. And there was a bed with soft bedding on it, and even a pad for Sambatis to sleep on at its foot. When Apphia's time had come upon her, it was Archippus who brought in the midwife; and shortly after there was a nursemaid to tend the infant. The nurse had an infant of her own which she kept close by in a small room prepared for her. She was a large jolly woman who treated both Apphia and Sambatis as if they were but older children. In due time another woman was brought in to supervise the household while Apphia recovered from her confinement. True, both of these women were slaves, but they had always been houseslaves and they took charge in no time, bending all of the other occupants of the house to their wills.

Never before had Sambatis enjoyed the company of women, but now she was initiated into the secrets of the sisterhood. One day they inquired about the blue bead that she wore for it still remained hanging from the leather thong her mother had laced it through. The leather was becoming thin and worn and was black from age and the dye of grease and sweat. Apphia found a stout linen cord dyed scarlet and the nurse plaited it into a chain with a skill which she had learned. The blue bead was securely fastened to it and Sambatis noticed how it emphasized her bronzed skin color as she admired it in Apphia's shining mirror.

She now was dressed in a simple undyed linen frock which reached from her neck to her ankles, leaving her arms bare. And as her diet improved her girlish body began to show round curves beneath the linen. The women noticed and approved. And when the tokens of womanhood appeared for the first time, they kissed her and reassured her and drove away her fears.

It was still her duty to sleep on a floor pad at the foot of Apphia's bed and be ready to care for her mistress should she wake at night and have some need. Often she dandled the baby Philemon, played with it, kissed it and cooed to it like a mother bird. Archippus was the only man who ever came into the women's quarters, and when he did he went straight to his sister and accomplished whatever business had brought him there. But he did not fail to notice the handmaid Sambatis though he gave her no greeting nor sign of recognition. Still the sight of her pleased him; but he put it from his mind for he had no time or inclination to become involved with the world of women.

Already in those early days, before the building of the house was completed, Archipppus had found his niche on the rock that overlooked the valley. The early shadows from its mountain backdrop made it a cool and comfortable place to escape the summer heat while he enjoyed the everchanging landscape of the valley below. He noticed that often in mid-afternoon Sambatis would walk down the distance from the house to the river bank. She would take off her sandals and stroll down the dusty path as though freed from all cares. For Sambatis the stroll was accomplished easily, though it is likely that the other women would do it only with difficulty, and Apphia not at all.

It was apparent to Archippus that Sambatis enjoyed a swim and took this opportunity to bathe unseen behind the rocks that held his treasure trove. At first he frowned and looked away, but soon knew he took pleasure in furtive glances that revealed her natural freedom.

He found some excuse to go down to the river himself, to examine perhaps if she had discovered his hidden wealth though he had no reason to believe that this was so. He secreted himself in a clump of bushes. The girl came down as usual, tossed her sandals aside and disrobed and for half an hour enjoyed splashing and paddling in the river. Then she came out, tossed her hair, put on her chiton and strolled back up the path. Archippus felt a pang, as though he had committed some offense. He examined himself but could find none. After all the girl belonged to him and he had the right to enjoy looking at her beauty as he might enjoy looking at some fine work of art, a marble statue or a skillfully contrived brass candlestick. He put it from his mind, but the next day found him again in his hiding place.

Sambatis swam about and then stood up. The sun gleamed on her golden skin and she shone like a sculptor's polished statue as she walked out of the water on to the soft river sand. Archippus stood up and met her. He was Praxiteles and she was Phryne. He touched her skin gently. It was firm and soft. The two lay down on the sand together.

The next morning when he arose from his bed to greet another day, he found his passion had not gone. He contrived some excuse to visit Apphia in her apartment. There his eyes met the eyes of Sambatis. No word was said. He transacted his business and took his leave without looking back. Up in his aerie he had a discourse with himself.

"Why should I feel this way? Have I some regret? The girl is, after all, only a slave. Not just a slave, but a slave who belongs soul and body to me. No, just body, for slaves do not have souls." His was the right to do with her as he pleased. There was no one who would deny him that. But a deep sadness came over him and mingled with the joy that overtook him in his thoughts of her. He had no explanation.

The meetings between Sambatis and Archippus were deeply secret. They did not even talk to each other; they simply took pleasure in each other's bodies. Certainly Sambatis did not speak of the affair with the other women; and Archippus made no mention of his activities. But somehow the women knew. The two slave women looked slyly at each other when they saw her, and suddenly Apphia began to dislike her. Even before they saw her wearing her blue bead on a golden chain. Apphia complained to Archippus that the girl was stupid and that she could not get anything done right. Furthermore she seemed unable to learn the simplest task. At last she had her trade places with her serving woman. Sambatis now slept outside the door of Apphia's apartment and not beside her bed. It was not long before her white garment showed a certain roundness appearing over her belly.

Apphia looked straight at Archippus and said, "She has been lying with the house boys. I knew it all along. And now she is with child."

Archippus was undemonstrative but asked his sister what she planned to do. "We will send her back to the fields. She is experienced there and some of the bucks will appreciate her charms."

Archippus said, "It is done." He had Stamnion take the woman to the field huts where the workers lived. Later, Archippus spoke to the overseer and said, "Treat her gently; do not give her hard work or burdens to lift. Let her wander where she pleases." The overseer seemed to understand and obeyed his orders. Archippus made no move to visit her.

Finally Sambatis' time came upon her. Even though it was her first child the birth was not difficult. The child was a squalling boy. Sambatis called the overseer and asked if he would notify Archippus of the delivery. The overseer nodded and Archippus somehow received the message. In mid afternoon he strolled down to the huts and found Sambatis there. She looked up with pleading eyes, but he did not look at her. He kept his eyes looking straight ahead and asked the overseer about the child.

"It is a boy," the overseer told him.

"Is the child healthy?" Archippus asked.

"He is in good shape," the overseer replied, "healthy and lusty with no demeaning mark upon him."

Sambatis rose in hope that Archippus would pick up the child, but he made no motion. He turned and walked away. He knew well that should he take the child up, he would acknowledge his responsibility.

Outside the hut, he instructed the overseer, "See to it that the child is fed and well cared for; and when he is old enough to leave his mother, send him to my house. He will be useful there."

"Yes, master," replied the overseer. "He will be Useful." And so
the babe was named, *Onesimus.*

Sambatis nursed the child and played with him. She patted him
and talked to him and cooed and he gurgled at her with pleasure. On
stout little legs he learned to walk and then to run. At last he would no
longer nurse, but toddled off to where the cookpot was steaming.

Sambatis took the golden chain with the blue bead from around
her neck and put it around the child's neck. She kissed him and he
waved bye-bye as she walked down to the river. In the bottom of the
river the River God smiled at her with his golden face. She pushed her
face down into the water to meet him. The black demons beckoned
her to come, and pulled her down to Acheron.

The overseer took the child by the hand and they walked up to the
great house on the hill.

"You had said, master, that he might be useful here; he's but a tad
but he will grow." There was a tear in the overseer's eye for he had
grown fond of the boy. Archippus showed no emotion. In an hour or
so he took the child to the women's quarters.

"He can be a playmate for Philemon," he said.

Apphia looked coldly, but her heart cautioned her to say nothing.
From then on Philemon and Onesimus played as brothers. When
Philemon rolled the ball, Onesimus retrieved it and rolled it back.
When they were hungry, Philemon sent him to the kitchen. At night,
Onesimus slept on a pad at the foot of Philemon's bed.

The Proper Education

My schooling was given me by my father, Philemon; so of the education of the two boys I have some knowledge. He taught my alpha-beta
in much the same way that they were taught. He was my school master for Christian parents kept their children close to home for safety's
sake. In my father's house there were no slaves; instead of memorizing myths, we learned Scripture, but we were taught with the same

methods that all childlren are taught, for when one is a child, he thinks as a child.

The year of Philemon's seventh birthday saw many changes in the household. It was not that in faraway Rome the Emperor Tiberius had died and had been succeeded by a relative named Caligula. The knowledge of that event took some months to filter into Colossae, and did not cause much of a ripple in local circles when it did. It was not that change was coming to Colossae. One could note that seven years had produced some local differences, but change came slow during that town's six hundred years of existence.

For Apphia and Archippus it was the year that the renovation of their house was completed. It had started with the shoring up of the south east corner foundation and the replacement of a wall. But at last almost every wall had been rebuilt; the whole plan of the house had changed.

Instead of one open megaron in the old Greek style which had not changed from the days of Priam, two peristyles graced the house, with fine painted columns all around. The front peristyle contained the pool and architectural landscaping. It was meant for impressing visitors. The back peristyle was more intimate and offered light relief from the darkness of the library and the two dining rooms, one for larger dinners and the other for smaller family affairs.

The house now fronted on a recobbled street, down one side of which there was a drainage ditch. A large door impressed the entering visitor, and that was protected from the street by a metal gate which was locked at night. The door opened on a widened corridor. The old corridor was scarcely wide enough for one person to squeeze through, and that person had to stoop if he were tall. (In the old days this was considered to be a protection from invaders.) Next to the door was the porter's cubicle, furnished in such a way that the door would be attended day and night. There was a new porter now; old Phryx had become too feeble to attend such duties.

On the other side of the door from the porter's lodge was a shop which was rented to a baker. In that land even wealthy families see nothing amiss in renting their streetside space to tradesmen. The family lives inside, privately; besides the rent is income not to be despised. This house had been the last house on the street which led outward from the city. The street had become unfashionable in its latter years, but with the restoration of the Archippus dwelling, some of the other property owners began to spruce up their deteriorating places; now there was not only the bakery, but across the way was the shop of a wool merchant, and next to that crockery and glassware were being sold. Not too far down the street a taverna stood; Apphia complained that it made it all to easy for slaves to slip away and waste their time, and it drew a noisy crowd. Still, all of this activity was good for property values. Still it was life inside the house, not outside, that marked the time as special. Philemon would soon be seven, and that meant it was time for him to be starting school. Apphia approached Archippus about it by telling him that the nurse who had been with them since birth needed to leave. Archippus was startled; nurses did not leave. Who was the first to recognize Odysseus on his return home from his voyages? It was his nurse, still faithful to her duties.

Apphia laughed and said that times had changed; Philemon did not need a nurse, and besides the nurse had children of her own to care for. Other duties could be found for her or she could be traded to a family who needed her special abilities. (Apphia did not say "sold"; it was unpleasant to think of profiting from the sale of one so faithful.) Archippus agreed and further noted that it was time to find a proper *paedogogus* to help the child to and from school and tutor him with his studies.

Apphia was not finished. The serving woman who had taken care of housework was elderly. In fact, her feet were swollen so that she walked only with difficulty; furthermore she had become slovenly and did not see that things were cleaned properly. All in all, she was quite unsatisfactory. Archippus suggested that they might look to see if there were any younger women among the slaves who could take over; but Apphia protested that they needed someone who was experienced in housekeeping and supervision. In fact, she was suggesting that they hire a free woman to take overthe job as housekeeper. A woman who could supervise the cleaning, one who could give orders to the cook and watch the boys who shopped for provender, a woman who could set up the weaving frames and get some semblance of a household textile operation so that cloth could be made and clothing fashioned and mended. . . . "Wait a minute," expostulated Archippus, "where will you find such a paragon?"

Apphia, it turned out, had been inquiring among her friends and had a novel suggestion. "We will find a Jewish woman. There is a large Jewish colony at Colossae on the back side of the city. Jews do not sell their children into slavery, but they often put them to work for wages as freemen. Their womenfolk are well known for their thrift and chastity. In cases of necessity they hire themselves out as household servants but do not break their family ties."

Archippus was intrigued but not convinced. "Wouldn't it be easier just to find a well trained slave woman? I am sure we could find someone if we inquire."

Apphia was emphatic. "Slaves are not good workers. They are lazy and ignorant. Mostly they shun responsibility. But worst of all, you can't get rid of them. Who will buy a worn out slave? There's old Phryx. He's become a family member, a family responsibility. He babbles and he slobbers; the porter refuses to have him in his room any more; and now I think we are going to have to diaper him."

Archippus sighed. It was a problem.

"Well, all I can say," Apphia pursued the subject further, "slaves are a headache and a nuisance. You can't teach them anything; they do as little work as they can get by with; if you beat them, they sulk and when worst comes to worst, they commit suicide and you have lost your whole investment." Her last words had a special sting. Apphia had never mentioned Sambatis to her brother, nor intimated that she had any knowledge of the affair. But now and then she had a thin stiletto with which she pierced his heart. Finally, it was agreed that Archippus would find a proper pedagogue for Philemon and she would take care of hiring a Jewess. Within the week Apphia proudly produced her candidate for housekeeper. She was a Jewish lady of poor but honorable family. She had been widowed before she was twenty, before she had any children. She had returned to her father's family and had helped with the rearing of her younger brothers and sisters; but now she was in her thirties; the brothers and sisters were grown, and her father wished to see her settled before he died and left her with no support.

Leah was indeed a paragon. She was experienced in the preparation and weaving of both flax and wool. She was an expert with the needle and could even embroider. She understood the preparation of meals and could give advice and orders to the cook; she knew how to choose select vegetables from the kitchen garden as well as how to buy them at the market. She understood how to launder and how to store and keep linens and woolens from moth and mildew. In fact, had Archippus desired a wife, he could not have chosen better.

It was agreed that Leah should have her own room in the house; that she could visit her family and have them visit her (all within discretion, of course). She would answer to no one in the household except Apphia herself. Not even Philemon or Archippus could give her orders. She would have the Seventh Day free because it was her Sabbath, but all other times she was on call. And she would receive a stipend of twelve drachmai per year.

Archippus also filled his part of the bargain. He returned one day with a sallow bandy-legged slave whom he had purchased at a good price for he was highly recommended by his former master. Archippus introduced him to his Apphia.

"He can read, dear sister; and he speaks impeccable Greek."

Apphia restrained her laughter. "What is your name, my good man?"

The new pedagogue replied gravely, "They call me Platon, madam."

"Platon?" Apphia's eyebrows lifted.

"Yes, madam. When I was young and learned to read, the other slaves in the household would come to me with their problems and I would give them learned answers. They began to call me their 'Platon,' and the name has been with me ever since."

"But why should we need a pedagogue who can read?" Apphia asked her brother. "All he has to do is walk Philemon to school. The school master will teach him to read."

Archippus replied, "He will be needed to help Philemon with his studies for many years. Besides, he is recommended as a good disciplinarian."

"Disciplinarian?" Apphia was aghast. "He will never lay a hand on my son."

"No, madam. I will discipline your son, if necessary, by putting the ferule to the other boy. When your son sees the other boy beaten for his mischief, he will be sorry and behave in a more acceptable manner."

"The other boy?" questioned Apphia.

"Onesimus," replied Archippus. "Such an arrangement is customary."

Apphia was silent. In her mind she was thinking, "Why should the poor baby have to learn to read, and at such an early age?"

Apphia could not see much use in reading. True, she had been taught her letters and could read signs and decipher notes. What else is there to read? Archippus had collected scrolls for his library but for all of her, the library seemed to be there just for show, and she had no cause even to read a grocery list.

It was decided that Philemon would not start to school until after Apollo's birthday. By this time the days would be lengthening and the worst of the winter's cold would be over. The day finally came; Philemon called his slave Onesimus early before sunup to help him wash himself and with his dressing. Onesimus was ready at the call. The two had a small breakfast, some bread, that had been set out for them the night before. The pedagogue was ready, carrying wax tablets and some styli with him. These he handed to Onesimus to carry, while he took Philemon's hand. The three marched out the front door eager in their excitement of the new adventure.

While there were a number of schools to choose from in Colossae, Archippus had determined that the one nearest to their home was as good as any other. Only a short walk from the house and on the same street, the schoolmaster had set up his business in an open shop which fronted on the street. The room, enclosed on three sides by the residence, was protected from street traffic by curtains hung in front. Other boys, accompanied by their pedagogues, were already assembling and looked warily and curiously at their new classmates. Seats were found on benches which were arranged in straight rows facing the teacher who sat in an armchair on a slightly raised platform. The pedagogues retired to the back of the room to benches prepared for them. They evidently knew each other and were engaged in their own conversations. Philemon looked around at his classmates, most of them seemed older than himself, but one or two he knew from previous acquaintance. Onesimus, too, looked around and recognized another slave boy or two, but obviously he was the youngest and the smallest of the boys in the room.

It was the law in Colossae that all boys should attend school and learn the basics of reading, writing and figuring. Slave boys too were sent for education, for their masters understood that an educated slave was greatly increased in value. Often the slaves came with their young masters and doubled in their duties as scholars and attendants. Girls, too, might be sent for training in the basic skills. There were no girls in the school which Philemon attended, but the rumor was that in some of the more progressive cities the attendance of girls was required.

The schoolmaster rapped for attention and the boys marked upon the teacher. He was a short dour man, wearing an ink stained tunic underneath his woolen cloak.

"Alpha, Beta," he said in a scratchy voice.

"Alpha, Beta, Gamma, Delta, He . . . " the students chanted back in sing-song style.

"Kai?" the master raised his tone.

"Kai Zeta, Eta, Theta," chanted the students.

It did not seem to make much sense, but the students seemed

to know what was required. The master frowned at Philemon and Onesimus who began to listen very hard to find out what was going on.

"Alpha, Beta," repeated the school master.

"Alpha, Beta, Gamma, Delta, He ..." the boys chanted with resignation, and Philemon and Onesimus moved their lips trying to remember the sounds that they were supposed to say. This was repeated line by line until at last only the more experienced were saying, "paronta *Phi*, te *Chi*, te *Psi*, eis te *O*."

The master rapped for attention and called the pedagogues forward. They were charged to drill their young charges in the basics while the school master worked with the older boys in a more difficult lesson.

"Alpha/Omega," said the master.

"Beta/Psi, Gamma/Chi, Delta/Phi," replied the students showing that they could recite the alphabetic names forwards and backwards at the same time. During this time Platon was attempting to get Philemon and Onesimus to repeat the first four names correctly, but the boys were becoming weary and Philemon's attention wandered.

"Pay attention," Platon warned sharply. Philemon yawned and Platon came down swiftly on Onesimus' shoulders with his stick. Onesimus blinked hard, trying not to cry.

"Why did you do that?" Philemon protested.

"Because, you did not pay attention," Platon stated simply.

Now the class was dismissed, and all the boys jumped up and ran about. Their pedagogues brought out cookies and sweet drinks and the new boys were sized up all around by their class mates. Recess over, the class assembled again, but this time with a different master who came to the front carrying a lyre. He got attention with a few chords, and the boys began to sing a song. All the while the headmaster who taught the letters munched upon his lunch, wiping the grease from his mouth upon his wide sleeve. All of the boys knew the song, for it was a simple thing such as nurses teach their babes.

"Alpha – hena, beta – duo, gamma – treis, tessera – delta," and they held up their fingers to show that they knew the numbers in the song.

Learning one's letters is the most important lesson to be mastered at school, but music and arithmetic are not slighted.

The morning classes were over; and the children all clamored with joy and ran home for lunch. The pedagogues were quite out of breath keeping up with them. Lunch and a nap; then it was time to go to the palestra. Afternoons the palestra was reserved for children who quickly fell to playing games of tag and hide and seek. But soon they were assembled into some kind of order, younger boys in front; older ones behind. The races began. The boys loved the races and they whooped as they ran round the oval track. The older boys quickly passed the younger ones, some even finishing two or even three laps before the youngsters finished one. Soon they were all sweaty and dusty, and thirsty too. The pedagogues brought out cups of clear water and raisin cakes for the winners. The losers made do with bread. At last they all went for a dip in the bath. Platon brought out a vial of oil and the two boys rubbed themselves and then scraped themselves clean with a strigula. Platon brought out their clothes, for during the play they had run about quite naked. Onesimus remembered to help Philemon on with his, and knelt and tied his sandals. At last Onesimus put on his tunic and sat down upon the pavement to lace and tie his own sandals. He could feel his little legs ache; after all, he was only five years old.

At home, Leah greeted them with an early supper. "How was it?" she inquired.

"It was fun," both boys chirped.

Alpha

A child's life is marked by school. It is an endless stretch of time, differing from eternity only in that it has a beginning and an end. The excitement of the first day of school swiftly recedes into the past. The school-room days of the present proceed slowly with tiresome regularity and never ending tasks of memorization and recitation. One hardly notices any change or anything new for the pace would bore the legendary tortoise.

When Philemon and Onesimus could say their letters backwards and forwards and forwards and backwards, they were introduced to the shapes of these letters. Philemon's sweaty hands tried to contrive an *alpha* that looked like an *alpha*. He pressed the pointed end of the stylus into the soft wax to make the first diagonal line. The pedagogue showed him how to make a whole row of diagonal lines /////. Then to make the diagonals in the opposite direction. \\\\\. Finally he hooked the two together /\ with a straight line in the middle /–\. Onesimus was trying it too, but his little hands were clumsy and making a whole line of AAAAA's made him tired, even though the master pressed a thin piece of reed into the wax to serve as a boundary. The pedagogue took the blunt end of the stylus and made the wax smooth again. The boy tried again to make a straight line of alphas. So with the passing of the days the young scholars became adept at recognizing an alpha even when it appeared between a kappa and a tau, K A T A. And at last they were drawing words. After this lesson, the master commanded them to make "big words," words so fantastic that no one would ever say them.

"Why not?" he asked "when you have mastered the letters you can write any word."

Philemon was bored. With stylus and tablet he was all thumbs. His attention was easily distracted by a fly that was crawling up the wall, or by a ray of sunlight that peeked uninvited through a hole in the curtain. Onesimus was practical. If Philemon's tablet did not have the proper letters on it when the master came by, Onesimus knew whose backside would feel the rod. So Onesimus leaned over and put the proper letters in the wax. Master Zaleucas knew as well as Platon what was happening but neither of them was willing to upset the classroom discipline to make a change. Furthermore, Master Zaleucas did not wish to risk losing a good tuition, and Platon was, after all, a slave who had a care for his own skin.

By the time that the boys were assigned to copying maxims and poetic passages on their tablets, a sort of elementary arithmetic was added to the curriculum. It was started with "finger signs." The last three fingers of the left hand represented the numbers one through nine, depending upon the extent the finger was bent toward the palm. Tens were represented by the thumb and first finger of the same hand. The right hand fingers were used to represent tens, hundreds and thousands. Tens and hundreds of thousands were represented by the position of the hands in relation to the chest, the navel and the thigh. A million was two hands locked together. Obviously the system required much practice, but for most youths it was more popular than learning the letters, for it involved movement and endless opportunities for joking. It is necessary to learn finger arithmetic when you are young, if you are ever to be successful in business and trading.

Archippus developed concern about his youngsters' progress in school. One day he found Zaleucas free of his teaching duties since the pedagogues were drilling the boys on their numbers. Archippus began pleasantly, "Do our boys have the capabilities required for learning?"

"Of course, sir. They are quite as capable as any boys are."

"I grant that this is so," nodded Archippus, "but I mean have they quickness of mind? Do they have any natural talent for learning?"

Zaleucas expounded, "It is falsely thought that some boys are incapable of learning because of dullness. The greater number are ready and quick in learning. It may be that one boy may surpass another in ability, but it is only a matter of more or less. There is no one who will not gain something by study."

The master had some fears that perhaps Philemon's family had noticed that the boy was not making much progress and find his teacher culpable.

Archippus continued, "But the slave boy is, after all, only a slave; and furthermore he is younger, so does he have the ability to keep pace with the other students?"

The master now began to sweat a little for the slave; he did not wish to lose his tuition either. "Quickness of study is natural to man," he replied. "Birds are meant to fly and horses to run, but humans inherit sagacity and understanding. Girls are said to learn as rapidly as boys, and slaves are as acute as their masters. A well-educated slave is a treasure for his master, even as a wife who can read and figure is a treasure to her husband."

"Is that true?" mused Archippus. "Certainly we seem to have some very dull louts as slaves in our household."

"Well, Onesimus is not one of them," the school master defended. "But if you want cleverness in your slave boy, you must cherish him and treat him with kindness."

Archippus looked relieved. Certain persons at home had been accusing him of being too light handed with the boy; for them, the lash was the better teacher of slaves.

Archippus inquired of Platon about the gymnastic activities of the boys. Platon was quick to tell the uncle that Philemon excelled in the foot races, being able to come in first of all his companions many times; and furthermore he was showing great progress in other physical activities. When asked about Onesimus, Platon could only reply that the boy was younger than his comrades and did not have the strength or the stamina.

And then he added apologetically, "The little fellow has a lot of burdens to bear." Archippus had the feeling that the burdens were more than the weight of school supplies and pairs of sandals.

Little more was said about the matter until one day Apphia flounced into the library and said, "My son Philemon is not learning anything at that school."

"How so?" asked Archippus without looking up from his books.

"How so? He can't read, that's how so."

"Why the school master himself told me that all boys can learn to read. Who told you otherwise?"

"Leah told me. She has tested him, and she says that he knows his letters but he can't read. And Leah can read very well. Leah says that it is well known that Onesimus completes all of Philemon's assignments and the result is that Onesimus is getting all the education and Philemon is learning nothing."

"And what does Philemon have to say for himself?"

"Philemon admits that it is so. He even smirked to my face when he told me. He doesn't have to learn anything because he will always have Onesimus to do it for him. Here we are paying out all that money to have Philemon educated, and what are we getting? A slave who can read, that's what we are getting."

Archippus murmured that he would look into the matter. Apphia went off in a huff. Shortly after Archippus summoned Platon into his study. Platon could only concur when Archippus said that they would have to remove Onesimus from school. But he reminded his master that the boy would be worth his weight in gold if he were to continue his education. In fact, Platon added that he himself would tutor the youngster if he were given the chance.

Archippus could only agree that Philemon must be put on his own so far as schooling was concerned. He was now twelve years of age and should be soon starting the next step of his schooling. Literary subjects, grammar and reading and especially oratory certainly required the elementary ability to read. If anything, Platon would have to tutor Philemon. There was yet time to figure out what kind of training would be best for Onesimus.

"In fact," announced Archippus, "I will attend to that matter myself."

The next day Onesimus was told that he would no longer sleep in the same room with Philemon, but that he would find his bed with the two houseboys Stamnion and Asterion. Then Archippus ran his fingers through his tousled hair and said, "Next week we shall have important guests at a dinner party, and you will be there to help serve. That will be exciting, won't it?"

Onesimus looked up in surprise and said, "Yes, master. That will be quite different."

Archippus awoke in the middle of the night. His first thought was "I must do something about the boy." He knew immediately that the boy was Onesimus, the slave who had brought him down from his aerie on the rock. The rest of the night was sleepless.

Archippus had paid little attention to the youngsters growing up in his house. True, two youngsters raced and whooped around the house and when they became too boisterous one of the women disciplined them. Customarily Archippus retired to his study which was off limits to intruders. When it was required he had made certain decisions about them but usually these were simply in concurrence with his sister Apphia.

Philemon called him "Uncle," and so also did Onesimus, since that was the only name known for him. Onesimus was slightly uneasy with the term after he was separated from Philemon and decided to follow the other slaves in calling Archippus, "Master."

After first light and morning chores, Archippus sent to have Onesimus come to his study. This was most unusual for few members of the household were ever welcome there, only Platon who was entrusted with cleaning the room and putting away the scrolls and the writing materials. Onesimus duly appeared. Archippus looked up and suddenly felt tongue-tied. He didn't know how to address the boy. "My boy, can you count?"

"Oh, yes sir," was the reply. And Onesimus began to count on his fingers as he had been taught: "Hen (one finger straight up), duo (finger bent), treis (finger down), and so he continued the counting exercise to ennea (with all three fingers down).

"Good," pronounced the uncle. "Can you write the numbers?" And he handed the boy a wax tablet and stylus. The boy wrote A-B-Γ-Δ-E giving the numerical name of each letter until he came to six when he said, "Squiggle, hex."

"Squiggle?" Archippus looked up in surprise.

Seriously the boy replied, "Yes, *pente* is *eta*. The next letter is *zeta*, but it is not *hex*; it is *hepta*." And the boy added with a mischievous grin, "That is because *hex* is a bad number."

"A bad number?" Archippus was surprised. "Are numbers good and bad?"

"Oh yes, *hen* is a good number because it represents the whole. It is a unity and stands for God Himself."

"And who told you that?" asked Archippus slightly amazed.

"Leah, told me; she knows all about numbers. *Duo* is a good number because it is one & one. It represents *male* and *female*. And *treis* is a very good number because it represents three unities: heaven and earth and sea. But the best number of all is *ennea* because it is three threes."

"Well," said Archippus, "I would think that *hex* is a pretty good number because it also has a couple of *threes.*"

"That's the point," continued the boy, "It is only two *threes.* and so it is an odd ball."

"I thought *hex* was even," teased Archippus.

"We're not talking about oddses and evenses," replied the boy sternly, "we're talking about good and bad. And *hex* is 'bad cess.' "

"Bad cess?" asked Archippus. "What is this 'cess'?"

"It's something bad, like bad luck. That's why we don't write it with a regular letter but we just make a squiggle. It's a Phrygian word. Platon told me."

"Platon told you that *hex* is a bad number?" inquired Archippus.

"No, he told me that *cess* is a Phrygian word," explained Onesimus. "Everyone knows it is a bad number."

Archippus had not heard of it. "Who is everybody?" he asked.

"Why, everybody. Asterion and Stamnon and even Leah. Every-one knows it is bad; that's why you see it on walls and doors. It means 'bad luck to go in.' It's even on your door here," And Onesimus ran to the doorway and found the squiggle drawn on the pilaster, down near the floor.

"It's the sign of the snake," he said solemnly.

Archippus straightened up. "Well, boy, don't let it be bad cess for you. You are welcome to come in and talk whenever you want." Onesimus scampered off, happy to be set free. Archippus sat down at his writing table, "Bad cess, eh? Well, what the digamma. . . . "

The next day Archippus observed Onesimus watching the fish in the peristyle pool. "What are you doing, boy?" he asked.

"I'm waiting for Leah," replied the boy. "We are going to the market."

"And you are going to carry her bundles?"

"Well, yes, that too. But Leah likes to go with me because I know how to make change."

"You can make change?" asked Archippus thinking that Onesimus had had precious little change in his lifetime to work with.

"Yes, like how many obols and chalci are in a drachma, things like that. You have to know things like that if you want fish for supper."

Archippus sensed a certain cockiness in the boy's attitude which pleased him. "Well, when you get back from your shopping trip, drop into my study and see me," he said.

Onesimus nodded and then he looked up in a panic, "Oh, I'm supposed to go help the cook." And off he ran.

Shortly afterward, Archippus summoned Platon who came to him with a certain amount of dread; for he was fearing for his future. Philemon was about to start to the Oratory School and would no longer need a pedagogue, and Onesimus had completed elementary education, obviating his needs for a pedagogue if he had ever had such a need. So Platon could see very little use for his special kind of services. He could be demoted to "house slave," doing odd jobs; but more likely he would be sold to some other family and who knew what they might be like. The master got to the subject quickly.

"It's about Onesimus. He seems to be unusually intelligent for his age."

"Oh, yes sir. That is certainly true," agreed Platon.

Archippus continued, "I find that he knows his numbers, and today I have discovered that he seems to understand the principles of geometry. So, what should we do with him? I mean, how shall we educate him further? What are we going to train him for?"

Platon enjoyed being consulted as an expert. "He would be very good at keeping financial records, sir. I understand that merchants and bankers employ such people for just that task. In fact, the emperor has a whole staff of such book keepers who practically run the imperial household."

Archippus nodded in agreement. "But to hold a position of such importance, one should be of excellent moral character. I mean, the responsibility lends itself to great temptation."

"That is true, sir," replied Platon "It would be quite a responsibility to train such a person."

"He really should learn philosophy," mused Archippus. "He has need for knowing the rules of rhetoric and the sciences of astrology and medicine."

"That is quite a prescription for such a little boy," said Platon gravely.

Archippus looked at the pedagogue squarely. "That is your responsibility and mine. From now on it is your duty to teach Onesimus everything that you know. And I will take it from there."

Platon was flushed with pride, "Sir, it is a great honor."

"Yes," replied Archippus. "But do not tell my sister. This is between the two of us. From now on you and Onesimus will live on this side of the house." Platon bowed in acknowledgment, and backed out of the room.

Onesimus had now became one of the houseboys. Some would have counted it a demotion, for he had formerly been a personal attendant to the young master of the house. For Onesimus it served as a maturation rite; he was no longer subject to the whims of Philemon; he left the constant eye of the women, now he had the company of his peers, other male slaves. They quickly called him *Useless*, just as Stamnion was called *Jug Ears*, and Asterion was nicknamed, *Scarface*. Perhaps they resented having to share already small space with yet another; still it was outside their competence to do anything about it, so they went about the business of initiating him into their company, while Onesimus began to accommodate to their way of life. The two older slaves were in their late teens having been brought into the house from the fields several years past. Both had placid personalities, a good quality for house slaves, possibly developed in childhood to save them from the physical deficiencies which made them the butt of field slave humor. Unlike Onesimus who had been brought to the house while still an infant, they had learned something of slave culture.

Neither Archippus nor Apphia had a stomach for the "slave trade." They kept slaves, for they understood no other way to live, but they did not buy or sell. They relied upon slave reproduction for their servant supply; from time to time they brought appealing youngsters to the house, but were likely to send them back to the fields if they formed annoying alliances with each other. Although "slave families" had no legal status, on the farm they were allowed to exist.

One day the two older boys consulted Onesimus on a household question that had been bothering them. Although Archippus was obviously the *pater familias* who bore the *potestas* in this house, and Apphia was equally obviously the *mater familias* who seemed to have a lot of *potestas* of her own—though everyone knows that women do not have *potestas*, the two seemed to be very remote from each other. "How could the two ever have cohabited long enough to produce the son, Philemon?"

Onesimus found that one easy to answer, "Archippus is not Philemon's father," he announced. The boys were stunned, "Well, who is he then?" "Archippus is Philemon's uncle," explained Onesimus. "He has the *potestas* of the mother's elder brother. In Roman law he has *tutela mulierum*, that is he is the woman's guardian because her son is too young."

The two slaves found this an interesting idea. "When he is older enough will Philemon have this *potestas*, as you call it?"

"Not unless his uncle gives it to him," replied Onesimus who had long since been rehearsed on this Catch 22 of Roman law. "Apphia is always telling Philemon what his position ought to be, and how he will inherit the house and the land when he grows up, but when Archippus hears of it, he says, 'Nonsense.' "

"And who will inherit all of this when Archippus (Apollo forbid) passes on?" asked Asterion who savored and remembered all family gossip.

"Unless Archippus should marry and have a son, Philemon will inherit," said Onesimus gravely.

"Then why doesn't Archippus marry?" asked Jug Ears who always believed in seizing the moment.

"I think because he doesn't want to make Apphia mad," replied Onesimus. "And, of course, he doesn't want her to marry again because there would have to be a settlement of the issue then, and he wouldn't be her guardian any more. So they both stay as they are, so they won't antagonize the other."

"Well," laughed Stamnion, "I think Philemon is no better off than any slave. He has a mother but no father."

"Of course he had a father," Onesimus defended. "His father died."

"No, he has an overseer, just like us. Look at us, all of us, we have no fathers."

This was contrary to what Onesimus had been told about life. "We all had fathers; someone had to be my father."

"Oh sure," laughed Asterion. "We are all of us Sons of the North Wind."

"What do you mean?" asked the youngster.

"It's as they say, 'A slave woman bares her ass to the North Wind, and he mounts her.' " Scarface and Jug Ears both laughed at Onesimus' confusion.

"But seriously," Stamnion asked, "Why doesn't Archippus get married. He doesn't have to ask his sister's permission."

"You might ask Archipor, over there," winked Asterion. Onesimus sensed that the two older boys had in some way turned against him, and the tears began to well up. "You're his catamite," said the slave; and both of the boys laughed raucously.

It was early afternoon, time for Platon to start the daily lesson with Onesimus, for afternoons were given over to Philemon's time at the palestra. Platon had determined that there was in Archippus' library the entire text of *The Iliad*. He savored the thought of having access to the whole epic. Archippus agreed to the lesson plan, for any education at all require a knowledge of Homer. They had started with the school master's technique. Platon read the first two lines of text and Onesimus practiced saying the two lines back to him. When he had those lines committed to memory, then Platon would show his charge the text. Onesimus would read the words he already knew; and then begin the laborious process of copying the text on some old papyrus leaves which Platon had scraped and made ready for the project.

"When we finish with this, you will have the whole of the Iliad for your very own," Platon predicted.

"The whole text?" Onesimus was wide eyed and frightened. He wondered how many years of this it would take to memorize and copy the entire epic.

"By that time, you will be a real amanuensis," boasted Platon. It was enough to make any little boy sigh.

When the lesson was over, Onesimus lingered in the library to straighten things up for Archippus who came in a little earlier than expected.

"And how is my boy?" asked Archippus genially. "Do you have any questions today?"

Onesimus looked up thoughtfully. "Yes sir, what is a catamite?" The next day, according to the master's express command, the household learned that Onesimus would become Archippus personal attendant and sleep on a pad in the master's room. And so by attempting to save the boy's innocence, he confirmed the opinion of his associates.

The Cult of the Household

We know only in part. It is difficult enough to explain the process of how a child learns to read and write, but it must be told; for it was well known to those who knew Onesimus in later life that he had a prodigious memory; it was not just a gift of the gods, in some way it was the gift of Platon who compelled him to memorize Homer's epic when he was twelve years old. It was not merely the work of Platon; every member of the household, shaped every other member.

Apphia did not think of herself as a religious woman; she rarely attended festivals and could not be bothered with pomp and processions. Her household was never on the list of those who had contributed toward a new robe for the statue of the goddess. However she did

have a small shrine on the wall of her bed chamber in which there
was a silver statuette of the goddess, a relic she had received from her
mother. Sometimes she was observed standing in front of the opened
shrine speaking silently in prayer. She kept an alabaster lachrymal
nearby for collecting her tears. She paid no attention to the devotional
habits of any of her servants or attendants, and she made no provision
for the religious instruction of her son. However, she encouraged him
to take part in such cultic activities as were common to boys of his city.
One household custom was observed by all. Everyone who lived in
the house whether slave or free, male or female, participated in story
telling. On long summer evenings in the cool of the peristyle most of
the household would gather, women sitting on cushions, men on their
haunches, and listen to one of their number spin a tale.

Old Phryx had been a famous story teller, and this is probably the
reason why he was tolerated long into old age. He had tales of olden
times in the kingdom of Phrygia when Midas was a glutton for gold.
When he told how the aging king grew ass's ears, he nodded toward
Stamnion, and the jug-eared boy blushed and hung his head while
everyone was convulsed with laughter. He told of the magnificence of
the royal city of Gordion, and how Alexander had in a single blow cut
the fabled Gordion Knot, so that Phrygia was no more than an outpost
of the Greeks. The family of Archippus and Apphia had Greek origins,
but a family does not occupy a territory for over three hundred years
without some admixture with the natives. Everyone in that room was
familiar enough with the Gordian cap, a woolen affair, pointed to cover
the ears of Midas.

When Phryx had completed his tale, Ifiti, Apphia's serving maid,
told the melancholy story of Iphigenia—how her father tried to sacrifice
her to the wind and the sea and how she spent the rest of her lonely
days at the altar of the Goddess who saved her, the very goddess who
protected the Phrygian lands.

Then Platon in the long winter nights told of the marvelous adventures of Jason who sailed into the Pontic Sea, seeking the golden
fleece. Platon warmed the cold nights with those adventures. Apphia

had braziers lit, and her couch brought in so that she did not become wearied with the tale. Even Archippus dropped by and seemed to enjoy the rehearsal of the old story.

When the spring festival came, Archippus suggested a wonderful holiday, and the whole household trooped to Laodicea where there is a theater in the Greek style. For a whole day they heard the actors strain their voices, and marvelled at the glorious costumes as they enacted the ancient drama of Medea. Apphia, Philemon and Archippus sat in a front row, next to the town dignitaries; the house-servants sat high up the hill side where the seats were hard and the sun was merciless, but they all enjoyed the performance, especially when the Witch Medea flew in her dragon-born chariot across the roof top. Philemon and Onesimus were wide-eyed with excitement, but Onesimus from his high position could see the backstage slaves sweating as they cranked the ropes.

One evening they turned to Leah and she responded with a tale from her people. She told how Judas Maccabaeus fought against the wicked tyrant who used an army of elephants against them. For days after the boys would dive under a table, brandishing sticks for swords, as they stabbed at the maddened elephants' undersides. Even the houseboys made a plea to go to a circus in a nearby town where there were real elephants baited by dogs; but Archippus coldly turned down the suggestion. Archippus had no truck with circuses.

Apphia begged for a good story about a good woman instead of battles and bloodshed; so Leah found another story about the beautiful Queen Esther. The women of the house found the tale charming, and the boys were already building a gallows in the courtyard upon which to hang any Mordecai who might come into their presence.

At last they wheedled a story from Archippus who told them of the Egyptian Queen Cleopatra and her lover who was a Roman Soldier. This was a true story and happened not so long ago, and on our very coastland.

Leah had not been in the house very long before she began to take Onesimus to the market with her. She had no children of her own,

and this little waif brought out her mothering instincts. She gave him
bundles of vegetables to carry for she pretended to need his help. And
when they got back home she would press a small copper into his hand
which was good for a cookie or a sweet at the baker's shop. One need
not think that the slaves were watched like prisoners. It is the Romans
who fear the results of the bad treatment which they dole out. There
were many ways for our slaves to escape for an hour or two, and two
innocent eyes often looked up and pleaded, "I didn't know you were
looking for me."

Onesimus sometimes begged for a story for Leah to tell him alone,
"a story about a slave boy, perhaps. Are there no stories for us?" Leah
told him of the boy Joseph, sold as a slave in Egypt, and how he at last
was almost as powerful as Pharaoh himself.

Archippus usually stayed away from the noise of the household.
He stayed in his library though no one could imagine what were his
interests there. It was there that he kept a fragment of *The Black Stone*,
a part of the very rock that the Phrygians had sent to the Romans against
the invading Hannibal. It was rumored that in the parchment scrolls
hidden in that room were magical spells for calling up the demons who
rule the streams and mountains, and that he also knew ways to conjure
up the spirits of the dead. No one had seen him do it, it is true; but
there had to be some reason for his need for privacy.

Archippus was a seeker after truth. In his late teens he had taken
leave of his father in a not entirely friendly way. He had gone off to
Rhodes to study, but he seemed to have been a lot of places that were
not on that island. He had, indeed studied; for he knew the works
of poets, and the rules of the rhetorician. He could look at the stars
and plot their journeys; he knew what plants were good for medicines;
and he could build a wall straight against a leveling rule. About these
things, however, he kept his silence.

In his early years the man had devoted himself to philosophy. At
first with the Epicureans he rejected the warnings of dour ethicists that
forbid dalliance with pleasure. He could quote:

"As for all the torments that take place in the depths of Hell, they

are here, in our own lives. There is no wretched Tantalus transfixed with terror at the boulder poised above him. In life mortals are transfixed by the fear of the gods and impending doom which may fall upon them by chance."

Then with the Stoics he struggled for a presentation of truth; but each time he thought that he had a grasp upon this truth, like a phantasm it drifted out of his hand. One must have knowledge to know truth; but even a child or a mad man is likely to say something true in the course of events. Yet even the wise man may propound something in his knowledge which is false. With such a philosophy one is not inclined to bandy words about.

There was Philo, the Jew, who proclaimed that the soul differs from the physical body; and he demonstrated three ways in which this was so. For the mind is the sight of the soul, which shines brilliantly with its own rays, and it dissipates the darkness which ignorance covers.

At last Archippus had returned home and found there the problems that hold families and communities together; but he suffered from the malaise of the philosopher, melancholy. Now he began to yearn after the boy and feel sorrow for him.

All these thoughts do not come in a day. Life in a family moves slowly, but soon enough it was time for Philemon to leave his primary school. He was enrolled in a secondary school which had been established for the noble youths of the city, though nobility is relative. The young men who studied under the grammarian in Colossae may well have been snubbed by a more sophisticated peer in Pergamon. Still he was becoming acquainted with the great poets and thinkers of time past. He was a middlin' scholar and preferred sports. He frequently came in second or third in the races; he was good at jumping, but he preferred throwing the disc or even the javelin; boxing and wrestling he did not particularly enjoy.

Philemon was growing tall and muscular, and standing naked, shining with oil, he was fit to be a model for any sculptor. His mother was proud of him; Archippus found him satisfactory; and his old school-mate Onesimus admired him. Indeed, Philemon and Onesimus remained on fairly good terms frequently sharing pleasures between themselves and household gossip. However, there always remained the sense of demarcation of class which neither one was willing to overstep.

Apphia noted that soon her son would enter the civil ephebic order. This was meaningful to her for it seemed that she had once almost lost this Hellenistic civic duty when she married into a Phrygian family, no matter how ancient or well-established. So one day she spoke to her brother and suggested that it would be appropriate to take a house in Hierapolis for the sacred season. Hierapolis was scarcely a day's journey; but there were certain sacred duties there which had been neglected and now ought to be re-established. She herself had made a vow to the Great Mother that she would visit the holy places, and she felt that Philemon should make himself properly introduced in certain cultic practices before he became an ephebe.

Archippus was amenable, remarking that he too would like to renew his acquaintance with the religion of his ancestors. Furthermore, he understood that Hierapolis had become a gathering place for some of the mystics of the East about whom he would like to understand more.

So it was that a considerable amount of furniture, draperies and utensils together with bedclothes and changes of wardrobe for each family member were packed and carried by both their slaves to a cottage in Hierapolis, close by a steaming pool. When all was settled only the family remained: Apphia and Ifiti; Leah, Philemon, Onesimus and Archippus, with Asterion to be the houseboy. Stamnion and the cook would stay to guard the possessions in Colossae. Leah and Ifiti would share the cooking in Hierapolis. It was an exciting time for all, for only Archippus had ever spent so much time away from home.

Hierapolis

Hierapolis was a pilgrims' town; the property-owning residents made their livings in ways that accommodate travellers. There were merchants who dealt in foodstuffs, but there were more tavernae than vegetable markets. A tourist can be satisfied with a beaker of beer and a cake more easily than a vegetable. There were merchants who specialized in cloth, purple wool, dyed with madder root which is set in its color by the wondrous waters found only there. Many sold pots and candles, shoes and caps, and knick-knacks from abroad. Most commonly seen were the shopkeepers who specialized in statuettes, particularly of the goddess and her train, and in small cups and dishes meant for sacrifices. One could buy rough miniatures of arms and legs, which had been healed though once broken; eyes and ears to accompany prayers for healing, and small rolled parchments with prayers and curses written upon them.

The town boasted of moneychangers who could change any foreign coin into the temple coins which bore the likenesses of Hygieia and Asclepias. With these, sacrifices and prayers could be bought in the precincts of the temples.

The narrow streets were filled with carts and donkeys, mules and even camels, and all manner of men and women scurrying about their business or simply gawking at the sights. The business of the town was religion, and the local citizenry fattened upon it from priest to hierodule. Lacking any other occupation, many of the locals rented out accommodations for the foreigners. There were innkeepers who offered unkempt cells with flea-filled sleeping mats; there were stables where provender could be had for pack animals and horses. Many who came pitched their tents outside the temple limits and set up housekeeping wherever they found space.

There were also those who offered houses where worshippers could live for a season in style. Such a place had been found by an agent for Archippus and his family. The house was near the bottom of a mountain which stretched upward to where its tree-lined summit met the sky. Shade from the mountain kept the house cool in even during scorching summer heat. In March one might need a cloak to keep warm. Near this hillside the Goddess Cybele had long ago made herself a marbled home with white terraces stretching down the mountain top to the valley below. Over the white marbles, cascades of warm water bubbled and flowed, not as a gushing torrent but quietly bathing the whole hillside in their steaming waters which collected in pools below where worshippers gathered to bathe their tired and broken limbs. The waters were channeled into fountains into which the faithful dipped their cups and hands for the these springs were powerful medicine. The Greeks had brought the priests of Asclepias to establish a healing center here with shrines to the great Doctor God and his goddess Hygieia.

When the terraces were bathed in the morning sunlight, the worshippers proclaimed the glory of the Goddess. When the terraces shone ghostly pale in the white moonlight, the worshipper felt the power of light throughout his entire body. There were times when to be there, and to see this sight was as though one walked on and through a cloud, so lovely were the terraces.

Some of the fortunate owners of houses at the bottom of the hill had pools wherein the warm waters had collected, and around them they had planted gardens and laid out furniture so that they could spend the day time absorbed in delight, and the evenings warming their bodies as in waters of the bathing pools.

Such a house had been rented for the family during the time of the equinox, which is the holy season when the soft breezes of spring banish the winter cold. The hills turn green and all manner of flowers begin to bloom. Archippus knew that the crowds would be pressing and the rents would be even higher than usual tourist charges. The summer heat discouraged many travellers, but in springtime, everyone feels welcomed, and the presence of the goddess encouraged the pilgrim to come.

Even before the household was settled Apphia, accompanied by Ifiti, climbed up to the upper pool to find the place where the waters fall over the rocky cliffs and down the famous terraces. For a while they forgot their roles as staid matrons and with eagerness of girls climbed over rocks and tree roots in search of freedom of their spirits. It was as if they might at any moment discover Kubaba, the ancient

Phrygian goddess, taking flight in her golden chariot. It was said that the Lady Mother's lions still lurked in the woodlands though few were privileged to meet with them. After this frolic, the ladies returned to their house, vowing that the next day, properly attired, they would visit the Temple that leads to the underworld, and beside the sacred pine tree they would weep for the wounded Attis.

Archippus viewed his sister's enthusiasm in good humor, and announced that on the next day he would show Philemon the monuments of the town, and that Onesimus should accompany them. Early in the morning, while it was still cool, the three walked through the monumental gate and down the Sacred Way. The buildings on either side were magnificent in the Greek Style. Predominant was the great temple to Apollo, though this god is known by many another name.

"Truly he is The Invincible Sun, the source of all life," explained Archippus in his best didactic manner. "If I were to worship any god, it would be He."

The boys stood in awe, wondering if they were to enter, but the uncle waved them on, "There will be plenty of time for that," he announced. "Today we will just see what Hierapolis has to offer." A great fountain, dedicated to the Nymphs, stood in front of the Temple; the boys let their hands play in the water and soon discovered that the water was not only warm, but it had an effervescent quality that stung their tongues and made their noses quiver.

Not far away were the Baths, a magnificent building, with the Gymnasium close by. Workmen were busying themselves with construction work here, for the Emperor Claudius had made himself the benefactor of the city and was making Roman improvements which would certainly work to the city's profit. Farther on, on a hillside that overlooks the entire Lycus Valley, was the theater. Here one could see in the distance the city of Laodicea on the opposite bank of the Lycus and to the north the juncture of the Lycus to the Meander River. Archippus stopped to give the boys a geography lesson.

By this time the sun was high and a summerlike heat was becoming obtrusive, so taking a short cut path outside the walls, they found their way home.

"You're on your own now," announced Archippus. "Onesimus, you stay with Philemon."

After a lunch the boys ran for the gymnasium.

"Who is this Attis that you should weep for him?" asked Leah of Apphia who was examining her wardrobe for the day.

"Who is he?" exclaimed Apphia. "He is the beloved of the Great Mother herself. He was wounded by the tusk of a boar and shed all his blood. When Kubaba found him she wept all her tears over his body, and the power of her tears brought him to life again."

"Well, if he has been restored to life, why are you weeping?"

"It's a symbol, dear Leah. Attis is the symbol of all mortals who die. Our weeping is for our own mortality. By weeping for Attis we may restore ourselves and our souls, like the soul of Attis, will be given a new life instead of death."

"And you believe this?" asked Leah in wonder.

"It is as the old hymn goes,

> *O Mystoi, be courageous and brave*
> *As now you see him wan and breathless*
> *Your tears will Lord Attis save*
> *Like Him you will be deathless.*

Archippus looked up from his note taking and commented, "I believe this same Attis is known to the Thracians as *Kurios Sabazios* which is in your language, Leah, *Yahveh Sabaoth*. Indeed the Romans equate Sabazios with Jupiter himself."

At this mention of the Lord of Hosts the color drained from the face of Leah. "Well, I never . . ." she muttered to herself and quickly left the discussion for her Gentile employers to continue by themselves. Apphia and Ifiti were completing their costumes by wrapping scarlet shawls around their shoulders. They had taken the pins from their coiffures and were dishevelling their hair, letting it fall loosely. They determined that they would wear their sandals until they came within sight of the sacred pine tree, and then discalce themselves to finish the course barefoot.

"No use bruising your tender feet too badly," commented Archippus wryly. "Have you kept your nails long enough to make the scratches on your pretty cheeks?"

Apphia looked at him scornfully. "A little less levity from you and a little more piety is in order if you want to save your own soul."

Her brother chuckled as the two women left. They walked through the great gate and down the Sacred Way until the road turned toward the cave called "The Jaws of Hades." In front of the entrance grew a lone pine tree, somewhat scraggly because it was almost stripped of its branches as high as a human arm can reach. Nor were they alone, for a great crowd of women was already gathered there, wailing and moaning. Some did indeed scratch their faces with fingernails grown long for just this purpose. Others poured handfuls of dust and gravel over their heads. Soon several *galli* came out of the cave with tambourines and hand drums, and chanted an absolution of forgiveness, while lesser *douloi* passed among them with baskets for their offerings of the temple coins. Leah took the time when the other ladies of the household were away to visit with some friends of her girlhood who now lived in Hierapolis. After catching up on their personal histories and relating her own station in life, they turned their conversation to other news of import.

"There are those among us who say that the Messiah has already come," someone began a new topic of conversation.

"Of course, there are those who say that," retorted another. "There are always Messiahs coming and going. What is special about this one?"

"Nothing unusual," reported the first speaker. "Except that this one came to Jerusalem at the time of Passover. It was when Pontius Pilatus was governor. And he was executed for treason; executed, I believe, in the Roman way, by crucifixion."

"That's barbarous," exclaimed Leah. "Only the Romans would torture a poor misled soul to his death."

"It's thoughtless too," added another. "Suppose the man had really been the Messiah. God would seek retribution, for as Scripture says,

'He is a jealous God'."

"I wouldn't have mentioned it, for it wouldn't have been news—except witnesses are appearing throughout all of Asia, saying that this Messiah rose from the dead on the third day after he had been officially executed," explained the first speaker.

"And with what proof do they deduce that," asked one incredulously, while the others smiled somewhat smugly.

"It's hard to say," replied the speaker, "But there is a man here in Hierapolis who is preaching this new doctrine, and he claims friendship with two or three persons in Ephesus who testify to the actuality of the event. They say they were actually present when it happened."

"Oh, well, the *goyim* will believe anything. Do any Jews believe it?"

"As a matter of fact, the answer is 'Yes'; there are some Jews who believe it. They say that the resurrected one was an Angel, Metatron perhaps, or the Angel that met Tobias on his way."

Leah replied thoughtfully, "I suppose God could send His angel to give us warning of things to come, but the Messiah is supposed to be descended from David's line; that would not be an angel."

"This may be a good time to test this thing," continued the speaker, "For it is almost time for the Passover; indeed our first Seder is tomorrow night, and we would be pleased, dear Leah, for you to be our guest. It is said that this Jeshua, this Saviour, was crucified on the eve of the Passover. Perhaps like Attis he will rise for us."

Leah was scandalized more at the levity than from the crucifixion on Passover Eve; but it was time for her to return home, so she put the matter out of her mind with no thought that anything would come of it.

Before another day had passed, Archippus realized that he had something of importance to deal with. Early next morning he and Philemon set out alone for the temple of Apollo.

"You are now sixteen," explained Archippus, "and soon your secondary education will be over. We must plan for your future."

This is what Philemon had expected, and their destination in the

Temple of Apollo was not unanticipated.

"We have not been a religious family," continued the uncle some-what slowly for he did not feel that he was on very solid ground. "But every young man must realize that it is necessary to pay some respect to the Gods and to recognize that he has a duty to his City."

Aware that his nephew was not listening very closely, Archippus strengthened his voice and spoke more clearly.

"If any City or State is to survive it must have laws and a leadership to practice them. Now leaders must have some basis for their beliefs and their decisions; if a city does not have such leaders it will fall victim to the whims of every demagogue who tickles its fancy."

Philemon nodded in agreement; it was the comment expected from schoolmasters and uncles.

"Well," continued his uncle, "certainly among the gods the one most worthy to be revered is Apollo. It is through Apollo that we have existence. I have come to believe that probably Apollo is the only God; these nymphs of lakes and streams, these oreads dancing on the mountain tops; these Poseidon-driven sea horses—these are all simply fantasies. Apollo, the Invincible Sun, is the source of power."

Philemon really had no argument, but he felt that he was obliged to show that he had assimilated some learning in the matter. "What about Zeus, the father of the Gods? Is he not said to be the ruler even of Apollo? And what about Cybele, the great mother? Certainly my mother Apphia has some ardor concerning her.?"

Archippus had anticipated the questions. "Zeus is merely another name for Apollo; as is Jupiter, as the Romans name him. They both mean 'The Day Spring.' But truly it is Apollo who ushers in the light and with it the day. Without light nothing would grow, and we would live in darkness and blindness, as do indeed the *galli*, the priests of Cybele who spend their days dancing in that dark cave down the street from here. They frighten women like your mother with their stories that only they can survive the noxious fumes of that place. Truly, the only thing that the fumes have done is to addle their brains. What, indeed, could Cybele, the earth Mother, bring forth if the Sun did not give out the life force?"

"Well, uncle, you speak most persuasively though I do not think that I have ever before heard you give much thought to the matter. Still, I suppose it is a useful exercise at my time of life. Is this a precursor to my going off to study in some distant city, as you did?"

Archippus restrained his remarks, for he did not wish to find himself in a discussion about his personal beliefs. "I have contained my thoughts in my study," he replied. "And, of course, your mother and I both anticipate that you will wish to continue your studies with some fine philosopher."

By this time they were approaching the Temple. They lengthened their strides as they took the high steps up to the level of the sanctuary. Inside they could hear the chants of the votaries echoing off the marbled stones.

"Apollo! Apollo! Apollo!" they sang in unison and beat slowly upon their drums. Looking down upon them was Apollo Himself; a twelve foot bronze representation of Apollo imposed his presence upon them. Archippus led his charge to a nearby booth where a scribe was waiting.

"You must ask a question concerning your future; if you are fortunate, he will write you a prognosis."

Philemon looked dubiously at his uncle, but received no message in his eyes. Archippus merely took some gold coins with the Hygieia stamp and put them on the scribe's table. The scribe pushed a scrap of parchment toward Philemon and gave him an ink stained stylus.

"What is to be my lot?" wrote Philemon on the papyrus strip. The scribe took the writing and disappeared behind a column. In a short time he returned and presented Philemon with a small rolled scroll sealed with red wax. Philemon looked to his uncle for advice.

Archippus covered his hand and whispered, "Take it home with you, and read it when you are alone."

The two watched the worship of the votaries for awhile; then they followed the story of Apollo and Cassandra who, when she betrayed Apollo's love for her, was given the double-sided gift of prophecy:

always to prophesy true, but never to be believed.

"A fate fit for any prophet," sniffed Archippus. Relieved that he had properly instructed his nephew in religion, Archippus went about his business for the afternoon and Philemon returned home. When he was alone in his room he broke the seal, unrolled the parchment and read: "Your fame will be useful."

From this he determined that in some way he would be blessed, but decided it would be best not to rely upon the blessing.

As he retreated from the temple, Archippus heard his name. When he looked around he saw there an old friend.

"Epaphrus, my old friend, how is it that I see you here?"

Epaphras, dressed simply in an unbleached chiton and not much more except for the sandals on his feet, smiled. "I belong here, my dear Archippus. It is you, I think, who are the visitor."

Archippus acknowledged the words. "In truth, I am a visitor in this city. We are making a kind of pilgrimage, you might say."

"Everyone in Hierapolis is making a pilgrimage. Are you, Archippus the philosopher, consulting the oracle about your next commercial venture? Or are you warding off a curse from one of your competitors?"

Archippus laughed genially at this joke. "As a matter of fact, my nephew is about to enter the ephebic order in Colossae and his mother had determined that he should be properly introduced to the God who ought to take note of the event."

"And where is this lad? I do not see him with you."

"I sent him home with his prediction. It will do him good to contemplate it in privacy."

"You mean, you do not want to accompany him in his discovery?"

"True enough, Epaphras. I used to dabble in some Oriental fantasies, but for the most part I have given them up. My sister, however, has come to your city to consult the Phrygian goddess. She feels that we are missing the kind of blessing known in old times. And as I grow older, I admit that the old religion has more attractiveness for me. The believers of Old Time may not have been wrong. In fact, we hear that the Emperor, Claudius himself, has favored our ancient Phrygian practices and beliefs. He has appointed Roman citizens as *archigalli*. He even aspires to that priesthood himself, if one can believe such gossip." "It seems unlikely that many Romans will accept this dubious honor. As for Claudius, we hear all manner of scandal about him. Do you mean that you would accept a belief on the slim ground that one such as Claudius proposes it?" Epaphras scolded.

"Though I do not abandon philosophy as my mother, I am willing to admit that there is some value in practicing old rites, for the old symbolisms give us insights into our lives. Claudius is our divine ruler, at least so we are taught; therefore I find it useful to search into his insights." Archippus searched slowly for words that might be politically correct.

"Ah yes, I appreciate that as a landholder you would favor rites meant to bring about the fertility of the earth and increase of crops. And here you are, swallowing down the whole cloth of some ancient superstition which will prosper your planting. I might point you to a specialist in ordures down the way who would give you a better promise of fine vegetables than the blood of Attis."

"It is not necessary to be so acerbic," laughed Archippus. "Belief in the old ways pacifies the mind and brings hope to future generations."

"The Old Age is gone," exclaimed Epaphras. "Have you not heard, my friend, that we are living in a New Age?"

"And what is this New Age of yours?" inquired Archippus.

"It is the Age of the Brotherhood of Man," stated Epaphras. "It is the age when all men shall acknowledge the one God who looks down upon and favors us all."

"Do you not believe in Apollo as the Invincible Light? I call to Apollo and even to Kubaba herself to charm my life so that I will not die tomorrow."

"No, my friend, I believe in the one God who has sent One in our Likeness to show us poor humans how we ought to live today without fear of tomorrow." Archippus looked hard at Epaphras to determine his sincerity.

"I perceive, dear friend, that you have some enthusiasm for a new kind of religion. I am busy today; but perhaps some other day I would have time to hear you out."

Epaphras smiled at Archippus, "You are hoping to escape me today, and tomorrow you will leave for home in Colossae. But you will find that I am there also. Good bye, dear friend. We shall meet again soon."

Onesimus was pleased to find himself left at last to his own devices while the master's household ran hither and thither trying to accomplish a lifetime of religious errands during a brief spring holiday. Outside the gymnasium he sat down on the bench where slaves often wait for their masters to call them. Seated beside him was a fellow strangely dressed in baggy woolen trousers and wearing the countrified woolen cap with which he had come to identify as belonging to rural Phrygia.

"Am I to identify you as a fellow Phrygian?" he asked.

"Indeed, you should so identify me," the fellow responded, "and I am proud to be one. Should you not be wearing a cap of liberty too, if you are a Phrygian?"

"I only know what I have been told," apologized Onesimus. "My friend Stamnion wears such a cap now and then, but the master does not care for it."

"I should think not," replied the Phrygian. "This Phrygian cap is known in the city of Rome as the Liberty Cap. For manumitted slaves, Phrygian or not, have taken to wearing it as a symbol of their freedom."

"Are you then a freed man?" asked Onesimus with awe.

"Only in spirit," replied his new found friend. "While there is one who rules over me as a master of my body, he cannot deny me my soul."

"How then, does he allow you to wear these as symbols of freedom?" asked Onesimus.

"For two reasons perhaps. I tell him that these garments are required by my religion, and the master has sworn not to interfere with the religions of his slaves." the slave chuckled.

"And the other reason?" asked Onesimus.

"The second reason is that the master is a rustic fellow who hasn't heard about what is the latest fashion in Rome."

Onesimus was delighted, "I think I shall get myself a Phrygian cap. My master also does not interfere with the religion of slaves. Perhaps that is being too affirming. My master doesn't even interfere with the religion of his own household; he does not believe in religion, he says. Hm, perhaps I shall get myself some trousers too. That will show up old Stamnion."

"Well, good luck to you," laughed his friend. "But don't blame me if you bring down a bucket of trouble around your ears. By the way, what makes you think you are a Phrygian? Your ears are not long, and you look like a Greek to me."

Onesimus bristled, "My mother was a Phrygian, and my father was the North Wind."

"Shake, pal," and his new friend ran off at his master's whistle.

And so passed, pleasantly enough, the days of a week. Apphia was resting in her own quarters, and Leah had gone off to another Passover celebration of some kind. Philemon had been invited to a supper at the house of a new found friend. As for Archippus, his bones ached from all the running around and he was happy to escape the madness for a time.

"Come," he called to Onesimus, "bring some oil and some of those soft cotton sheets and we will seek the warmth of the lower pool."

Onesimus was trying on the jaunty peaked cap he had purchased for himself. He decided not to introduce it at this moment. "It would probably shrink in the hot water," he said to himself.

The bright moonlight lit their way down to the water. They walked into it rather gingerly for the bottom of the pool harbored the ruins of what had once been a small marble temple. The temple had fallen during one of the frequent earthquakes some years before and the water covered the ruin. The owners of the pool had made no effort to restore it, but left it as a charming underwater shrine for those who ventured to swim into it. By day this was a pleasant adventure, but at night it was a bit more hazardous. The two glided through the warm water to a place where a casement rose a little above the water and made a convenient pillow for their heads. Here they lay floating in the soothing waters. It was a moment of delight.

"Have you been enjoying yourself in Hierapolis?" Archippus inquired.

"Yes, indeed, it has been quite pleasant," replied Onesimus, "though there are many things I do not understand."

"And what is it that troubles you?" asked Archippus.

"I really do not understand about religion," said the boy gravely. "I have read something of the gods in Homer, and now and then I find them mentioned by poets and story tellers; but in that context they are remote, whereas here everyone seems to find gods at their fingertips and can bring them up at their command."

"You speak right about that," said Archippus. "And I find myself sorry to say that you have not been instructed in religious matters, or duties. In fact, neither Philemon nor you have had any such training. It is an oversight which I ought to correct."

"Well, who is Kubaba? She certainly is not in The Epic." Onesimus was a little petulant.

"Kubaba is the Phrygian name for The Great Mother. The Romans mispronounce it into *Cybele*. And many of the surrounding peoples call her name *Astarte* or *Ashteroth*. She is the one called *Artemis* by the Greeks. Her symbol is the new moon, and she travels about in a golden chariot drawn by lions. Her worshippers claim her as the Mother of All, and so at this time of the year she is called upon to make the crops grow well."

Onesimus was confused and uncomprehending, "And who is this Attis, then?"

"Attis is her lover, though some say that he is her son. Still others claim that Attis is her husband. He also goes by the name of Adonis, which is to say, "Lord." At a certain point in the story Attis is out in the woodlands and is attacked by a ferocious boar who gores him with his tusks. So Attis died of his wounds, poor godling; and now his priests cut down a pine tree to represent his dead body. Wrapping it in a net woven of violets and other sweet smelling herbs, they carry it to its resting place in the earth. So now the women wail, and the *galli* flagellate themselves, offering their own blood in a senseless orgy. The neophytes in a fit of madness castrate themselves with flint knives until enough blood has flowed to revive the pine-tree. Then suddenly the dead Attis springs up, horny as ever, and goes chasing after Kubaba—who is, I believe, his mother, or is she his wife?"

Onesimus was even more bewildered and unbelieving. His naivete was contagious and Archippus was soon laughing at his own demonstration.

He continued, "Yes indeed, Kubaba is that same whom others call Leto and Leto's son is Apollo himself. The genealogy of the gods gets a little confusing at times."

Onesimus wondered, "I have learned that Leto means *death*, and Apollo is appropriately named *Destroyer*."

Archippus agreed, "Indeed, there are many double meanings. Leto's other name is Hecate and she presides over the dead. Upon my word, there is that *hex*, that incomplete six. Out of the mouths of babes, . . . excuse me, my dear boy, my mind was wandering. Yes indeed, there are hidden truths that need to be opened up. We must not forget the Old Ones."

"You have found the meaning of Squiggle?" asked Onesimus and both of them laughed.

Onesimus became serious, "If Kubaba is a Phrygian goddess, then perhaps I should be worshipping her."

"Why you?" asked Archippus.

"Because I am a Phrygian," proclaimed Onesimus.

"And what makes you believe that you are a Phrygian?" asked Archippus in wonder.

"Because of this," said Onesimus, showing Archippus the blue stone which he wore usually under his tunic, but now his nakedness did not hide it. "My mother gave me this; the overseer told me so. Phrygians draw power from the stones of the earth and this is precious." Onesimus suddenly put his hand over his mouth realizing that he might be endangering the stone.

Archippus thought a moment and replied, "It may be true that your mother was Phrygian, but you also had a father."

"My father was the North Wind," stated Onesimus.

"That is a ridiculous statement," snorted Archippus. "Your father like any other father was a man."

"It is a way we have of explaining it," said Onesimus simply. "We slaves may know who our mother was, but we have no way of knowing our fathers, so we blame our birth upon the vagrant wind."

Archippus reached over and took the boy by the hand. "My dear son, I am your father."

Onesimus looked at him uncomprehending. "That blue bead, is it not upon a golden chain? It was I who gave the chain to your mother."

Onesimus felt a sudden chill upon the water and he shivered as he turned away.

"Dear son, have I ever treated you in any other way than a father should? I know that others may have accused our relationship as being other than virtuous; but you know that I have acted always as your father."

Tears formed in Onesimus eyes and slowly he swam away to the poolside, leaving Archippus alone.

The family returned home after their too brief holiday. In retrospect the events had not proved as exciting as the prospect. They had expected sounding brass, but had heard only the tinkling of a cymbal.

For whatever expectations there had been for the holiday in Hierapolis, there was a feeling of unfulfillment, as Apphia expressed it to Leah.

"I had thought that I might find myself there; I had hoped that we could restore some of the excitement that seemed to fill our ancestors. We would sing the old songs, dance the old dances, make sacrifices and chant the old prayers. Well, we did it; but nothing happened. It was as though we were play acting, and not living real life at all. I had hoped for Philemon's sake that we could inject some spirit into our lives; but nothing happened."

Leah murmured her sympathy. She had already heard from Philemon. "It was so silly. All those fake priests, they call them *galli*, hopping around and yowling like sick dogs to the gods. And there was my mother standing there barefoot with her hair hanging loose, pretending to tear at her skin with her fingernails. Of course, when it was over, there wasn't a mark on her. And the temple agents all standing around with their hands out for whatever coin they could get."

"I'm sorry you didn't have a better time of it on your holiday," sympathized Leah. "I had thought that you and your young pals were quite active."

"Oh, that," shrugged the young master. "There were a lot of us there with our parents, mothers especially. And they do have a pretty snappy gymnasium. There's a fair race track; but the theater really didn't have very good shows—old Greek stuff, you know, the Classics. Even the Comedies were old. Swimming in the pools was pretty good, but Archippus wouldn't let me go to any of the real parties. Gad, but he is a fuddy-duddy. He wouldn't even let Onesimus attend me; sent me out with old Asterion to keep me out of trouble, he said."

Leah smiled to herself. Her own observance was that there was plenty of devilment for a young man to get into, though Asterion was hardly the man she would have picked to keep the young master out of it. As for herself, she hurried off to visit with her family and friends as soon as she could find free time.

Quickly she apprised them of all the news from the Jewish community in Hierapolis. Of the latest Messiah they didn't seem to have much news, but there were those who tried to put the story in perspective.

"There was a man whose name was John," began an elder thinking backward slowly as the words came to his mind. "He was a strange man, wearing only an old sack for clothing, a sack that rasped his flesh for it was woven of camel's hair. He girded himself with a leather belt; his feet were bare and his appearance betrayed him as unkempt and uncombed. This Johannan was holding forth on the far shore of Jordan, near to where it enters the Salt Sea. Truly it is a barren land and forbidding in its landscape, far away from any settled town. Still crowds of people flocked to see him and to take in what he had to say.

It wasn't long before the authorities in Jerusalem took note of it and sent the temple police out to investigate, not wanting any incidents against law and order.

The captain came up to John and said, "Just who do you think you are?"

And John was an insolent fellow who blabbed back, "Well, who do you think I am?"

And so they played out the guessing game. One said, "Are you the Messiah?" That's always the first question; if you can get them on that, you don't have to go any farther. You can take the joker in right then. But this Johannan was canny.

"No, I am not Messiah," he said.

A second agent took over, "Are you Elijah?" Well, he looked like Elijah, what with the shirt of camel's hair and the diet of locusts and wild honey. It was a good question. Half of the inhabitants of Judah are expecting Elijah down from heaven any day.

But Johannan says, "No, I'm not Elijah."

So the third guard came straight out and asked, "Are you the prophet?"

And the cagey old geezer denied it. Said he didn't know anything about messiahs so how could he prophesy about him? They asked him other questions too, like what was he doing. But he just kept saying that he was washing away people's sins in the river water, because everyone is filthy with sin. He claimed to be washing the sins away and telling his people to go back home and behave themselves. The police couldn't fault him for that so they left him alone. But everyone knew that he was really saying that the "Long Expected One" was on his way and that he would soon be here. And from what I hear, there are those who say that this Messiah did appear, teaching people and working miracles. But when I hear that, I usually drift away. I have enough troubles of my own without getting myself entangled with Messiahs and false Elijahs. However, there is a little group of believers not many houses down, who are followers of this very Johannan."

Others of Leah's family nodded agreement, but no one else was willing to speak of it.

Leah went back to her place of employment feeling confused and not a little unsettled.

Still there were other things to talk about. The slave Onesimus had grown quite cocky of late. He had taken to wearing a woolen Phrygian cap, even during the day; and evenings he was seen lolling about with no work to keep him busy and wearing of all things, woolen trousers, which came down almost to his ankles where they were tied to keep them from dragging on the ground. The house slaves were interested even to the point of admiration, and kept asking Onesimus what it meant. Asterion said that it was the fashion among some of the slaves that they had met in Hierapolis. It is true that Stamnion had affected such a cap now and then, but never so openly.

Old Archippus said nothing about it and seemed to tolerate the actions of his slave.

Platon, when questioned, shrugged and disclaimed any knowledge of his student's actions. "He is studying his lessons and is developing into a talented calligrapher," he explained. "The rest of it is none of my affair."

Meanwhile it was noted that Onesimus frequented the slave huts near the river, and often went down and spent the evenings with young friends there. Archippus yearned after the boy, but said nothing for he feared losing him should he become too antagonistic. So far there had been little conversation between them.

Platon had undertaken to rearrange the files in Archippus' library. From odd corners and shelves, from table tops and piles on the floor, he had collected scrolls. Other papers too, of various shapes and sizes and of seeming importance or unimportance he was collecting into little piles to be dealt with when the time came; but first came the scrolls, for their represented a sizable investment which the master failed to acknowledge or care for. He identified the obvious, and whenever Archippus entered the room, Platon would run to him with something as yet unidentified. Now he had found a work that seemingly had been a part of something longer, but he could not find where it belonged. To be sure, Platon had limited knowledge of only a few works; nevertheless, he was industriously applying himself to the job, and was extending his own learning. He presented the scroll to Archippus who began to shuffle around through some loose pieces inside.

In a short time Archippus sat down as he perused bits and pieces, musing more to himself than anyone else.

"I haven't looked at this in years. No, not since that disastrous dinner party that I gave for the Roman legate." Then he chuckled to himself, "I was certainly more politically naive in those days," and looking up at Platon, he clucked, "You know, I actually thought I could recreate a philosophical symposium and impress a couple of Roman idiots with my learning and gentility."

"It must have been a good try though," responded Platon with a certain amount of admiration.

"No, hardly. Even Apphia knew I was acting the fool. But don't you know what this is?" Platon nodded negatively. "Well, put these scrolls together in the right order—so, and so, and so—" and he began shuffling short pieces of papyrus together rearranging them as he went, "Put them in the right order, and here you have a wonderful work of your famous namesake."

"You mean it is a work of Plato?" asked the would be grammarian.

"Yes, indeed. It is called *The Symposion*, and it is all about a dinner party attended by Agathon and Socrates, and the ill-fated Alcibiades."

Platon took the scroll eagerly, "You mean the time when they all gave speeches about Love? Oh, sir, I should like to read that . . . "

"Not so fast," laughed Archippus. "I think I shall spend the afternoon reviewing it. When I am finished, you shall certainly have it. And I shall expect a critique from you. I value your opinion."

"Oh, sir, you do me so much honor," and Platon beamed at the compliment and almost shook in anticipation.

Archippus sat down at the table with the papyri spread out before him.

"Ah yes, here is where I became misled," he mused.

dots for my proposal is that we should deliver a full-dress

oration in praise of love, each one from left to right, and
Phaedrus must begin first, since he is in the first place . . .

Archippus read the words slowly and aloud to himself; for the words
were in no way separated into their entities, and there were no marks to
show where a speech began or ended. Many times the reader pointed
to the letters with his finger; while Platon leaned over his shoulder
peering hard to see what the master was reading.

> *Of Love Hesiod had said one thing, but Parmenides "con-*
> *trived Love the first of all the Gods."*

"Hesiod is an ancient authority," said Platon.
"But Parmenides was the better philosopher," responded Archip-
pus.
Platon hastened to agree.

> *Love is most ancient among them, being most ancient, he*
> *is the cause for the greatest good for us. For I cannot say*
> *what is a greater good for a man in his youth than a lover,*
> *and for a lover than a beloved.*

"Ah, yes, Platon; in my innocence I thought we could invent pretty
speeches such as this at our own banquet."
"And did you, sir?" asked Platon.
"My dear man, the guests were a Roman soldier and a political
appointee."
"That must have been quite disappointing, sir. But I understand."
And both of them laughed.
"But look, there is more.

> *If any device could be found how a state or an army*
> *could be made up only of lovers and beloved, they could*
> *not possibly find a better way of living, since they would*
> *abstain from all ugly things and be ambitious in beautiful*
> *things towards each other; and in battle side by side,*
> *such troops although few would conquer pretty well all*

the world. For the lover would be less willing to be seen by his beloved than by all the rest of the world leaving the ranks or throwing away his arms, and he would choose to die many times rather than that . . .

"Hm, an army of lovers, what an idea." While Archippus paused, Platon read on—

There must be two Loves, two goddesses. One is older, and motherless, daughter of Heaven. We call her Heavenly Aphrodite. The younger is the daughter of Zeus and Dione, whom we call "Common." And the work of this Aphrodite is called Common love, and the other is Heavenly Love . . .

Archippus picked up the work again,

Common Aphrodite is truly common and works at random, and she is the love which inferior men feel. Such persons love firstly, women as well as boys; next when they love, they love bodies rather than souls. . . .

Archippus stopped. "Leave me now awhile, Platon. I need to read this again and more carefully. I had wholly forgotten what is said here and I need time for review and even contemplation."

So Platon left the room and Archippus continued to read, even when the daylight waned and he had to light lamps which did not give off enough light to brighten the fading letters.

When Platon came in the next morning, he found the scroll rolled up but still in the middle of the table. He could not resist. When Archippus came by he noted his scholar hunched over the unrolled parchment. Smiling he tiptoed out of the house and sought the sunny street outside.

The warren of alleys and streets in that part of Colossae reached a knot in the Portico of the Nereids. Here there was a colonnade of arches that gave protection from the hot sun. Benches were conveniently placed for resting and small gatherings. In the center there was a fountain decorated with statuettes of maidens who poured the water from the water jars. Children played games marking the pavements of the portico; women came down from their crowded apartments to fill their own water jars; and men gathered for company and conversation. Archippus often resorted to this place to find companionship, nor was he disappointed on this particular morning. Scarcely had he found a seat when Epaphras spied him from across the square.

"My old friend, there is hardly anyone I am more desirous of seeing on this fine morning," called Epaphras.

"I thank you for your words," called out Archippus. "I am sure the gods have arranged our meeting on this fine morning."

"And what brings you to that conclusion?" asked Epaphras.

"My reading, my dear fellow. Only last night I labored long over a book which I am sure that you must know. I was renewing my acquaintance with Socrates in Plato's famous *Symposium*. I remembered that the last time we met we had a few words about love and friendship, and now I am all boned up on the subject and ready to take you on."

Epaphras laughed, "I fear you will take unfair advantage of me. I have not read this work. Tell me, what thesis do you expound?"

Archippus proceeded, "One speaker points out that there are two goddesses of love, one the Aphrodite of base love, and the other the Aphrodite of noble love. Therefore, I would take it, *love*, as we understand it, is not one thing."

Epaphras professed some interest so the speaker continued.

"Base love, I would take it, is such as we find men professing for women, and many times for boys. It is carnal—physical, I take it; and yet necessary, if we are to continue our race."

"To be sure," responded Epaphras, "but perpetuation of the race does not require the carnal knowledge of boys."

"Of course not," Archippus defended himself, "Still it is the same physical urge which brings man and boy together. It is *eros, paideros*, we call it."

"This is not a universal practice, you know," said Epaphras wryly, "though it seems so among the Greeks. You say Socrates advocates it?"

"Well, no, I do not say that. There has been some hint that there may have been such a relationship between Socrates and the handsome Alcibiades; but of Alcibiades there has always been much gossip. The *Symposium* does not suggest that Socrates was a pederast. But actually, I did not mention base love in order to praise it; I mentioned it in order to differentiate it from noble love."

"Which is?"

"The elder Aphrodite. It is the expression of love and admiration that a man develops for a fine and handsome boy, one who is well born and needs a noble example upon which to model his life. Likewise the boy develops an admiration or 'love,' if you will, for his lover. This love ennobles both of them. It causes men to be brave and act heroically, for they would not demean themselves in the eyes of their loved ones. And it causes young men to strive for the honor which inspires their lovers. This kind of love is the very essence of honor and glory for the state or the city, if you understand me."

"I have heard the theory," confessed Epaphras, "but there are points which are lost on me. Let me suggest that *love* is not a goddess, as you say, or even two goddesses. It is, instead a spirit, a virtue, or a quality that is found in human beings. I am surprised at your attribution to a goddess, for in the past you have renounced belief in the gods, as they are generally known."

"Well, so I have," admitted Archippus. "After all, this attribute, as you call it, is commonly given the name of a deity and worshipped as such. In this way Zeus becomes the personification of Justice; Apollo personifies Intelligence; Athena is Wisdom—"

"And Dionysus is Drunkenness, and this Zeus of yours is a seducer," interjected Epaphras.

"Well, of course, we can't explain all of the folk myths in this way," defended Archippus.

Rather than get into an argument, Epaphras turned the conversation away, "I think we need to consider a third kind of love. Love, you know, is not so much an attribute as it is a *passion*. It is a compulsive feeling, and I do believe that all of us experience it. Love is not limited to men of noble upbringing, you know. Yes, I mentioned base love. It is the passion men have for women, and I believe that even slaves feel it, or even dogs . . . "

Archippus winced. "You need not be ashamed of women or of slaves—or even dogs, my friend. For this passion is known and experienced even by God himself; and this God I would explain to you, if you would give me the time."

"Perhaps it would be better if you explained your third kind of love to me first. It seems as though it would be easier than trying to explain the gods," said Archippus uneasily.

"Well, first of all, do not the Greeks call this *base love* by the name of *eros?* I believe they make him out to be a boy, the son of Venus Aphrodite and Mars, to show how love and war are at war with each other and yet love. At the change of a vowel Eros becomes Eris and so every after we have a love/hate relationship between men and women."

"So, I have heard," agreed Archippus.

"And this admiration or friendship between two noble men is often referred to as *philia*. It is such a thing as father and son might have, or two brothers, or two heroes."

"Of course. For such a reason we name our towns *philadelphia*, brotherly love." I think such a distinction is helpful. Tell me now, about the third."

"Well there is a word that the Jews have. It is something like *aghav*. It means 'the passion of men for God, and the passion that God has for men.' The Jews of Alexandria have hellenized it as *agape*. It is of this kind of love that I wish to speak."

"Say on," returned Archippus.

"It was out of this feeling, this passion, that God created the world, and then created mankind. He created us as an expression of his need or feeling. Perhaps it was like a hero doing brave deeds to create admiration in his beloved. At any rate, there is only one such God, and I have heard the philosophers of the great schools expressing this opinion. That God has many of the attributes that you suggest: justice, righteousness, wisdom—all of these attributes belong to God."

"I have heard of this before, and in part I am in agreement," nodded Archippus.

"Well, human kind was created by God; but in some ways we humans have imperfections and have not entirely pleased God."

"So I am told," agreed Archippus.

"God could have destroyed his creation, but instead he looked upon it with sympathy. He longed for man's salvation, and at last he conceived a plan," continued Epaphras.

"Now, wait," said Archippus. "You are committing the same error as others do. You have made God into a man."

"Exactly," replied Epaphras. "I could not have explained it better myself."

Envious, Boastful and Arrogant

Teenage Rebellion

Archippus soon noticed the change in Onesimus, but he chose to ignore it. It made him a little proud to know that his own offspring did not lack in spirit, that indeed he could be rebellious, remembering his own youth. However, there was some danger, for rebellion in a slave was not countenanced by the law. Slave owners were expected to keep their slaves in tow; slaves who went beyond the power of their owners to discipline them were subject to the death penalties, whether the owners were willing or not. Onesimus understood this too, but was quietly testing how far his master/father could be pushed.

He still reported on time to Platon for his lessons and was diligent in his study. Platon, for his part, tried cautiously to admonish him, but Platon, too, secretly admired the boy's audacity. It was far beyond anything he would have tried. Onesimus continued to seek out Leah, if only to listen to her talk. She bantered with him, but also warned him.

"You could take a step too far, you know. You seem to have the old man in your power, but there are others to be concerned with in this household, you certainly understand that."

Onesimus laughed, "I am your servant, ma'am. Have you any errands for me to run? Any chores to be done? Your slave awaits your command."

Leah smiled and said he had a tongue like Jacob. As Onesimus grew more bold, Philemon seemed to grow more cautious. Onesimus came upon him one day while he was taking his ease in Archippus' aerie.

"You're up here contemplating your inheritance, aren't you? See the fields and the orchards down there. One day they will all be yours, and those little ants pushing their loads up that ant-hill, You'll be their master also." Philemon looked at the trousered Onesimus (for he wore his costume quite openly now).

"I don't understand you any more. I used to think of you as my brother, and now—well now you have let those trousers and a cap come between us. You're a Phrygian and I'm a Greek, so lets declare a civil war. Is that your game?"

"You're a Phrygian as much as I am," sneered Onesimus. Philemon did not bear the insult lightly. "I am a Greek, and a citizen of this city," he protested. "How do you dare name me as a Phrygian?"

"Your father was a Phrygian, and you know that. But he was a traitor and accepted foreign rule; that's why he owned this land. He danced to the ruler's tune; does that make him less a slave than the rest of us?" Philemon's face grew red as he tried to restrain himself.

"My father was accepted as a freeman, a native of this land; and my mother was of an old Greek family."

"So," taunted Onesimus, "my mother was born free, a native of this land, and her own countryman, your noble father, enslaved her. But my father was of a fine old Greek family." Philemon winced; he had heard the accusation before, but usually in whispers.

"Then why don't you honor your father?" he asked.

"My father does not choose to honor me," Onesimus replied, "So I will choose my mother."

"You are more hot-headed, than you are wise, my dear cousin. It's likely you will have to pay to your regret."

"I've already earned my keep in blows from you, dear master," and Onesimus walked away.

Philemon shook his head. He had retreated to the aerie to contem-

plate what the future held in store for him, and sensed that the seas
were stormy.

Archippus Asserts Himself

Apphia went to her brother's study.

"What brings you here?" he asked pleasantly enough.

"It's time that you suppressed the scandal that you are countenanc-
ing," she said coldly.

"And what scandal is that?" he murmured not glancing up, for he
sensed what was on her mind, and he was not ready to reply since he
had not made up his mind.

"That slave boy of yours. He seems to be quite your favorite,
and you are letting him show your weakness to the entire household;
Phrygian cap and trousers and all. You'll have the Roman guard down
on us . . . and, I've tried so hard to keep us in good standing with the
best families."

"Madam, the Roman guards don't give a fig for how our slaves
dress; and we'll be in good standing with the best families as long as
the money holds out."

Apphia drew herself up, "You forget where the money comes from;
I own this property and as soon as Philemon comes to his majority,
he will own it. Furthermore, the slave Onesimus belongs to me, for
he was born to Sambatis who was my personal slave, given me by my
husband."

Of all of this Archippus was acutely aware, but he had not before
this moment allowed himself to state his case openly.

"It is true, dear sister, that the land and fields in the valley belonged
to the family of your late husband, who had mortgaged it heavily and
was about to lose it, and maybe that is why he chose to drown himself."

Apphia grew stony white.

"However, since I was the male heir of our father, the house descended to me for he was intestate at his death. By law I became
the overseer of the entire property, and of you and your son also, if

memory serves me right. Philemon will never become the heir if I do not attest him, not even upon my death."

"That is not the agreement that we had," expostulated Apphia.

"Woman, you cannot make contracts," Archippus' face grew purple and the veins stood out on his forehead. "Onesimus is my son, the child of my begetting, and I shall determine who will be my heir."

Apphia fled in tears; never before had she seen such explosive behavior in her brother; he had always been acquiescent. After the outburst the house remained quiet, almost as though nothing had happened. Within the week Leah noticed that the little shrine in Apphia's chamber had been removed.

"Kubaba does not hear my prayers," Apphia said simply.

Other Gods

"There are other gods," responded Leah with dignity.

A few days later Apphia approached Leah with unusual timidity.

"Leah, you always seem to remain calm, even when everything seems to go wrong."

"The Lord watches over the innocent."

Apphia nodded, "Who is this Lord of yours? Can I know him?"

Leah suddenly felt apprehensive. As a Jew in a gentile world she had been careful not to speak of such things. Yet she fully believed that her God was the God of all, Jew and gentile alike. Suddenly a thought came into her mind. "I have been invited to a meeting, and some of my friends are going. A famous man is coming to our city and he is going to speak about a prophet of new thought. Both Jews and Gentiles are invited. Maybe we could all go together and find out what it is about."

A meeting to hear a speaker; Greek women had few opportunities to go beyond their walls, and a meeting to hear a man talk of religion seemed daring indeed.

"How can we do this?" she asked. "Can you go to a meeting by yourself?"

Leah, to be sure was not that daring, but she usually could find a cousin or an older woman to accompany her. "There would be two of us together," she suggested. "Maybe Archippus could go with us."

Apphia shuddered, "I think not," she said.

Leah was struck with an idea. "Why not ask Philemon. He is tall as any man; and he should be proud to accompany his mother."

The suggestion did not fall on a deaf ear, and before long Apphia announced that she had wheedled Philemon into acceptance. Not much later the two ladies and their escort were walking down a street in a part of the city that Apphia and Philemon had never before visited, but the Ghetto was well known to Leah. They found the house which proved quite spacious on the inside and were graciously given chairs to sit in, though most of the visitors sat on benches or the floor. As they were watching the other attendees make their entrance, Apphia gasped as she saw Archippus accompanied by Epaphras coming through the door. Such a possibility had never entered her mind, and she was frightened beyond belief.

Philemon patted her hand and waved at his uncle. "Now, mamma, it's all right," he encouraged her.

Epaphras seated Archippus in an honor seat at his left, then appeared again with a short balding gentleman who sat on his right.

"It's Paul," whispered Leah who seemed to know what was going on. Apphia was too nervous at first to note what was taking place, but in a short time the speaker, Paul, was talking quietly in a friendly manner from his seat in the front of the assembled guests. She became a little more composed as the talk progressed, and was able to remember later something of what Paul had said.

Paul's Sermon

I am beseeching you, to conduct yourselves as worthy of the vocation to which you are called. Be humble and gentle, bearing one another patiently, bearing one another in love. At last we will all come to meet the unifying faith and knowledge of the Son of God, THE PERFECT MAN, who is the standard of manhood.

No longer are we infants, tossed by waves, whirled about by every doctrinal gust, caught by the trickery of men who are are experts in deceit. By speaking the truth in love we shall grow in every way toward him who is the head, The Messiah, who is at work fitting and joining the whole body together. HE PROVIDES FOR THE NEEDS OF EACH SINGLE PART, enabling the body to make its own growth to build itself up in love. This is what you must do.

Do not conduct yourselves as the Gentiles do with futile minds. Because of their refusal to know the True God and because of the stoniness of their hearts, they have excluded themselves from the life of God. . . . One does not become students of the Messiah by this kind of thinking. Seek for truth in Jesus.

You must listen to him and become disciples in his school.

> *Strip off what belongs to your former behavior,*
>   *Instead become new in mind and spirit*
> *And put on the new man created after God's*
>   *likeness,*
>   *with true righteousness and piety.*
> *Put away the lie. Let everyone speak the truth*
>   *to his neighbor,*
>   *for we are members of one body.*
> *At times you may get angry, but do not sin in*
>   *your anger.*
> *Let not the sun set on your fit of temper.*
> *Do not give the Devil any opportunity to seize*
>   *you.*

Do not let foul talk pass your lips, but say what is right and useful to the listener. Do not grieve the Holy Spirit of

*God and every kind of bitterness, passion, anger, shouting
and cursing shall be taken away from you with every other
kind of malice. I beseech you, Be good to one another.
Be warm hearted and forgive one another. For God has
forgiven you.*

Apphia found herself nodding her head in agreement, and Philemon noted that his uncle had been wiping his eyes with his handker-
chief. After the sermon, Epaphras dismissed the visitors with thanks
and told them that they might come again to hear more. Archippus
joined his family on the way home, but little was said for all were lost
in thought.

In this way the family first became aware of the new thinking.
Perhaps none who were there could remember the words that the
great Apostle taught, but they were restored to us by one who became
beloved of Paul. *When the perfect comes, the imperfect will come to
an end.*

The Weaving Room

For the women of Colossae, and indeed for all in Lower Phrygia, their
living quarters contained a weaving room. Apphia had been instructed
in the weaving arts from her childhood. Her mother and grandmother
were both known for the evenness of their work. At least twice her
grandmother had been chosen to weave the new garments which would
grace the statue of the goddess for the new year. So it was by no means
unexpected that when Apphia and Archippus reconstructed the family
dwelling, a special room for weaving was included. The first room was
small and opened toward the family peristyle and therefore rather dark
and cramped. In those days the three or four women of the household
would gather. Apphia set up the loom for herself and instructed the
others in the preparation of the wool from the carding through the
spinning. Within a short time, she had found another loom and began
instructing Sambatis in the art. Her accusation concerning the stupidity
of Sambatis referred to the girl's ineptness with the loom.

Weaving was traditionally woman's work, and women, whether well-born ladies or born in slavery, practiced it as a trade. Well-to-do households established weaving on almost a factory basis, and many a freedman's family had acquired that status through the unremitting work of the mother. The sheep of Phrygia were raised for their long fine coats. When they were shorn, the wool was given a preliminary washing and then sold on the open market for carding and spinning. When Apphia's work began to prosper, she and Archippus determined to produce their own sheep and acquired experienced herdsmen to keep them on nearby hills for grazing. These sheep were discouraged from pasturing too much among the thorns and brambles which tangled the wool and damaged the long shag.

Within a few years, brother and sister decided to enlarge the weaving room and built an annex toward the back with windows that overlooked the valley. The light was not only pleasant, but it also helped to improve the quality of the product. By this time, Apphia was finding women born on the farm who were amenable to learning the art. Often as many as ten women would live in the women's compound, staying there day and night. The weavers would bring their small children with them for care while endlessly they carded, spun and wove the wool. The product was sold to wool brokers, but the finest of the household was taken to the dyers of Colossae who produced the products for which the city was famed.

The finest purple was *sea-purple*. The dye was obtained from mollusks brought all the way from the great sea. The richest color was so deep as to seem black, though it had a shimmering quality in the sunlight. Other purples were made from the madder root which produced all manner of crimsons, maroons and rose. The dyers carried on their trade in another part of town where those who chose to live there became impervious to the odor.

Besides the wool, Apphia worked also with linen and turned out a fine unbleached product. Some of this finally went to the fuller who made it gleaming white. It brought a good price, especially from wealthy Romans who indulged it for their native garb. Linen and purple wool woven together was Apphia's own specialty, and she began to be wealthy in her own right. She was delighted when Archippus brought her long white cotton threads from Egypt and the women turned out fluffy cotton sheeting.

As young children Philemon and Onesimus had played in the weaving room. When the children became too boisterous they would be sent outside to play and the cook would bring them cookies and sweet drinks made with the juice of wild berries or of apples. Although the long days at weaving were tiring, the women who worked there were content, for they were protected from the unwanted attentions of the laborers, and here their children found a haven of safety.

Erotion

Among the children was Erotion, a delicate girl, some years younger than Onesimus. Erotion's mother had been born on the farm where she had been a favorite. Her child's father was the overseer, who claimed both mother and child as his own, though being a slave, he could not legally possess a family. It was not the habit of Archippus to interfere in the domestic matters of slaves, if he could help it. The overseer had long since proved to be a strong but peaceable man; few dared to challenge his authority. Erotion's mother had become a weaver, but she often did not remain with the other women at night, having the liberty to return to her husband. By the time the child was six, she was put to the spindle. At ten, her nimble fingers were trained to the loom, for the small fingers were deftly tying threads and making almost invisible knots. The overseer preferred that she stay in the women's quarters where she was safe from the glances of the laborers.

Apphia watched her grow into womanhood and had determined that she would give her to Philemon when he reached his eighteenth birthday. But when that time came, Philemon was training for the foot races. He accepted his present with some embarrassment and paid no further attention to her. Erotion was no little piqued by this, for she was accustomed to being petted and praised.

Onesimus was aware of the slight; furthermore, when he looked at Erotion, his heart seemed to beat faster. He lost few opportunities to speak to her sweetly, pat her hand softly, and brush by her hair with his lips. It was not unknown that the two could often be found together in shaded recesses of the house in the afternoon, though Apphia kept the doors to the women's quarters locked after sundown. Onesimus' actions may have come to the ears of Philemon, who did not appear to care. The affair also was marked upon by the overseer who was then in terror for his daughter.

"The lad with the Phrygian cap has an eye for my Erotion," he complained to Archippus, who remained unruffled by the news. Archippus thought to himself that his son was beginning to react in a normal way to his world, and that perhaps there was hope for him at last.

It was to Erotion that Onesimus confessed his secret thoughts. He had despaired of manumission, for Archippus showed no sign that he had such a thought. He feared that Philemon would claim Erotion for his own once he lost interest in the games which Onesimus thought of as ephemeral. And so, he told Erotion, he was determined to flee, to run away and find his freedom in some far place where he would be unknown. Then he would make his fortune and at last return to claim Erotion for his own. Erotion knew that the dream was impossible and the plans preposterous. She kissed his lips and stroked his shoulders and begged him to take her for his own; for should she be found with child, Philemon would want none of her, and she felt that she could handle her father's anger.

But Onesimus would have none of it, though he kissed her mouth and pressed her close to him. "No," he replied, "I will father no slaves. The only rebellion that we can have is to refuse to beget our kind."

Archippus Reviews His Life

Onesimus was not the only one in the house whose heart was besieged by love. The meeting at the house of Nympha left Archippus with a certain sadness. As he retraced it in his mind he could discover no reason for his feelings, but at last his mental meanderings took him to his meeting with Epaphras and their discussion about love.

"I think," he thought to himself, "there is no one who loves me." Indeed, there were those who respected him, as well as those who depended upon him. There were even those who feared him; but he could think of no one who loved him. "Certainly, Apphia does not love me." Apphia could depend upon him, and had depended upon him when she had troubles; but, at times, it seems that she could barely tolerate his presence. She was such a nag that he had almost permanently removed himself from any place where she might be present.

"My nephew, Philemon, tolerates me," he mused. Philemon respected him as a youth respects an aging uncle. His uncle had never expressed any feeling toward him, so he saw no need to cultivate his feelings toward his uncle. He assumed that he should treat Archippus in a mannerly way, always making a civil reply when confronted. Behind his back, Archippus was aware that he was mimicked and even ridiculed.

There was no one else in the household to love him. There is an adage, "Twixt slave and master there is no friendship." It is a maxim to be upheld. A master who relies upon a slave for love, subjects himself to all kinds of abuse. That a slave should love his master is unthinkable. It was this attitude that so long had restrained Archippus from acknowledging Onesimus. It was love that Archippus was seeking when he confessed his relationship to Onesimus. He had hoped that Onesimus would love him. That Onesimus turned against him brought an ache to his heart. It brought an ache, not bitterness. In bitterness, he could have turned Onesimus out; the ache was born of his own yearning for love and his own sense of inadequacy. He felt the inadequacy of Plato's hero who could do no cowardly deed in the fear that his lover might find him a failure.

Outside the household, there was no one. True, he was respected in Colossae as an upright citizen and a gentleman. His business associates found him cold and calculating; it was said that he was a master of the sharp deal. As for women, in his society they were unthinkable. It was with shame that Archippus remembered Sambatis, that once he had fallen captive to the younger Eros. As he reviewed his situation in his mind, he was turned to think not of who loved him, but of whom he loved.

"No," he thought, "I do not love Apphia. I do not enjoy her company. I wish her no ill; in fact I wish her well, but no, I do not love her." With such reasoning he discovered that he did not love Philemon either; he was a very shallow youth; it was difficult even to plan a proper education for him. He thought of other household members. He had always distanced himself from the household slaves; he would not even chasten them.

Leah was a pleasant woman, but obviously not of his class. Platon was fawning. Only Onesimus was left. Was the feeling he had for the boy love? Had the passion he had felt for the boy's mother been love? "No," he could not admit to any feeling of the ignoble love. And how could he have a noble love for a boy who was not his equal, who could not return feeling for feeling.

Archippus had truly tried to close the gap between the young slave and himself by giving him the best of education. He had plans that the day would come for manumission; there were certain legal difficulties but he felt they could be overcome. But now, the boy himself presented the biggest obstacle. He did not look upon his natural father with reverence or awe, let alone love.

He examined his mind as if in a mirror, and found only a dark image there. Archippus' mind drifted back to Paul of Tarsus.

"Be gentle, be kind to one another," he had admonished.

Archippus could think of himself only as gentle and kind. He never punished a slave physically; he always called upon some one else to do it, out of his hearing if possible. He had certainly dealt gently with Apphia. He remembered his visit to the Temple of Apollo with Philemon. That was a kind thing to do, he reminded himself. He also thought of how eagerly he had abandoned the young man at the end of the visit. Certainly, he had treated Onesimus with the utmost kindness. Who else would lavish such attention upon a slave? And with no affection in return? No, kindness was not the answer.

Archippus determined to find some kind of solution to his problems. He called for his chlamys and his street sandals and went out for a walk, to search for Epaphras.

Epaphras was found at his usual place in the Portico of the Nereids, bundled against the cold with his back to the wind. The autumnal chill sent fallen leaves down the narrow streets and water from the fountains splashed wet and cold across the cobble stones.

"Good friend," called Epaphras, "What are you doing out in this kind of weather?"

"I was looking for you," responded Archippus, "but what are you doing here?"

"I was waiting for you to come," said Epaphras simply. Archippus, taken aback, began to wonder what kind of seer he had bargained for when Epaphras explained, "Someone always comes; someone always comes. What problem draws you to me?"

Taking Epaphras by the elbow, Archippus drew him into the shelter of a nearby taverna out of the cold and the wind. Suddenly he was seized with an unaccustomed shyness and could scarcely find the words to speak.

Epaphras sat quietly sipping a little warmed wine, mulled with blackberry juice. Finally Archippus blurted out,

"Nobody loves me."

Epaphras searched his comrade's face to see some sign of sincerity or insincerity.

"It is true," sighed Archippus, "I have searched a list of all my acquaintances, and no one loves me, not one; and—" he paused a moment, "I have also found that I do not love anyone either."

"I believe," Epaphras replied after a few moments of silence, "that the last time we talked we were speaking of love."

"That is why I came to see you."

"Exactly what do you mean by love?" asked Epaphras, more stalling for time than for making an analysis.

"I mean there is no kind of passion in my life; there is no thrill of excitement; my heart does not beat faster for anyone; and, worse yet, I arouse no feeling in the thoughts of anyone else."

"And this passion, as you call it, that is what you call 'love?' It sounds much like the inferior *eros* that you were describing in our last talk."

"That is true," replied Archippus. "But I also lack a visit from the elder sister. No one looks to me with admiration, no one comes for guidance; nobody casts a fond glance in my direction. Quite the opposite, they snicker behind my back, and mimic me to their friends. Unless I call for them specifically, they leave me strictly alone. Perhaps the loneliness is worst."

"Who are they?" asked Epaphras. And Archippus proceeded through the list that he had rehearsed for himself earlier.

"And who is this Onesimus whom you name? I do not remember meeting him."

Without explaining himself further, Archippus revealed the whole story of Sambatis, the boy Onesimus, of his education, of Platon and Leah and Apphia and all his household.

Epaphras nodded his head in recognition at the main points, "Yes, it is because of sin," he kept saying. "It is an uncleanness which causes your malady; and not yours alone, for this whole generation seems to suffer in the same way and is seeking atonement."

"What is this atonement?" Archippus looked up in dismay. "Is there some sacrifice I have neglected? Some potion that I can buy? Some piece of parchment to hang over my door?"

"Not so fast, my friend. There are some things that cannot be bought at any price, and surely the wisdom of the ancients has taught you that. Our beloved Paul has said,

> *We have been called to freedom, but we have used our freedom for self indulgence, and make ourselves slaves to one another. The whole law is summed up in the commandment, 'You shall love your neighbor as yourself.' But this generation bites and devours one another to the extent*

of entirely consuming one another.

I say, Live by the Spirit and cease to gratify the flesh, for what the Spirit desires is opposed to fleshly desires which prevent you from living as you really want. If you live in the Spirit, you will be led away from the sins of the flesh—all of things which you have practiced and are still practicing: Fornication and impurity, idolatry, sorcery and those enemies of state and household, strife and jealousy, quarrels and dissension and even drunkenness and carousing.

"Stop, stop," called Archippus. "I admit to perhaps a few of these sins—the fornication of my youth, and even to trying out idolatry and sorcery, though I have more or less abandoned any hope in them. As for strife and jealousy, I absent myself where it is going on. And no one has caught me drunk or carousing since my youth."

"This may be so," admitted Epaphras, "but they are the stigmata of our society, and few can escape the results of the sins of the age. No one is without sin. Do not be deceived, God is not mocked and you will reap what you have sown. You sowed your own flesh, and now you reap corruption."

"What must I do?" Archippus was close to weeping.

You must sow to the Spirit and from the Spirit you will reap eternal life. Do not be weary of doing good. Do not give up. Whenever we have an opportunity, we should work toward the good of all, and our best opportunity is given us in the family of the Faith.

Epaphras was drawing a crowd with his oratory. Archippus remembered an appointment and fled back into the wind.

The Story Spreads

It was a day on which Leah had taken for visiting with her friends and her family. She wrapped a sturdy woolen shawl around her shoulders. It reached almost to her knees. And winding a woolen scarf around her head and throat she braved the wind and walked down the miles to the ghetto. There at her sister's house she found a group of women in the weaving room. They welcomed her and quickly fell to talking of their recent activies. Quickly they remembered Paul. "He was just passing through on his way to Ephesus. It was not a planned meeting," explained one of the sisters.

"My husband says that the man is an apostate," one woman remarked by way of disclaimer.

"No, I think he is quite sincere," cautioned another. "He really believes that Jesus was the Messiah."

"Was?" smiled another raising her eyebrows.

"I meant *is*," the speaker went on correcting herself. "But we seem to be getting the stories of different speakers. Apollos came first and told us about John; and indeed he baptized some of us. And then Paul and his followers came and told us about this *messiah*, and we were confused". But both agreed about Jesus.

"I think we need to hear this thing out further. Don't forget, Jesus said that we were quick to stone the prophets and not to listen to them."

The first lady got up and wrapped her shawl about her. "I think it is dangerous to speculate when we are talking about apostasy," she cautioned; and she walked out. Two or three others walked out with her.

Leah looked with questioning eyes to her sister, "What do you think?"

Her sister whispered to her, "I, for one, have been baptized. Come, let me tell you about it."

Nympha had been summoned to the house on the hill, the house of Archippus. She was met by Ifiti who motioned her to silence and led her into the women's quarters of the house. In a room partly shuttered off from the family peristyle there was a brazier burning for warmth. Apphia and two of the weaving women were sitting on cushions. Apphia welcomed the visitor and motioned her to sit.

"Tell us about Jesus," said Apphia.

Nympha expressed no surprise for she knew what she was expected to do.

"It was my angel who brought me to the Master," she said. The women drew close. One whispered that she too had an angel. Nympha told how Jesus, the prophet, had gone into the desert to pray, the southern desert, mind you, where there is no water and the searing sun causes the heated winds to bear down upon the traveler like blasts from a furnace. Jesus stayed there forty days, fed and kept alive by the angels.

"Who are these angels?" asked one of the weavers.

"They are all around us, good angels and bad angels, but if we are faithful, the good angels will protect us," replied Nympha.

"I think I have found an angel who is better than Kubaba," said Apphia.

On another day some young men, friends of Epaphras, met with Philemon in the palestra. They talked long and sincerely about their new-found peace of mind. They talked of the times and showed how the days in which they were living betokened the end of the age. They had come to the belief that they were indeed living in the last days of all and that before another emperor would come to rule the Lord Jesus would come in glorious majesty floating down on a cloud. Then the evil of the earth would vanish into everlasting fire, but the faithful would be drawn upward into the heavens and live in sinless splendor.

These things do not happen in a moment, but when spring came again Archippus and Philemon went with a small group of devotees down to a shallow place in the Lycus and were baptized. At the same time Nympha came to the house of Apphia, where guarded from the wandering glances of men, Apphia and Leah and two serving women were baptized in the pool of the family peristyle.

Change is Slow

The little group of converts were very circumspect about their new beliefs. Already there were rumors that the cult of Jesus was politically incorrect. In the first place, its Jewish origins were suspect. The Romans found the Jewish colony difficult to rule. The Jews were prone to proselytize; this in itself did not disturb the Romans greatly for Asiatic cults abounded in the capital, and even emperors had accepted the practices of Hierapolis, but the Jews were known for a dogmatism that rejected all competition. On the other hand, the Jews were rejecting the cult of Jesus, chiefly because it was heretical. For people who have an heretical leaning, these feelings generated a kind of delicious excitement. Furthermore, not all of the newly baptized understood what they had taken on, and they needed time to converse among themselves as to the meaning of their new beliefs.

The household slaves paid little attention to the extrinsic beliefs of their masters. Platon, who might have become aware of new thoughts and philosophies, was too involved with the newly discovered treasure trove of Plato's *Dialogues*. He and the master had some brief conversations about the philosopher which lifted up the pedagogue's spirits.

Among the Slaves

Leah, whose status was always somewhat between the slaves and the family, now seemed to be drawn closer to the freeborn than to the workers. Least of all affected was Onesimus, who as a slave had once been privy to the secrets of the household, but now through some rebellion of his own he had absented himself from the proximity which he had once enjoyed.

Archippus had seen rather little of Onesimus during this time. He had been wrapped up in his own thoughts and was pursuing his own problems. He had told himself that the boy needed space in which to find himself; furthermore, he had been deeply hurt by the boy's rebellion. He still referred to Onesimus as "the boy," as did the rest of the family although by now everyone tacitly understood the true relationship.

It is not uncommon, of course, for a master to be the father of a slave. Sometimes the relationship is acknowledged; other times it is unaccepted. At first Onesimus was relieved that his father was undemanding. Indeed his style of dress went unacknowledged, and furthermore there seemed to be a rather generous amount of spending money allowed him. But this very fact began to be a source of worry; it seemed as though his father did not care, or even did not bother to notice the statement that he was making.

What frustrated Onesimus even more was that the slaves did not pay attention to him. At first he would stroll down to the fields where the farm laborers were working. He meant to show that he was one with them, and that he understood their problems; but he lacked even the language to communicate with them. His education threw a barrier between them. They laughed at him for the way he dressed and the way he talked. The meaning of wearing native Phrygian garb was totally lost on those whose entire wardrobe consisted of the one tunic that they were wearing.

Onesimus had through his childhood maintained a casual relationship with the overseer who had first brought him up to the master's house. Now the overseer saw him as a threat. He feared that he might be blamed for being the benefactor of this delinquent. And when it became apparent that Onesimus had an interest in his daughter, the man was beside himself with fear and anger. He had been pleased when he had learned that Apphia had given the girl to Philemon, and had hoped that certain benefits would come from the relationship. So he sternly warned Erotion to watch her step and not accept any advances from Onesimus, even though he was well aware of the relationship of Onesimus to the master.

One day Onesimus found Stamnion taking his ease in the porter's room.

"Well, how is Archipor comporting himself today?" he bantered. He knew well that Onesimus had a particular dislike for that nickname. Onesimus struggled to keep his composure and retorted that his jug ears needed cleaning out so that he could hear the call to freedom.

"Freedom," snorted Stamnion, "now what have we to do with freedom? Is it freedom to starve, or freedom to court a whipping that you're talking about?"

"One would think that two slaves could talk to each other about their common plight and work toward their mutual good," replied Onesimus.

Stamnion laughed, "Listen to the fancy big talk; you sure got a lollin' tongue."

Onesimus turned red, "You'd think that slaves would have more sense than to make fun of each other."

Of course, slaves do make fun of each other. They play rough games, and make cruel jokes. If one slave receives a beating, either justly or unjustly, the others join in laughing at his discomfort.

The overseer who was a more kindly man than most was known to pick a culprit from the herd, and then invite the others to jeer while the unfortunate was lashed. It is in the same way that school boys seem to find amusement when one of their number is flogged for some misdeed. Never is there the feeling that "but for the grace of God, there go I."

Stamnion turned serious. "What are you doing with all this freedom talk? You, of all people. You are within reach of manumission, and none of the rest of us can even think of it. You and your talk of being one of us. You could inherit the whole lot, but you're playing such a fool, that you'll get yourself crucified for it. Why this talk of being a Phrygian, when you are as Greek as Philemon himself. And then there's this stuff about the girl. Man, he could nail you down. He could rip up her belly in no time at all if he found out. And probably all the rest of us would get it too."

Onesimus turned white and tried to control his rage. At last he said, "I understand how you feel. I am about to leave this damned house forever and the lot of you can, can . . . " and he did not finish his sentence for fear of the words that he was about to say.

Stamnion jeered, "You're going to run away? Why you couldn't get as far as a morning walk before they'd catch you."

Onesimus stamped off and ran headlong into Philemon. "You leave the girl alone," he snarled.

Philemon, whose mind was lately filled with good will toward all, and whose lips were evermore praising the King of Heaven nowadays, was astonished. "What girl, what are you talking about?"

"You know what girl. Your mother gave her to you; but you just keep your hands off. She is mine, you understand?"

No one had ever talked to Philemon in that way. He was taken quite off his guard. "Why you little bastard," he yelled, and hit his cousin square on the jaw. Then he said, as he helped Onesimus to his feet, "Take the girl, and good riddance. I sure don't want her."

Earthly Possessions, Given Away

That night Onesimus put a little bundle which he had readied on his back and fled along the river road. Before dawn he had travelled farther than he had ever been on the river before.

Judging that it would be safer to travel by night, Onesimus found himself a place under an overhanging rock somewhat removed from the path. He was physically tired from his long unaccustomed walk, but more than that, he was emotionally exhausted from the events of the preceding day. Suddenly he was awakened. A huge ugly face was looking into his.

"Aha, an' wot do we have here?" asked the face. "A nice slavey boy run away from his master, eh?"

Onesimus was too startled to reply.

The burley blackguard had begun to go through his small pack. "Ah, and sure, ye've stolen some of master's money, haven't ye?"

Onesimus struggled to get some words out, "No, no, that's mine," but his accuser was counting out his few pieces of silver and chortling,

"Well, m'lad, this will come in handy." Onesimus wondered what would come next, expecting at the very least a blow from a massive fist, but the brigand said, almost gently, "No, I'll not hurt ye; they'll soon catch up with yuh and ye'll be nailed for it by them. No need for me to shed yer blood." With a bound, he leapt over the surrounding rocks and disappeared before Onesimus could catch his breath.

It took Onesimus some time to reconnoitre his situation. He looked at the sky and saw that the sun was now low in the West. He did not recognize the landscape. Considering everything, he was quite lucky. Only the money was gone, and there had not been much of that anyway. The brigand had not touched his bread, and now he realized that he was hungry. He munched on the loaf and found an easy access to the river for a drink. The threat of being caught by now had become real, and Onesimus realized that he must be wary, for life goes hard for a runaway slave. As night came on, Onesimus continued his trek, keeping closer to the tree lined side of the path and in the shadows. When dawn came, he found a well sheltered place and slept fitfully during the day.

At moonrise he started on his way again. By this time he recognized the emptiness in his belly. Not too far along he spied an orchard and carefully stole into it, to find a tree with newly ripened figs. He managed to scrounge a few, but the barking of a dog drove him back to the pathway. As dawn began to glimmer in the East he started to look for a sleeping place, when he suddenly stumbled over the body of a man. The man, aroused abruptly from sleep, took one look at Onesimus, stood up, and felled him with a blow.

Onesimus grew bolder this time and shouted, "Is that any way to treat a fellow countryman?"

His assailant stood over him and replied, "Ye' ain't no countryman o' mine, young fella. Ye be one of those Greeky boys wot com' an took wot's ourn." He seized the pack that Onesimus had been carrying, "Here, I'll have that. And those sandals too." When he was finished with stripping the boy down there was nothing left except the thin tunic to cover his nakedness. All was gone, even the blue bead on its golden chain. Before the sun was fully up, the thief had disappeared. Onesimus sat down upon a rock and wept.

After a nap, Onesimus decided that he must be on his way, even if there was danger of being seen. Without his sandals he had to take greater care of where he stepped. Just before sundown he stumbled into a small camp, and quickly realized that the campers were two soldiers. On impulse, he bolted and started to run, but the two men were too quick for him and soon had him spread upon the ground.

"Yer a runaway, aren't yer?" Onesimus nodded.

The soldiers poked and pinched him.

"Well," said one jovially, "there's nothing to fear. We won't take you back to your master. He'd whip you and hang you on a tree, wouldn't he?"

Onesimus could do nothing but nod his head.

"Now, lookee, we'll take you down to the town, and sell you to a new master. That way, yer old master won't find you and give you what you deserve."

Onesimus looked glum.

"Who knows," said the second soldier, "You might even like your new master better than your old one. And besides, you ain't got much choice. No matter how you cut it you're still a slave."

Onesimus nodded.

"And we'll be richer for it," laughed the soldier.

By midday they were approaching the outskirts of a considerable city; Onesimus could see that it was much larger even than Hierapolis. By evening the soldiers reached a house which they had in mind. There they dickered a bit before turning Onesimus over to the largest woman he had ever seen. She felt him all over and when she lifted up his tunic, she laughed at what she saw. Then she prodded him ahead of her into the house.

"Here, bring this boy some porridge," she called; and a half dressed woman put a bowl in front of him. Onesimus, though by now he was half starved, hardly had stomach for the food that was given him. His new mistress pushed him over to a straw filled corner where he fell asleep exhausted.

The House of Women

Onesimus awoke to the sound of tittering girls. He rubbed his eyes, looked around, and found himself surrounded by scantily dressed females, standing around him and laughing. Still dazed, he struggled to sit up; the girls pulled him up by the arms and tried to brush the straw from his tunic and his hair. They seated him on a stool and began to wash his wounds as they clucked sympathetically. He was suffering from a blackened eye and cuts across his face. He had difficulty making himself understood through his swollen lips. His feet and arms and legs were scratched and cut, but he did appreciate that someone was caring for him. At first he decided that he was in woman's quarters, but saw no signs of weaving or other women's work. A stalwart biddy brought him a bowl of gruel, foul tasting, but food. He grimaced as he gulped it down. Then two of the younger women peremptorily removed his tunic before he could protest and put a long yellow gown in its place. One woman combed his tangled hair and two others brought in rouge pots and a tray of umber paste and began to paint his face with reddened cheeks and darkened eyes. Suddenly grim realization came upon him and he tore himself away from them shouting, "No, No."

By this time the women were screaming with laughter. He was no match for the many who piled upon him, pushing him this way and that, and sitting on his belly and his legs. Suddenly the large woman of the night before returned and clapped her hands. The others scurried away while she took charge. Standing over him, she too was convulsed in laughter. Her fat jowls waggled and tears came from her squinty eyes. Her obese buttocks bounced obscenely as she walked around him surveying what she saw. But finally, observing the terror on his face, she said,

"Do you object?"

Onesimus nodded agreement.

"Don't you know where you are?" she snapped, all seriousness now.

Onesimus nodded disagreement. She turned to the girls.

"Leave him alone for now. You can force a woman; but you have to be tender with a boy. They are obstinate creatures."

Returning to Onesimus, she said,

"You can make a lot of money this way, you know. Old men pay well; soon you will have enough to buy a gold chain to put around your neck, and earrings for those pretty ears." Onesimus felt for his gold chain and blue bead before he remembered that they were gone.

"Well," she announced, "Until you come to your senses you can make yourself useful. What's your name?"

"Onesimus," he blurted out. And again the girls screamed with laughter.

"Here, Useful One," the madam said. "Take the bucket here. There's water at the well outside. It will be your job to keep us supplied."

A Life in the brothel

Onesimus took the bucket. The well was not far away. His day had begun, as many more would follow. One might imagine that a youth so carefully educated as Onesimus would have quickly started planning an escape from the unpleasant circumstance in which he now found himself. However, his reaction was as one drugged or recovering from a long and stressful illness. He was a portrait in a picture stepped out of its frame with no relationship to anything or any surroundings known before. The journey and its mishaps had drained his self esteem. His former life had provided him with no values with which to judge the present situation. He was now on foreign soil unable to relate anything known to the unknown. The first demands upon him were the performance of simple physical chores, not beyond his physical abilities; carry water, carry wood, wash pots. The girls found him likable, and also safe. The madam found him amusing; he became her pet, dog or cricket in a cage.

For a time Onesimus did not care. The stress and anger from the old life drained away, like pus from an excised abscess, and now his brain was resting. Later there was new feeling when he became more and more aware of his new circumstances. He understood the nature of the business of the house. He continued to refuse to become a working participant, and the madam ceased her urging. Managing her great bulk used up most of her energy; her new slave was helpful in running errands, in mending things that were broken, and in bringing in necessities that used up the little energy that she had. For the most part she used her size for enforcing her demands; the sight of her looming body was threat enough for most. The girls feared her and quickly acquiesced to her orders; unruly customers shied away from even the thought of tangling with her.

The women of the house had little urge to undertake more than their profession required of them. When they were not engaged in their trade, they spent their time eating, making up their faces, and doing up their hair. Otherwise they slept. They were known only by their first names; Rhoda, Chryse, Poppy, Phylla and Xenia. It soon became apparent that they were older by a dozen or more years than Onesimus, and they played with him as though he were a little brother.

At first Onesimus wondered why there were no children in the house; there seemed to be ample opportunity for producing them. Soon he learned that pregnancy was unwanted, and indeed a catastrophe. Most of the girls considered themselves to be barren, sterilized by bygone obstetric mishaps. It was known that the madam possessed a potion which would end the unwanted outcome of a night's amours. It was a vile stuff that caused the unfortunate woman dreadful cramping and pain before the dead foetus was ejected, even if it did not bring about the death of the unwilling mother.

Poppy was the unfortunate one. She hid her unexpected condition as long as possible by wearing loose gowns and turning herself away from a frontal view by the madam. But at last the hidden was revealed and the dreaded medicine was administered to the wailing woman. Within hours the brat was delivered, looking more like a dead rat than a human infant. It was thrown into a bucket and given to Onesimus to disposes of. He tossed the contents of the bucket into the streetside trash heap, and the dogs converged to eat the bloody contents. Even though he had seen enough of life to cure him of ordinary queasiness, this turned his stomach.

Poppy did not recover. Each day betrayed new weakness. At last a midwife was brought in who announced that no doubt some of the foetus had not been expelled, and so she performed her surgery which caused Poppy to scream so passionately that two burly customers were driven away. Still Poppy grew weaker. Onesimus helped her sit up so she could take a sip of water.

"Dear one," she pleaded. "There is a magician in this town who is well known for curing such illnesses as mine. If I could only go to him."

Onesimus inquired further.

"His name is Sceva" agreed Rhoda, "He and his troop walk the streets of the city and for a price they will invoke the names of deities who cure ailments that others find incurable."

Onesimus, volunteering to find him, walked farther into the crowded streets of Ephesus than he had ever been before. At last he found one who claimed to be a 'son of Sceva'.

"Bring the woman here, and do not fail to bring five drachmas with you. Be here at sunup tomorrow and my father Sceva will heal her."

Onesimus returned with his news. Somehow five drachmas were produced. Onesimus and Rhoda helped the ailing Poppy, half walking, half carried, to the appointed place. The son of Sceva took the money and Sceva himself, dressed in the fanciful garb of some religious, stood up tall with raised up arm and pronounced, "Satan, avast. Satan, begone, I abjure you in the name of God Jesu, and his minion Pavlo."

There are some who say that a grey rat skittered down from beneath Poppy's dress. She said she felt better and was at peace. That night she died.

It was then that Onesimus deemed that he must become better acquainted with his surroundings and plan to remove himself from his captivity. Opportunity presented itself rapidly enough. The madam announced that she was in need of certain potions that could only be procured from a learned man who lived in a house not far from the harbor; but, alas, there was no way that she could get herself to that place. Onesimus suggested that she send a message.

"How does one send a message to a learned man?" she demanded. "No one can understand what I want except myself."

"You could write it down on a tablet," he said simply, "and the tablet could be taken to him."

"I write it down? Nobody here can write." and she laughed ruefully.

"I think I could write down what you tell me," offered Onesimus.

"You, you can write?" she roared in disbelief. Onesimus produced a piece of a broken pot and took a piece of charcoal from the fire pit.

"Try me out," he suggested.

She pronounced a few words and he wrote them down. "Well, read them back to me."

He read. The others crowded around in astonishment. The madam took him to her room and after rummaging around found an old wax tablet. Onesimus fashioned a stylus from a wooden peg and then wrote the message she wanted sent. She then gave him directions about finding the place, and he wrote them too.

"You come back quickly and I'll give you two leptas," she promised.

Onesimus went on his errand, carefully taking note of where he was going and where he had been. To his surprise he found the recipient of the message without much difficulty. The alchemist went to the shelves of his shop and found the ingredients stored there. He mixed them carefully, and ground them together. Then he gave the *pharmakon* to Onesimus, along with a lepta, and told him to hurry to his mistress. When he returned she hugged him impetuously and gave him three leptas,

"You are indeed Onesimus," she said.

From that day, Onesimus had more freedom. Often he wandered the streets of Ephesus discovering its many alleys, dark warrens, and silent groves of cypress trees. These were secret places where fugitives might rest undiscovered, and take quiet refuge. Sometimes he would catch shadowy glimpses of others like himself. They might sometimes sit together and quietly discuss their fate, or even banter with each other with crude joking over what seemed to be the universal condition of mankind. And so Onesimus began to develop his plans for faring alone in that city, the second largest in the world. Slaves milling about the streets caused little comment. Many were on assigned errands, and some perchance were merely absent without leave intending at some point to return to their rightful owners. The authorities could not press the matter too hard; had they done so the city would have become a blood bath. If caught, the recalcitrant would simply claim that he had intended to return; the city police, themselves civil slaves, might return them to their owners. Most owners had more prudence than to demand punishment.

Late one afternoon, Onesimus was lazing in the small shade of the bordello's courtyard when Rhoda slipped up behind him. Back to back, both pretended not to notice the other.

"Onesimus," she whispered, "I must leave here tomorrow morning if I ever leave alive."

"What is your plan?" he hardly moved his lips.

"I will meet you on the other side of the river fountain. Be there and stay until I come. If I leave by day, everyone will be sleeping and they will not notice I am gone until nightfall."

Shortly after daybreak, Onesimus strolled from the house into the alley way that was just coming to life with the morning business. Not long after, he was joined by a woman veiled in a rusty colored garment.

"Where to now?"

"To the great temple," she whispered.

Onesimus had heard of the place though normally he did not seek out his adventures in that direction. There were always crowds coming and going there, and Onesimus had been more interested in finding lonely spots where one might hide. The temple was far down by the harbor. The broad boulevard ran straight toward it, and now, as always, it was crowded with visitors and traders. Onesimus and the lady he guided were unnoticed in the press. They walked as fast as she was able, but Onesimus had to hold himself back to stay with her. Outside the temple walls all sorts of peddlers had set up their stalls filled with knick-knacks to tempt the tourist. Purveyors of food carried their trays of fruits and cakes and hawked their wares. More permanent were the shops set along the temple walls, but this was not the time for sight-seeing, for they were caught in the crush of those who were pushing themselves through the gates. At last, inside the temple, the veiled woman sat down at the foot of a great column, exhausted and panting. Onesimus crouched down beside her.

"What is it that brings you here?"

"The old woman," she said with a grimace, "she would be my death. By now she must know I have been withholding some of the fees."

"Why would you do that?" Onesimus asked without surprise, for he had already surmised the reason. "I had to get away; I can stand it no longer; so I have been saving up some money, little by little. But last night I knew that I had been discovered."

"What will you do now?—"

"I am safe here in the temple. It will give me time to make my plans. Please go back and pretend that you have not seen me."

The Great Temple

The temple bounds provide asylum, for murderer or thief or runaway. But one cannot live for long in the temple. The temple guards often make a sweep at night and chase away the loiterers. Onesimus left

Rhoda as she bade, but took the opportunity to wander about that great edifice—first among the wonders of the world. He found himself in a forest of great columns of polished green marble. A man could not encircle the girth of one with both his arms. And there were lesser columns, of twisting swirling shape with branches of golden leaves and fruit swirling around them. High above, the painted ceiling imitated most naturally the sky, in the east at dawn, in the west at sundown. Farther and farther was he drawn into this wondrous magnificence until at last he neared its most sacred sanctuary. Behind the purple curtains was the holiest sight at all, to be glimpsed only when the curtains were opened for a moment; and that, only when the astrologers foretold the propitious time.

As he stood there in the marble gloom, a brass gong sounded; a chill ran through his body, up his spine and to the nape of his neck where he felt the hair stand straight out. Awe overcame him and suddenly the curtain opened. Silence broke into that noisy place and became an audible presence.

The goddess stood revealed. Belief was suspended at the sight. The black figure seemed to step out of her niche and yet she remained unmoved. Slowly the curtains fell down around her and there was nothing there. Onesimus felt his chest exploding within him; he could hardly breathe. He went down on his knees and closed his eyes to recreate the sight that only he had seen. A lethargy overcame him; in his mind he ran his hand over that black body, feeling the softness of the breasts of women, many, many breasts, warm and supple to his touch.

At last he came to himself; it was as if the whole room came to life again, charged with the excitement. The chant went up: "Great and Powerful is Artemis of the Ephesians."

He had seen the Great Mother, Cybele herself, the Phrygian Kubaba. He thought of Apphia tearing at her face with her claw-like fingers.

"I must escape from here," he thought, and tried to find his way out through the crowd.

"I ought to find Rhoda and bid her goodbye."

By now he was thoroughly lost. Pushed forward by the press of the crowd, he went through another gate, far from the one which he had entered.

Once out on the great highway, he headed toward the city and before long found himself in the center of its commerce. In times before he had avoided that part of town, if only because he knew that Archippus sometimes came there on business. Nearby was a grassy park, hedged around by barbered bushes. Inside there was a statue which almost rivaled the great black one that had fallen from heaven, for it was as ridiculous as the other was awesome. There stood erect an enormous phallus, projected by a tiny man, the ugly god Bes.

"This is the capital city of Madness, it believes all things," cried Onesimus outloud.

When night came, he was far from the place that he had called home, but no longer did it matter.

Onesimus Freed

Onesimus claimed his freedom. One might claim that he was not civilly free, but such an argument would involve us in the philosophical question of what true freedom is. It was at this time that he became responsible to no master; no one called for him; no one sought him; no one knew of him at all. He attributed this change in fortune to Artemis. Daily he sought her temple and found refuge for a few hours of sleep in some unvisited niche behind a great column. He was not alone; the temple was filled with beggars and cripples and fugitives, many of whom bore the marks of their unhappy condition. By this time he had identified the place where he had left the runaway Rhoda, but never did he see her again. More importantly, never again was he present at an epiphany of the Goddess though there were times in the temple when he realized that it had happened.

He subsisted on crusts that he found or cakes and fruits pilfered from the food purveyors who had their tables outside the main gates.

Now and then he would pick up coins dropped by careless tourists. He observed the pickpockets, and occasionally practiced their art. Wisdom suggested that his needs must be supplied by some method less dangerous, so soon with newly purchased inks and bits of papyrus and with styli sharpened from reeds, he set himself up as "a writer of letters," just outside the south east gate where the mobs were not so large and there was shade from the afternoon sun. The very first afternoon brought a few customers for his service and left him a little richer than he had been in the morning.

Early the next day he had a visit from a scar-faced man.

"Demetrius would like to talk to you," was the message. Already he was familiar with the name, for "Demetrius, the Silversmith" seemed to have booths bearing his name at all of the main entrances to the temple. He also had a shop in the center of the City, near to the Great Library.

For sale in these shops were clay miniatures of the goddess, flags and ribbons and other knick-knacks of the same sort that Onesimus remembered from Hierapolis. However on the high shelves in back of the counter were statuettes fashioned of silver and even a silver replica of the great temple. Most of Demetrius' trade was in flimsy tourist stuff, but the silver work showed that Demetrius was an accomplished smith. More popular than expensive religious wares were the rings and bracelets, earrings and pendants set with colored stones. With these the little shops did a thriving business.

However, Demetrius did not rely upon his art to increase his fortune and his fame; his reputation came from work more sinister. Onesimus was not unaware that his setting up shop at the temple gate might bring him some notice. He had already thought of how he should react to a call from Demetrius.

"Tell Demetrius that I would welcome him as a client," he would reply. Rumor had it that Demetrius did not suffer competition, but Onesimus could not see how his little business would offer competition to the shops of Demetrius. He knew he would be expected to pay a protection fee; he also knew that he had almost nothing to pay it with; but his faith was that the Goddess would help, because he was a Phrygian, if nothing else. Onesimus was surprised when Demetrius himself stood in front of him within the hour.

"How may I serve you, Sir Demetrius?" asked Onesimus bowing slightly.

"Well, what exactly is your business?" asked the merchant.

"I, sir, am an accomplished amanuensis. I can fashion a fine prayer to the Goddess on vellum with colored inks."

"Do you sell many of those?" asked the silversmith.

"Oh, about as many as you sell from your stock of silver temples," replied Onesimus suavely.

Demetrius laughed showing his white teeth. "But what do you do for pennies?" he asked.

"I write letters for the unlettered, sir. For a few pennies I will write a letter for your aged mother and tell her that you are faring well. For a little more, sir, I can compose a pretty poem for a lady, suggesting a romantic tryst in a sheltered garden."

Demetrius studied the youth for a few minutes. "I might be able to use a man like you," he admitted. "Look here, usually I demand a fee from those who do business in these bounds; after all, you need protection from the bullies who would knock over your stand and steal your inkpots. And do not think that I have no secretaries to write at my bidding, but there are sometimes other things that need to be written. I have reason not to trust all of my business to one secretary."

"Of course not, sir," replied Onesimus. "But I am very discreet."

Turning quietly to Onesimus, the smith confided, "You know I am 'The Temple Guardian.' "

"So I have heard, sir; but I have not heard what a temple guardian is."

"I am a special protector of the Goddess," Demetrius confided in a whisper. "Her welfare is my welfare."

"I too have been favored by the Goddess," murmured Onesimus. "Indeed, she has looked down on me and smiled."

"I will call upon you when I need you," said Demetrius abruptly, and as he departed he tossed Onesimus a silver coin, which the youth deftly caught.

During the afternoon the aspiring business man wrote a few letters, earning enough to go into the town and lay in a supply of wax tablets, used papyrus sheets and powders for erasing them, with still enough left over to buy his supper in a taverna.

That he had no place to live was of little concern to Onesimus. At night the solid citizens bar themselves within their houses. Persons of importance do not go out at night, and certainly never alone. Anyone who finds reason to be abroad after dark goes with a band of servants carrying torches and cudgels to provide for his safety. The only light for the streets and alleys at night is the light of the moon; for Diana smiles down compassionately upon the night people who came out of their holes and hiding places to transact such actions as are needed to keep themselves alive. Onesimus quickly adapted himself to the role of night person.

In a small grove behind the Odeon there is a spring which falls into a pool. There during the day, children come to play; veiled girls with their duenas walk about, and old ladies find relief from the summer sun. At night the place is deserted, for such dark recesses are threatening to the innocent. Onesimus had discovered this pool one night when Luna's beams were falling upon its waters. Nightly he would come and enjoy a refreshing bath and perchance wash his clothes which soon dried in the fragrant breeze. Now and then some other visitor would share his privacy, but rarely speak.

One night while he rested on the grassy turf beside the pool, a man stopped by, produced a cup, filling it from the waters of the spring. Pretending sleep, Onesimus watched the intruder sip his drink. He then stretched out his hands in prayer.

> *I pray that the God of my Lord Jesu,*
> *the Father of Glory,*
> *give me a spirit of wisdom,*
> *and his revelation as I come to know Him.*
> *Let my heart be enlightened,*

with the hope to which he has called me.
O the riches of his glorious inheritance!
O the immeasurable greatness of his power
Given to those who believe . . .

The stranger lapsed into silence and stood quiet bathed in moonlight which made him a figure of silver such as might be fashioned by
a silversmith. After a time of silence, he turned to Onesimus and said,

"And you, my friend, do you too worship the Great God in this
fragrant night?"

Onesimus was startled for he had thought himself unnoticed. "I
often worship the Goddess," he stuttered, "but I came here only to
wash myself from the day's dirt and filth of the city streets."

"Rather wash your soul in this clear spring, than to pollute it with
your flesh."

"I have little time for my soul nowadays; it is difficult enough to
keep my flesh alive," retorted Onesimus.

"How do you keep your flesh alive? You appear to be young, well
sinewed, and fair faced. You cannot have been battling with the world
for long. I would think that you would be home in your bed instead of
prowling about at night."

"I have no home, and I am not a prowler," replied Onesimus
somewhat testily. "I have simply fallen upon evil times."

"I did not come to question thee, nor to accuse thee," replied the
stranger using an old-fashioned familiar form. "You will pardon me, I
thought that perchance you were another one of our community who
worship the Great God of Heaven. There is redemption through his
Son, Jesus the Christ."

"I have heard of this Jesu," replied Onesimus, "but the one who
cried for healing was not healed; are you perhaps from the tribe of
Skeva, who sells healing salves and prayers for Jesu and Paulo?"

"No, my son, I do not sell healing nor prayers. I do not rejoice in
such wrongdoing; I rejoice in the truth. My name is Paul and I can
only give what has been given to me. If you give me the time, I will
tell you of my redemption and pray for your salvation."

Onesimus eyed the man warily. "I don't have the time now; but if you need a letter written, or a scroll on which I may inscribe your prayers, you may find me at the South East gate of the Temple, for there I ply my trade."

"Your trade, sir?"

"I am Onesimus, the Amanuensis, at your service."

"I shall not forget," replied Paul, the man from Tarsus.

A Day in The City Of Ephesus

When morning came, Onesimus tardily set up shop. Having no master behind him, he worked when he was moved to do so. Before long Demetrius was standing by.

"I have been waiting for you; you should tend your business more promptly."

Onesimus eyed him with surprise. It had not occurred to him that a man of free enterprise should have responsibilities to anyone.

Before he could make a smart response, Demetrius continued. "I have here a list of names. I want the following message for each one.

> Demetrius summons you and your followers to assemble
> on The Arcadian Way, near the Great Theater at the Ninth
> Hour.

Onesimus looked up in surprise; there were 16 names on the list.

"I'll have my messenger pick up your message for delivery within the hour," Demetrius called as he departed.

Onesimus selected medium sized ostraca for the job, matching them as nearly as possible in size and shape and busied himself with his assignment. He was finishing the last one when the messenger came up and scooped the messages into a leather bag.

"Be careful, they break easily," Onesimus warned the messenger who was already on his way.

A short time later a new customer arrived. He was a short unimposing fellow, wearing a small back pack from which he took a small papyrus sheaf.

"Remember me?" he asked.

Onesimus recognized the voice of the man with whom he had been speaking the night before, but in daylight he seemed much slighter than the man who stood with him in the moonlight.

"You are Paul," Onesimus remarked in surprise.

"Indeed I am; and I am here to order a small job which your skill will accomplish in no time."

The paper in Paul's hand contained a few lines of writing. "I would like this written on a good piece of parchment in your most elegant hand. I will leave it as a gift for my good host in this city. I will return before dusk; I am now on my way to meet with Alexander who has some knowledge of the ways of this place."

Onesimus cleared away the dust of the ostraca and began to prepare some inks suitable for parchment. He read the writing left by the customer:

> *O the depth of the riches,*
> *and the wisdom and knowledge of God.*
> *How unsearchable are his judgments*
> *and how inscrutable his ways.*
> *For who has known the mind of the Lord.*
> *Or who has been his counselor.*
> *Or who has given a gift to him, to receive a gift in return.*
> *For from him and through him and to him are all things.*
> *Amen*

Onesimus recognized that the author had given him a bit of poetry, and he toyed with the manner in which he would inscribe its poetic style. While he considered the task ahead, the messenger of his earlier customer returned and gave him a small leather bag with some coins.

"Demetrius thanks you; The tribes are already gathering."

"The tribes?" Onesimus inquired.

"The guilds, I mean. The league of Silversmiths. They are going to have a riot. Go up the Arcadian Way. You'll see quite a parade."

"Why would the silversmiths riot?"

"Why? Because Demetrius told them to riot, that's why."

"But there aren't enough silversmiths in this whole city to have much of a riot," protested Onesimus. "You don't have to be a silversmith, idiot. The silversmiths' guild is one of the strongest in this town; everybody who is dependent upon the guild will turn out and riot because Demetrius has ordered it. He is the Temple Guardian."

"Is that a City Office?"

"No, no. You sure must be a fresh onion around here. Demetrius calls himself by that title because he has power, the power to get all of the guilds together. You belong to the guild; you ought to know."

"I belong to the guild?"

"You work for Demetrius, don't you. You pay your dues. That's why he rewards you so well for scratching messages on pieces of old pots."

Something began to stir in Onesimus' mind. "Why are we rioting?" he inquired.

"We're showing our dislike of the Jews. They come here preaching their 'One God' stuff, and dissuading people from worshiping at the temple. Obviously that's bad for business, your business, my business, and the whole city's business. But I've got to run. See you on the Arcadian Way."

Onesimus tried to put his mind to his latest order. He turned the paper over on saw a note on the back, "For Alexander. Arcadian Way."

Something clicked. Paul was a Jew; he could tell because he talked about God in the same way as Leah used to talk. He was going to meet with Alexander and the note suggested that Alexander lived on Arcadian Way. That was the long street that went up to the amphitheater. Suddenly it came to him that Paul, his customer, was in some danger; and that he himself was the unwitting source of that danger. Quickly he put his writing materials away, and sprinted out toward The Arcadian Way.

The guilds were already assembling. Urged on by loud leaders who carried megaphones with them they were chanting, "Great and Powerful is Diana of the Ephesians," as they converged upon the theater entrance. Rocks were being thrown and garbage was pelted about. Onesimus watched as two men were being dragged from a nearby house. The crowd shouted, "Down with the Jews. Away with the God-Fearers."

Onesimus ducked behind the house where a small group of men were gathered. He recognized Paul who was shouting, "They already have Gaius and Aristarchus. Those men are not Jews; they are Macedonians."

But the words of Paul could not be heard above the crowd. He was struggling to free himself from those who would restrain him.

"I must save them," Paul was shouting.

A tall man came out of the house and approached Paul. "You must hide yourself at once. Let me handle this affair."

Onesimus stepped up authoritatively, took Paul by the arm saying, "Paul, sir, you must come with me. They are after your hide; they will tear you limb from limb."

Alexander looked squarely at Paul; "Go with this man; it is my job to prevent an uprising, not to abet one."

Reluctantly Paul allowed Onesimus to take him by the arm and lead him away.

The crowd ignored Paul, for they only recognized Alexander as a representative of the Jews. The rioters were pushing themselves into the great amphitheater. When they saw Alexander brought forward they shouted all the louder,

"Great is our Artemis, Protectress of the Ephesians."

Alexander, a citizen of Ephesus and a Jewish Community leader, was unable to be heard by the rioters. Finally the City Clerk gained enough order to be able to speak to the unruly mob.

"Men of Ephesus, Who does not know that our great city is the Keeper of the Goddess Artemis in her temple. Who does not know that her statue fell as a gift from heaven. These signs are not denied and no one here has gainsaid them. The Goddess herself demands that you quiet yourselves and do nothing rash. These men whom you have seized are not temple robbers; nor have they blasphemed our goddess. If Demetrius and his Guild have any complaint, let them come before the courts. Bring your charges to the Pro-Consul. This matter must be settled according to the regulations; for we run the danger of being charged by Rome for causing a riot and a disturbance."

The crowd's energy was depleted at the mention of the Roman pro-consul and glumly but peaceably the mob dispersed.

Onesimus had steered Paul to the little park behind the great Library which was now deserted because the citizens were busy elsewhere. There they met face to face in the shadow of the god Bes.

"Hideous monument," shuddered Paul. "What will the Ephesians think of next?"

"I hardly think the Ephesians can be credited with its invention," laughed Onesimus. "But what am I to do with you next is more apropos."

Paul shivered though the late afternoon breeze was quite warm.

"I must get back to them and save them somehow. They must not suffer for me."

"And who might 'they' be?" inquired Onesimus.

"They are Gaius and Aristarchus, Greeks like yourself, and they have been faithful followers. How could they be taken for Jews?"

"I am not a Greek, but you have taken me for one; so I suppose that an Ephesian could mistake a Greek for a Jew."

"But you are not a Jew, surely."

"No, I am proud to say that I am a Phrygian."

"Ah, one of the Galatians; I am proud to know you; and you must hail from no mean city."

The face of Onesimus clouded. "I come from Colossae, sir."

Paul smiled, "I visited Colossae once; I stayed at Nympha's house."

"I am sorry; I do not know the lady. But then," he smiled lightly, "I am not one of the privileged classes."

Paul replied, "I really could not say that I travel with the privileged classes; I am a tentmaker by trade; while you are a learned scribe."

Onesimus felt a sudden panic. "I fear, sir, that your writing will not be ready as I promised. When I turned over your page and saw where you were bound for, I closed up shop and ran to save you from—"

"Save me? From what?"

"From the riot, sir. You see, I felt responsible, for I had barely finished writing the notices to all of the guildcaptains."

"You wrote them? Why?"

"Demetrius came and commissioned them, sir. And since I am beholden to Demetrius for my space, I obeyed his wish. Besides, I was paid well," Onesimus hastened to add.

"Then why did you want to save me?" asked Paul.

"Because you are my friend," Onesimus replied simply. "I do not have many friends."

The sun was setting over the mountains when they saw the figure of Alexander entering the park.

"I have been searching for you," he addressed Paul. "I must put you under arrest for instigating a riot."

"But he did not instigate the riot," protested Onesimus.

Paul put his finger to his lips to motion quiet.

"It will be house arrest," continued Alexander. "No whips and chains, but you must not leave your dwelling." He and Paul left Onesimus alone. Onesimus looked up at the statue and relieved himself.

Lessons On Freedom

Next morning Onesimus set up his writing table at his usual post; he again looked at the assignment which Paul had given him and determined to separate the lines in the manner of verse.

"It has a poetic ring," he thought, "even though it does not obey the rules of rhetoric. Each line should begin with a letter in red; that will make it an outstanding gift."

He leaned diligently over the work when shortly, he was approached by one whom he recognized as a henchman of Demetrius.

"You were not here yesterday afternoon."

"Was anyone?" asked Onesimus without looking up. "I thought the whole world was gathered at the amphitheater."

"Oh, you were there then."

"And why not?" laughed Onesimus. "I wrote myself an invitation."

"Well, Demetrius will appreciate your interest, I am sure. But I'm here for the weekly collection."

Onesimus had been certain that was the way it would be, though up to now it had not been mentioned.

"How much does Demetrius expect?" he asked casually.

"How much have you got," the bully insinuated himself close to Onesimus' face.

Onesimus stood up. "I have only dealt with Demetrius himself, sir; you, I do not know."

The bully backed away, looking at this slight youth with some amazement.

"You must be new around here; you don't understand how we work."

"I understand sniveling slaves quite well. I don't deal with slaves; I deal with their masters." Onesimus surprised himself when he heard his mouth speaking the words of Archippus in the voice of Archippus. That the slave retreated surprised him. He sat down shakily trying to think of what he would reply to Demetrius, but by the time that he had finished his work, Demetrius had not shown himself.

Third meeting with Paul

Now the problem was to find Paul. Somewhere in this huge city, Paul sat in a house, under arrest. Onesimus packed his writing materials in a box which he put in a place he had found for safekeeping, and started for the Arcadian Way. For a time he stood in front of the house which he identified as Alexander's when the doorkeeper came out. He asked a casual question and was happy to hear a Phrygian tongue which said, "No spik da Greek."

Onesimus whispered back a reply in Phrygian and the slave smiled broadly asking in perfectly good Greek, "What is your pleasure, sir?" Onesimus inquired the whereabouts of Paul the Jew who had been the object of yesterday's fracas. The doorkeeper obliged him by giving quite adequate directions. Shortly afterwards Onesimus was rapping on a door which was opened by Paul himself. He was no less happy to see Onesimus than Onesimus was to see him.

"I have finished your scripture, sir," and he unrolled the small parchment.

Paul examined it with interest and delight, "You are a fine artist, young man."

Onesimus beamed as he replied, "You are an excellent poet."

Paul smiled. "No, I have never learned the rules of meter; my education was in Hebrew, the sacred language of the Jews. I do well enough simply to get my words into Greek."

"I found them inspiring, sir."

"It was the work of the Spirit," replied Paul simply. "But now I must pay you. How much is your charge."

"It was my pleasure, sir; and I have few such pleasures now. That was pay enough. Besides, if you pay the customary fee, Demetrius will soon relieve me of it."

"And what is Demetrius to you? Are you his slave?"

"I am a free man; I was born a slave, but now I count no man as my master."

"You are a freedman, then?"

"No, sir, no one has freed me; I have freed myself. And I do not intend to be the slave of Demetrius either."

Paul quickly caught the drift of the speech.

"And I was born a Jew; I bear the mark of the Jew; but in Christ I am free. Still I am a Jew, for a Jewish speech controls my tongue, and the law of Moses remains in my mind."

"What do you mean then by saying that you are free in Christ? Who or what is this Christ?"

Paul could not have been happier at the question; he jumped fully clothed into the conversational waters. At the end of an hour he had described his meeting with and conversion to the Living Lord. By sundown he had elucidated his life as a Pharisee and his early education with Gamaliel. A boy appeared with some bread, some cheese and a sausage and Paul produced a skin of wine. The two shared the meal.

"But you must know that this sausage is made of pork, and Jews do not favor pork."

"This is true," replied Paul; "but that is what I mean by being free in Christ. I know that nothing that goes into the body through the mouth will affect the soul. God made the pig as well as He made me. That the pig is not kosher to eat is only a fancy of the Jews. Do I offend you by eating this sausage?"

"No, of course not," replied Onesimus. "I have eaten sausage all my life; but it would have offended Leah."

"And who is Leah?"

Onesimus began to tell Paul something of his earlier life, carefully editing the more identifying parts of it. It was late before the tale was finished.

Paul looked up with concern and said, "You must stay here the night. The city is dangerous after dark."

Onesimus laughed, and Paul laughed too realizing that the city belonged to the night people. For the first time since he had left the brothel Onesimus slept under a roof.

In the morning, Paul was serious.

> *Each person should conduct his life as the Lord has assigned him and as God calls him. When I was called I was a Jew, and I make no attempt to hide the marks of my Jewishness. You are a Gentile; I would not expect you to undergo circumcision, for circumcision is meaningless. Not being circumcised is equally meaningless. It is the recognition of God's law that is meaningful. Let each person remain in the circumstances under which he was called. Perhaps you are called as a slave. Then, that should not bother you. Even though you have become free, you are able to make use of what you achieved as a slave. When a person is a slave and is called by The Lord, he becomes the Lord's freedman. When a freeman is called by The Lord, he becomes the Lord's slave. The*

Lord has bought you and me with a price. Do not sell your soul into the slavery of men; but there is no reason to change your civil status. You belong to the Lord.

Onesimus looked at Paul seriously. "I understand what you are saying. Up to now I have been behaving quite haphazardly, and have considered myself subject to no one. Let me think about these things awhile."

Paul rose and bade his guest farewell. "Come back to share my evening meal and spend the night. During the day I have work to busy myself with; but night sometimes brings bad dreams to the lonely."

Onesimus wandered the streets of Ephesus alone with his thoughts. Late in the afternoon he returned to the Great Temple. He stood among the milling crowd and heard the hollow sound of the gong. Right in front of him the curtain was raised and he looked on the black statue; she had turned hideous with her sagging breasts. Far away he could hear the chant, "Great and Powerful is our Artemis, Queen of the Ephesians."

The curtains fell back covering the statue. Onesimus had not even knelt. He had seen her naked and she was a black stone.

Great and Powerful is Diana of The Ephesians

Again Onesimus set up his writing tables and awaited the smile of Fortune. But Fortune had abandoned him. Onesimus more often than not found himself alone with his thoughts. Sometimes she sent him unlettered country fellows who wished to send a few words of reassurance home. Onesimus counted them happy that they could still count someone as friend. When a few pennies came his way, he was assured that Demetrius and his henchmen were not far off and quite aware of how many pennies he had collected.

Notwithstanding the paucity of customers and the rapacity of Demetrius, the poverty of Onesimus was abetted more by his former condition. Slavery is a poor training school for private enterprise. Onesimus was not one to put in long hours; he did not drive a sharp bargain; he dawdled over assignments which he enjoyed, such as the one which Paul had given him, sometimes neglecting to charge for his work. He could be grudging over hack work, and a surly attitude frequently kept a customer from returning.

The Apostle to The Gentiles

A New Household

Before sundown, Onesimus could be seen packing away his writing materials and starting for the lodgings of his new-found friend, Paul, the man from Tarsus. On his way he would stop at the market, passing up the vegetables for cheeses, sausages from the country, a variety of fish, and always freshly baked bread. Thus laden, he would return to Paul whose small kitchen supplies tended toward vegetables and fruit and frequently new vintage wine, all the products of faithful followers who did not forget him. For often there were guests who stayed long hours while Paul laid out his views on life and love and death, never forgetting to allude to his Lord Jesus and giving him the thanks and the glory for the Spirit that dwelt within him. He showed the faith to remove all mountains.

In this way Onesimus was drawn closer to Paul. At length he went less and less to his writing tables; at last he brought the tools of his trade to Paul's lodgings where he found many assignments from his new master. Paul chided him for acting in a slavish way:

> *Don't you know that if you yield yourself as an obedient slave, you become the slave of him whom you obey? Now you should thank God that you who were once a slave to human master, and therefore to sin, in Christ you are set free from sin, you become the servant of righteousness. For Freedom Christ has set us free; stand free; do not*

submit to any kind of slavery.

And again Paul would admonish him,

> *You are running well. Who can hinder you from obeying the Truth. A little leaven will leaven the whole loaf. I am confident that the Lord will have the same view as I. Let the one who is troubling your mind will have to bear his own judgment. In Christ you are free.*

Such words encouraged Onesimus, and at last he ventured to attend the meetings of the community which Paul so frequently addressed. He became recognized as one of Paul's household, and as a special helper of Tertius who had remained with Paul through many hardships and had helped him with the planning of his schedule and the composition of his letters. Tertius was especially grateful for Onesimus nimble fingers, for his own often ached from the years of inscribing the letters, and his eyes had begun to grow dim when the daylight faded. Onesimus was quick with the pen, and while attending Paul's meeting, he would write down new sayings that fell from the inspired lips and help incorporate them into the new works which were always in the making.

Paul

Some of the visitors were well acquainted with these thoughts; they were companions of an inner circle, but to those who remained outside the circle, Paul remained gracious, gradually drawing all manner of persons to himself while allowing them to retain their own identities.

There were times when Onesimus felt that he had traded Archippus for Paul. Paul was a new master, for whom he would do anything. But Paul was not a man whose ways and thoughts were easy to discern. He seemed set in his purposes, yet eager, if not enthusiastic, to take on the suggestions of his friends. There was no doubting his aim to spread the good news of Jesus Christ as far as his feet and his influence could carry him; but he was severe in his judgment of those who opposed him.

Onesimus was awed when he considered the extent of Paul's travels, for he had been as far away as Arabia; he knew Jerusalem and Damascus and had sailed to the islands. He had established churches from Macedonia to Corinth, and even spent time in Athens where he talked with the great philosophers. Even now he was planning to go to Rome and beyond to farthest Spain. He had seen more of Phrygia than any Phrygian that Onesimus had ever met!

There was no doubt that Paul was a gentleman, well educated and a citizen of Rome. How then could he ply the trade of tent-maker? That was heavy work, with coarse cloth, unfit for gentility's hands. Yet he was at home with rich and poor alike; he spoke as gently to a slave as to a freedman; he was polite to women and to men; and he ate with Jew and with gentile, and with no apologies.

Of his hopes and fears, of his disappointments and ambitions, no one was privy. He seemed to have no personal life. Onesimus could discern no family but the rather scattered acquaintances who came to and went from this house, though some of them, like himself, slept and took their meals there. Although he seemed to know people of importance, he expected no honors nor gain from them. He did not gossip and yet in no way did he act in strange ways that often cause others to tell tales behind a great man's back. He seemed to enjoy all foods, but did not complain if they were lacking. He could nap anywhere; but also he could remain awake all night talking excitedly about his cause. He accepted without comment the customs and habits of all whom he met. In fact the whole of this man was concentrated upon the one great concern of his life—spreading the word of an almost unknown Jew who had lived decades before this time. The house arrest was lifted and at last Paul could be seen about the city again. Yet this did not change the way in which his household lived. As he had said,

> *I am all things to all men. I am a slave to all in order to win them all. To the Jews I am a Jew; But I do not consider that I must follow the law of the Jews; To the Greeks I am a Greek, not subject to the beliefs of the Greeks. For the weak, I am weak; for the strong, I am even stronger. I am*

all things for all people. Yet I am not free, for I remain
under the law of Christ.

At the suggestion of Tertius, Onesimus began to write Paul's con-
tinuous commentary down in the form of short notes to jog his memory
of Paul's sayings. Tertius had complained that Paul would start a letter
and then stop quickly, telling his scribe to continue with the conversation that they had this Tuesday past. Now it was possible to quote
something out of the notes of Onesimus as well as the memories of
all. For Paul was constantly writing letters, sometimes dashed off in a
few minutes; sometimes continuing day after day with new and fresh
thoughts.

Onesimus thus bathed in the teachings of Paul began to search for
questions. The whole community knew of the man Jesus, who had
lived and taught in Samaria and Judea within the memory of many.
But Paul regarded Him as more than a man, and about that Onesimus
was curious. Who was this Man-God to whom Paul was so attached?
How was He to be explained?

Paul never ceased to tell the story of how he had met this Christ on
his way from Jerusalem to Damascus. But this was an encounter with
the Eternal, such as Onesimus had experienced once in the Temple of
Artemis. When Onesimus had seen her earthly form, she was no more
than an ugly stone.

"Jesus was no more like an image, than Artemis is like a woman,"
Paul expostulated. "Jesus was a real person, born of human parents,
with brothers and sisters and neighbors who knew him. And yet that
earthly body was only a receptacle, such as a jar into which one may
pour wine."

"Jesus was a wine jar?" Onesimus joked.

In the hand of the Lord there is a jar,
and the wine is red,
It is full mixed,
and he poureth out of the same.

Paul frequently proved his point by quoting Scriptures.

Onesimus replied,

> *There are two jars that stand on the door-sill of Zeus;*
>   *they are unlike for the gifts they bestow:*
> *a jar of evils, a jar of blessings.*

Paul looked up; "and whence comes that scripture?" he asked.

"It's from Homer, sir; it's in The Iliad."

Paul's brow wrinkled a moment; and then he smiled. "You are a scholar, sir. And I applaud you." The others present noted this with some amazement. Paul was usually too engrossed with the argument to stop for plaudits.

> *Well, let us continue. What I mean is, God filled the cup that was Jesus, but Jesus poured out that power, for as a man he would not be exploited as a god. He emptied himself, as it were, and took the form of someone lowly, like a peasant or a slave with human likeness. He was humble, and he was obedient; he even accepted death like a sheep led to the slaughter.*

There was silence in the room. Onesimus felt a shiver of cold. Paul broke the silence. *"Then God exalted him."*

The others in the room took up the cue and quietly sang,

> *God raised him up on high,*
> *And gave to him the name*
> *Above all other names.*
> *To him all we below*
> *And all in heaven above*
> *Do bend the knee and know*
> *The blessed name of Love.*
> *Let every tongue declare*
> *That Jesus Christ is Lord*

Paul smiled; he had set the words to a tune he had known since childhood. Afterward, Onesimus kept humming the tune to himself.

Somehow he had become part of their community; he was able to talk and follow the conversation.

One day while Onesimus was munching on some bread, he remarked thoughtfully. "There are many stories of gods becoming men."

"Yes?" said Paul, raising his eyebrows.

"In the story of Baucis and Philemen, Zeus and Hermes in the form of travelers meet with these two old people and are so impressed with their piety that they turn the couple into trees so that they will not be separated by death."

"Trees do not die?" asked Paul with a smile.

"Well, yes, they do," replied Onesimus, "but that was not the point of the story."

"Then you admit that it was a story."

"Then there is the story of Athena, how she became an old weaving woman and challenged Arachne to a weaving contest."

"Yes," answered Paul, "Who won?"

"Athene, of course; but then, she was not humble."

"And I suppose, my young scholar, that you could think of many more instances," said Paul pleasantly.

par "Yes, I suppose I could," agreed Onesimus.

"Do you believe these stories," asked Paul.

"Well, no, as a matter of fact, I don't," admitted Onesimus.

"That may be the difference. I believe my story. In the depths of my soul I have faith that it is so."

Onesimus pursued the thought. "We must admit that an all power- ful, all-knowing God could become a man, if that is what we desire."

Paul looked up, "Yes, you admit that now, do you?"

"But," continued Onesimus, "Can a man become a God? That is, can a man die, and come to life as a God?"

"What are you thinking?"

"I am thinking about the Emperor. It is said that when Julius died, astrologers found a new star in the heavens. He had been translated from earth to the heavens."

Paul pursed his lips, but refrained from speaking as Onesimus continued.

"And when Octavianus Augustus died, the Roman senate declared him to be divine."

"The Roman Senate could just as easily declare you to be divine," retorted Paul.

"I do not deny it," Onesimus continued, "But the present Emperor already has priests and necromancers preparing him with ceremonies for his translation."

Paul burst into rare laughter, and soon all the room was filled with laughter. Finally Paul spoke up and said, "Onesimus, I think it is time for you to prepare for your translation."

The Baptism

Spring had come, and with it the season of the Passover. The New Community had out of respect for the Death and Resurrection of the Savior left off any of the old remembrance of unleavened bread. However, they did celebrate the time.

"Clean out the old leaven," ordered Paul, *"you must become fresh dough, and you are still unleavened. Our passover lamb, Christ, has already been slaughtered. We shall celebrate the festival but not with old leaven which is the leaven of evil and wickedness, but with our unleavened bread of purity and truth."*

The first day of the week would be celebrated with a feast. In order that new followers could participate in the feast Paul arranged for a baptism of those who had been learners, attending regular meetings. Paul inquired of Onesimus whether he wanted to be one of these, and Onesimus did not hesitate to agree; he had been fearful that the teacher would not consider him as yet fitted for the ceremony. Early in the morning of the Jewish Sabbath a small crowd gathered at a sandy beach where the river turns to go behind the Odeon. Paul had composed a new hymn for the occasion and the community began singing for the neophytes.

We give thanks to our God and Father,

> *and continually we do pray*
> *To keep faith in Christ, Lord Jesus*
>   *and love for all this day.*
>   *we hope with them for heaven.*
> *For we have heard truth's worth,*
>   *Glad news, new-brought to all the earth.*

They continued quietly chanting:

> *From that day when first we heard*
>   *Grace came through His own word,*
> *We prayed his wisdom to discern,*
>   *that we would know and do his will,*
>   *and with his love our spirits fill.*
> *O may we bring forth pleasing fruit*
>   *and grow in the goodness of God.*

The seven neophytes went into the water, allowed themselves to be immersed, and came out of the water shaking the wetness from their naked bodies. Quickly fresh garments were brought and they were dressed, laughing and happy amid the congratulations of the community which they had joined. With them they united in song.

> *Given the power to endure with joy*
>   *strengthened by the might of His glory,*
> *We give thanks, for the Father favors us*
>   *as heirs of his heavenly light*
>   *translated into His kingdom of love.*
> *We are delivered from the reign of darkness*
>   *redeemed and forgiven by his blood.*

On Easter morning the neophytes joined with the community and drank of the cup of blessing. Onesimus demanded from Paul the words to the hymn which Paul remembered by chanting the meter.

When the first week of exaltation was over, Paul said sternly to Onesimus, "Now is the time that you must put your life in order."

The Return

Onesimus had long since confessed the state of his former life to Paul who at the time seemed to pay little attention to the story. Now the apostle told him that Archippus was a member of the community in Colossae, and that the house church now met in the very house which he knew so well. That Philemon, Apphia and Leah were also members thoroughly astonished him, especially when he learned that all of this had taken place under his very nose while he, in his rebellion, had kept himself aloof.

"It was God's will," Paul reassured him; "God was saving you for his own purposes. But now we must find the key to unlock the treasure which you have to give the world."

"How are we to do that?" Onesimus wondered aloud.

"Epaphras has reported to me that Archippus is much concerned about you. It should not be too difficult for you to make amends."

"The problem has always been," Onesimus measured his words slowly, "that no one seems to know whose property I am, whether I belong to Apphia, Archippus or Philemon." He proceeded to tell him the story of the relationship.

"Well, then, we have a choice. Shall we have Apphia free you, or Archippus?"

Onesimus considered the question. "I think it should be Philemon. I offended him the most by striking him. Archippus feels guilt because he is my father; and Apphia would do it only out of duty."

"Philemon it will be then," agreed Paul. "Get a tablet ready and we will formulate a letter which you can copy properly when we have it done."

"Start with the usual introduction: *"Paul, a captive of Christ Jesus and Brother Timothy; to beloved Philemon, our co-worker, and to our beloved sister Apphia, and to Archippus, our fellow soldier and messmate, and to the whole church which meets at your house: Grace to you and peace from our Father God, and of The Lord Jesus, the Christ . . ."*

Paul stopped to give Onesimus instructions in composition. "Notice how I address these persons. I am the *captive* of Christ, Timothy is my *brother*. Philemon is *beloved*, that puns on his name, Apphia is my *sister*, and Archippus is a *fellow soldier and mess-mate*. We are all in this together. And notice how I turn his whole household into a *church*."

"*For you I give thanks at all times and make mention of you in my prayers, because I have heard of your love and of the faith which have toward the Lord Jesus and all the saints. I pray that the sharing of your faith may bring about the knowledge of all the good we may do when have received Christ. For, my brother, I have derived much joy and comfort from you love because the hearts of the saints have been refreshed through you.*"

"You might notice how careful I am in speaking to Philemon, for up to now he has seemed somewhat indecisive about the faith."

"*Accordingly, though I am bold enough in Christ to command you to do what I require, yet for love's sake I prefer to appeal to you. I, Paul, an ambassador and now a prisoner also for Christ Jesus, I appeal to you for my son Onesimus, whose father I have become in my imprisonment.*"

"*I know that he was useless to you but now he is indeed useful (Onesimus) to you and to me also. So I am sending him back to you, and in doing so, sending my very heart. I would have been glad to keep him with me, in order to serve me on your behalf during my imprisonment for the gospel. Still I prefer to do nothing without your consent, in order that your good deed might be voluntary and not something forced upon you.*"

"You will see my strategy in calling Archippus a fellow soldier and mess-mate. And as a 'fellow soldier in Christ,' perhaps I may outrank him a little; at least I have seniority. But you also see that even though I subtly reminded him of that, I do not trade on it. I am now an *ambassador*, that is, one who acts as an intermediary between a runaway slave and his master. You understand that, don't you?"

Onesimus nodded in agreement; this is what would get him off with a light sentence, or even save his life.

Paul continued, "And now is a good time to recall my own civil status, for as a prisoner of the state I am in a worse position than you are; yet you have done me a great service. So now is the time to bring up your name, and its meaning, *Useful*. You must understand that letter writing can influence the feelings of your correspondent even more than if you were speaking face to face. For the reader can scan over and over the words and probe the meanings that may possibly be conveyed."

"Perhaps this is the reason he was separated from you for a while, so that you might have him back forever, no longer a slave, rather more than a slave. He is your beloved brother and mine too, but so much more to you, born in the flesh, and to me born in the Lord Jesus.

"So if you consider me your partner, welcome him as you would me. If he has wronged you in any way, or owes you anything, you may charge it to my account.

"I Paul, am writing this with my own hand: I will repay you. And I will say nothing about your owing me, even your own self. Yes, brother, let me have this benefit from you in the Lord. Refresh my heart in Christ. Confident of your obedience, I am writing to you, knowing that you will do even more than I say. One thing more, prepare a guest room for me, for I am hoping through your prayers to be restored to you.

"Epaphras, my fellow prisoner in Christ Jesus sends greetings, and so do Mark, Aristarchus, Demas and Luke, my fellow co-workers. The grace of the Lord be with your spirit."

"You should note well how subtly we weave in the ideas of human slavery as opposed to slavery in Christ. And, of course, he will remember that all along he was your *beloved brother*, in the physical sense, and now you become *brothers-in-Christ*. Then just so that he may not get off by feeling that he has in some way been cheated financially on the deal, I offer a payment. We know that he could not graciously accept the payment. Please notice, my dear Onesimus, that letter writing demands great finesse and observance of all due propriety."

Onesimus nodded again in admiration. He realized that now he was receiving lessons from a master teacher. Having dutifully inscribed the letter in a fine hand, Onesimus gave it to Paul for signature. Paul signed it and gave it back.

"Now you must deliver it," he said simply.

The next day found Onesimus, accompanied by Tychicus, on his way back to Colossae; not, however, taking the low road along the river but taking the well traveled high road which scales the hill tops for bandits cannot swooop down on a high road. Paul had arranged for them to join with a group of travelers, for there is security in numbers. In general the travelers were a merry group, but Onesimus became withdrawn and silent. His way from Colossae had been in a mood of fear and anger. Now, he was no longer angry but the fear had not left, for his imagination played over the possible reception he might find on his return. In the middle of the third day with Colossae in sight, panic almost overcame him; he could scarcely restrain himself from turning in flight. Tychicus tried to allay his fears, but according to plan left the group when they came to Laodicea. Onesimus pushed on and finally left his new-found friends outside the city gates. At the Fountain of the Nereids he stopped to wash his face and adjust his back pack. Home was not far away.

As he neared the house he saw Stamnion sweeping the walkway outside the entry. "Aye-yee, a ghost," screamed Stamnion, who fled into the house.

He walked into the house as Stamnion returned with Philemon who appeared to be utterly dismayed.

"Is it you, brother?" stammered Philemon.

"Of course it's me; who else would it be?"

Philemon drew in his breath, "We believed that you were dead."

He burst into tears and Onesimus involuntarily threw his arms about him to hold him as he wept. Startled by the break in the customary silence, Archippus came running up and stopped short when he recognized his son. He seemed to be at a loss for words. Slowly they walked into the peristyle and sat down on a bench there.

Onesimus loosed his back pack and produced the letter which he gave to Philemon.

Philemon read the letter in silence and handed it to Archippus to read. While he was reading Apphia came running in. Seeing Onesimus she drew in her breath and went over to Philemon. When Archippus had read the letter, he stood up and said quietly "Of course we welcome you, my son."

Then, he unfastened a gold chain that he was wearing and put it around Onesimus neck.

It was now Onesimus' turn to be amazed.

"Where did you find it?" he gasped.

"I found it for sale in the collection of a street monger in Ephesus," replied Archippus. "I was certain you would not willingly part with it, so I assumed you were dead."

"It was stolen from me," Onesimus replied quietly and he told them briefly of the theft.

"This is truly a sign from God."

Philemon had now recovered himself for he stood and grasped Onesimus by the hand, "I welcome you as a brother in Christ."

The tears came again and Archippus said, "My son that was lost has returned to me."

By this time Asterion and Stamnion had come with Platon into the room; and Leah came in wiping her eyes on her apron.

"Prepare the fatted calf," called Archippus. That evening the whole household, master and slaves, mistress and weaving women ate a joyous meal together each one serving the other. All were eager to congratulate Onesimus, and all wanted to hear about Paul of Tarsus who was greatly revered by them all. In the middle of the evening, Epaphras came in.

"I have heard the good news, and I know that I must rejoice with you, for here is proof that love never ends."

Unnoticed during the festivity, Onesimus approached Epaphras and whispered, "I have a letter for you also," and he gave him another letter from his packet.

During the passing days there were many questions to be answered and much to be explained.

"Paul says that he will be coming; will that be soon?"

Onesimus had no answer to that question but Philemon replied, "There will always be a room in this house that remains prepared for Paul, no matter when he comes."

Everyone was eager to hear of the returned son's adventures. Onesimus could not tell the story of the mishaps on the way to Ephesus enough, though by this time the bandit was more cunning than ever, and the blackguard was larger. The soldiers almost became supernaturally demonic.

"And how did you fare? How did you make your living?"

Onesimus told about his adventures as a street scribe.

Platon was pleased, "Do you mean you could actually subsist by writing letters?"

Onesimus nodded in agreement, but there were parts of the tale that he kept to himself. For his part, Onesimus, too, was eager to hear all that had happened. He was still non-plused about the conversion of the whole house to the new faith.

"Are the slaves also Christians?" he wondered. "Do Stamnion and Asterion worship with you?"

Archippus acknowledged that they did not, however should they desire to become followers of our faith, we would welcome them, he hastened to add. Onesimus questioned Epaphras whom he had seen now and then at Paul's lodgings.

Epaphras admitted that he knew of the family's loss of Onesimus; indeed, he felt that their loss was an essential part of their acceptance of the gospel. But as for himself, he had somehow never made the connection between the disappearance of Archippus' son and the acceptance of a convert in Paul's household. In due time Onesimus had reacquainted himself with everyone. Still there was one missing. One day Philemon volunteered.

"I suppose you are wondering about the girl." Onesimus nodded agreement.

"Mother sent her away, and I have not heard about her since. I must admit that neither have I inquired."

The Church was soon to meet at the House of Archippus and Apphia. It was to be a somewhat larger than usual gathering. Nympha's household would also be present, as well as visitors from Laodicea. Epaphras would be the speaker. Rumors went around that Paul would be there also. Onesimus rehearsed a group of singers in the song that had been sung at his baptism. Onesimus added a verse of his own creation:

> *Christ is the ikon of God, the Invisible*
> *The First Born of all Creation.*
> *His word produced the heavens*
> *On earth, the visible and unseen.*
> *He created Thrones and Kingdoms and Powers,*
> *He is above them all; All things subsist in Him.*
> *O Ye who are born of the earth,*
> *O ye, who dwell in heaven,*
> *Once alienated in mind*
> *and in wicked works overcome.*
> *By his flesh pierced in death*
> *Be raised holy, without blame or reproach.*
> *Given the power to endure with joy*
> *Strengthened in his glory.*

Epaphras read the letter which Onesimus had given him.

> *In our prayers we always thank God, the Father of our Lord Jesus Christ; for we have heard of your faith and of the love that you have for all the saints because of the hope laid up for you in heaven. You have already heard of this hope in the words of the Gospel that has come to you. It is bearing fruit and growing in the whole world. For this reason since the day we heard it, we have not ceased praying for you and asking that you may be filled with the knowledge of God's will . . .*

I rejoice in my suffering. In my own flesh I am com-
pleting what is lacking in Christ's afflictions for the sake
of his body. His body is the Church. I am its servant
according to God's commission, given to me for you, to
make the Word of God fully known. For it has been a mys-
tery hidden throughout the ages. But now it is revealed to
you, his saints.

Epaphras paused while the worshippers meditated and then congratulated one another.

I am struggling for you, for those in Laodicea, and for
all those that I have not met. I want to encourage their
hearts and to encourage them in love. I want to assure
them that they know God's mystery: that in Christ are
hidden all of the treasures of wisdom and knowledge. Let
no one deceive you with other arguments. I am always
with you in spirit and I rejoice to see you strong in your
morale and firm in your faith in Christ.

So continue to live your lives in Christ, rooted and
established in faith, as you were taught. Beware that you
be taken in by false philosophies and empty traditions of
the elemental spirits of the Universe, as you once believed.
The whole fullness of deity dwells bodily in Christ's body.
You were buried with him in your baptism and you were
raised with him through faith in the power of God. It is
God who made you alive, forgiving all trespasses. He set
aside all previous legalities, nailing them to the Cross.
He has disarmed rulers and authorities, triumphing over
them as a public example.

Epaphras stopped his reading and waited for wandering minds to
catch up. He wanted to make sure that what was coming next would
be heard by all, for there were those present who had difficulties in
abandoning their old beliefs.

> *Pay no attention to those who would take you to task in matters of food and drink. Forget the festivals of new moons, sabbaths, and old gods. These are only shadows. The substance belongs to Christ. Put aside self abasement, scratching of faces, false tears. We do not worship the angels, or dwell on night visions which puff us up with human thinking. Hold fast to the Head of our body; our growth comes from God.*

They listened attentively, some covering their eyes, some shaking their heads.

> *You no longer belong to the world, for in Christ you died to the elemental spirits. There is nothing in the old regulations of 'Do not touch! Do not handle! Do not taste!' These things are perishable; They are simply human commands. They may have the appearance of wisdom but they are of no value.*

The sermon seemed over long to those who were not accustomed to such words, but when Epaphras pronounced,

> *If you have been raised with Christ, seek the things that are above where Christ is, seated at the right hand of God. Set your minds on the things that are above, not on things that are on earth, for you have died and your life is hidden with Christ in God. When Christ who is your life is revealed, then you also will be revealed in glory.*

Then they all called out "Amen" and a cheer went up, even from those who had not joined with the little church before.

At last Epaphras closed the reading,

> *Tychicus will tell you all the news. I have sent him to you for this purpose since I cannot come at this time. He comes with Onesimus, our faithful and beloved brother who is one of you. They will tell you how it fares with us.*

Aristarchus greets you and so does Mark, the cousin of Barnabas. If he comes to you, welcome him. These are the people who have been a comfort to me in Ephesus. You should know that Epaphras is always wrestling in his prayers on your behalf. He has worked hard for you and for those in Laodicea and Hierapolis. Luke, my beloved physician, and Demas also send their love. Give my love to the brothers and sisters in Laodicea and to Nympha and the church in her house. After this letter is read to you, send it on and let it be read in the other churches.

Finally, this is my word to Archippus. "See that you complete the task that you have received in the Lord."

At the end of the letter in a less formal hand was written,

I Paul, write this greeting with my own hand. Remember my chains. Grace be with you.

When Onesimus heard this, he wept; the others all came to him and comforted him as he touched the signature of his beloved benefactor.

New Life

5 The next day their rulers, elders, and scribes assembled in Jerusalem,
6 with Annas the high priest, Caiaphas, John, and Alexander, and all who were of the high-priestly family.
7 When they had made the prisoners stand in their midst, they inquired, "By what power or by what name did you do this?"
8 Then Peter, filled with the Holy Spirit, said to them, "Rulers of the people and elders,
9 if we are questioned today because of a good deed done to someone who was sick and are asked how this man has been healed,
10 let it be known to all of you, and to all the people of Israel, that this man is standing before you in good health by the name of Jesus Christ of Nazareth, whom you crucified, whom God raised from the dead.
11 This Jesus is 'the stone that was rejected by you, the builders; it

has become the cornerstone.'
12 There is salvation in no one else, for there is no other name under heaven given among mortals by which we must be saved."
(Acts 4:5–12, NRSV)

1 We declare to you what was from the beginning, what we have heard, what we have seen with our eyes, what we have looked at and touched with our hands, concerning the word of life—
2 this life was revealed, and we have seen it and testify to it, and declare to you the eternal life that was with the Father and was revealed to us—
3 we declare to you what we have seen and heard so that you also may have fellowship with us; and truly our fellowship is with the Father and with his Son Jesus Christ.
4 We are writing these things so that our joy may be complete.
5 This is the message we have heard from him and proclaim to you, that God is light and in him there is no darkness at all.
6 If we say that we have fellowship with him while we are walking in darkness, we lie and do not do what is true;
7 but if we walk in the light as he himself is in the light, we have fellowship with one another, and the blood of Jesus cleanses us from all sin.
8 If we say that we have no sin, we deceive ourselves, and the truth is not in us.
9 If we confess our sins, he who is faithful and just will forgive us our sins and cleanse us from all unrighteousness.
10 If we say that we have not sinned, we make him a liar, and his word is not in us.

2:1 My little children, I am writing these things to you so that you may not sin. But if anyone does sin, we have an advocate with the Father, Jesus Christ the righteous;
2 and he is the atoning sacrifice for our sins, and not for ours only but

also for the sins of the whole world.

(1 John 1:1 – 2:2, NRSV)

36 While they were talking about this, Jesus himself stood among them and said to them, "Peace be with you."
37 They were startled and terrified, and thought that they were seeing a ghost.
38 He said to them, "Why are you frightened, and why do doubts arise in your hearts?
39 Look at my hands and my feet; see that it is I myself. Touch me and see; for a ghost does not have flesh and bones as you see that I have."
40 And when he had said this, he showed them his hands and his feet.
41 While in their joy they were disbelieving and still wondering, he said to them, "Have you anything here to eat?"
42 They gave him a piece of broiled fish,
43 and he took it and ate in their presence.
44 Then he said to them, "These are my words that I spoke to you while I was still with you—that everything written about me in the law of Moses, the prophets, and the psalms must be fulfilled."
45 Then he opened their minds to understand the scriptures,
46 and he said to them, "Thus it is written, that the Messiah is to suffer and to rise from the dead on the third day,
47 and that repentance and forgiveness of sins is to be proclaimed in his name to all nations, beginning from Jerusalem.
48 You are witnesses of these things.

(Luke 24:36–48, NRSV)

Shortly thereafter Archippus called the two young men into his library. That the three of them should be conversing together on equal terms had always seemed most unlikely. Even now they were on edge. Archippus dismissed the slave who usually stood by to act upon his wishes.

"I have called you together because I want you to understand my dilemma," the host began. "You probably know the circumstances, but we have never discussed them, and certainly not in each other's company. You, Philemon, are my nephew." Philemon nodded. "And a very special nephew, for you are my widowed sister's son. As the maternal uncle, I have held authority over you in your minority. According to Roman law, and we are under Roman rule, I hold the *patria potestas* that controls this family. It might be expected that upon your reaching your majority, I might emancipate you and allow you to claim your patrimony. I see that you smile at the thought. The problem is that your patrimony is as yet undefined. Your mother, my sister, is still alive and very capable. When I brought her to this house, our father's house, she was scarcely more than a child, but she has matured and has become a competent woman, able to conduct her own affairs and direct her own business. Nevertheless, according to the law, she is still my ward."

Philemon frowned; it was impossible for him to think of his mother as the *ward* of his uncle. Apphia ran the household with a firm hand.

"Now the laws of inheritance are clear. Our father left no will that could be found. Therefore his property descended to me, his only son. I am the owner of this house in which we live. Apphia's husband, your father, was also an only son, but you were not yet born at the time of his death. So his property descended to your mother. According to the laws of inheritance, you should become the owner of these lands. However, as the years have gone by, we have purchased more lands and added them to the original farm. I fear that we did this as a joint venture, and we have made no determination as to which of us is the owner. In simple terms, I am the one who has the authority to say, for technically I am the *pater familias*. I confess that I have always avoided any confrontation with my sister. In fact, that is why she is not here now."

Philemon spoke up. "As I understand it, uncle, were you to die at this minute, stricken before our very eyes, I would become the *pater familias* with the control and ownership of all of this property, house and lands alike."

"You understand correctly," replied the uncle grimly.

"Well, don't be so serious," Philemon smiled, "I have no intention to murder you in your bed. As a matter of fact, I much prefer that you have to deal with my mother than that I should have to do so."

Archippus looked flustered, wishing that he did not have to deal with either mother or son. Turning to Onesimus, he changed the subject. "Onesimus, I have always wanted to have a son of my own, to be my proper heir. I could have married, but I have to confess that I did not want to face the prospect of a legal confrontation with my sister. It has been comfortable living here; I certainly could not bear the thought of living in the same house with two mistresses of the household. A man who would do that must be out of his mind. Of course I knew and accepted that you are my natural son. However, your mother was a slave. This determined your status. Society winks at this relationship, and does not even allow me to acknowledge that I am your father."

Onesimus fidgeted in embarrassment.

"I have always had in my mind that at some point I would manumit you and give you your freedom. But you must understand my problem. Your mother belonged to Apphia, and therefore you belong to Apphia. I cannot manumit you without her consent."

Onesimus nodded agreement. This was how he had presented the problem to Paul. This was why Paul had written his letter to Philemon, for Paul quickly deduced that the ownership of this slave would descend to Philemon.

Philemon turned to Onesimus, "I would wish with all my heart to grant your manumission."

Archippus said quietly, "That would be very desirable. If you granted manumission to Onesimus, then I could adopt him and make him my heir."

Philemon was startled, "Then why not manumit him yourself, if you want him for an heir."

Archippus returned with, "Because the law does not allow a man to adopt his own freedman; otherwise I would have purchased Onesimus from your mother and freed him long ago."

Onesimus said calmly, "I am a slave; whose slave I am cannot be determined by me. If I am freed, I become a freedman. Again, I cannot choose whose freedman I shall be. I cannot even choose the conditions under which I should be freed, whether to remain in this household as a free employee or leaving this household and making my own living. I know, however, that Christ is my true master; whatever my earthly fate, my life is bound up in Christ."

Archippus replied, "I am proud to have such a son."

Philemon reddened and said, "I will have to speak with my mother about this."

Within a few days the whole household was gathered together in the peristyle. Leah and the household slaves together with the weaving women looked on. Epaphras had come as a witness with Tychicus. Archippus and Apphia were seated in chairs on a dais. Philemon sat just below his mother; Onesimus sat just below Archippus. Platon stood at a nearby table with parchment and writing instruments.

Archippus stood stiffly and said, "Apphia, for twenty denarii, one denarius for each year of his life, I purchase from you the slave Onesimus."

Apphia stood, "I accept the sum and transfer the ownership of the slave Onesimus into your authority."

Both then signed the ownership contract which Platon presented. When that was done, Archippus stood and taking Onesimus by the hand said, "Onesimus, faithful slave, I grant you this day your freedom. Onesimus Archippides Paulus, on this day you are a freedman of this City with all of the duties and privileges that pertain to that status. We will sign the documents that outline this agreement."

They went to the table where the contract of freedom had been drawn up. Onesimus saw the terms of freedom.

> For past labors performed he was to receive 100 gold drachmas, no mean sum for a young man to have to start life with. He agreed that for the following three years and as long thereafter that he should desire, he was to live in the house of Archippus and render the services that he was equipped to give, for a reasonable fee.

His status was obvious, Freedman of Archippus.

The small audience applauded as Archippus put a fine purple cloak over his shoulders. Apphia presented him with a linen scarf. Philemon kissed him on both cheeks and put a gold signet ring on his finger. Onesimus stood and thanked his benefactors and addressed them all.

" ... and I am especially honored to bear the name of Paul, my father-in-god."

The tears came to his eyes as he thought to himself, "Under the terms of the contract, I may not return to serve Paul for three years. In the days that followed it seemed to most that not much had changed. The slaves had seen one of their number manumitted. Some saw the manumission as a positive change; there had been no such act in their memory; others could say that they knew of no other slave who was the master's son. For Leah, little had changed. Onesimus and Philemon still wandered into her kitchen and munched on cookies while joking with each other.

Leah said, "They are both my sons, and we are all God's children together."

Onesimus came more frequently and began to learn Hebrew letters from Leah while she told him stories from the Scriptures, as she had heard them. Apphia, feeling a little more secure in the matter of Philemon's inheritance, renewed her weaving work and considered opening a shop in a long-vacant street front space. There she would sell clothing already made and ready for wearing to wealthy customers.

"I am certain there will be a market," she told Archippus, who fretted over the thought of his sister employed in such non-aristocratic fashion.

"Well, of course, I wouldn't wait on trade myself," she retorted. "Perhaps your freedman would like to be a shop-keeper."

Archippus refused to respond to the little dig. However, Archippus seemed to be much freer, as though a weight had fallen from his shoulders. He took Onesimus and Philemon down on a tour of the farms where they examined the crops and looked over the slaves. Onesimus pointed out that many of the slaves were badly in need of clothing and that sandals would protect their feet. "It would certainly be cost-efficient," he remarked. "Many slaves cannot work at all because of foot injuries from rocks and thorns."

Archippus required a list of needed garments and sandals from the overseer. They also examined some boundary stones, along with hedges that had been planted marking off newly acquired property from the old property. Both young men made mental notes of what might possibly come down to them.

When they were alone, Onesimus asked Philemon, "I have not seen the maid Erotion. She does not seem to be among the weaving women. What has become of her?"

"I gave her back to my mother; I really was in no need of female companionship at the time. Mother was angry with me about it because she thought that having the girl would finish up my education in that department. Shortly afterward she disappeared, but I never asked where. I am sure mother found a proper place for her, for we all were baptized about that time, and mother was very careful that her women were well treated. Mother never brought it up again. I think because it didn't seem proper for a Christian to take a concubine." Onesimus was careful not to mention the subject again.

Epaphras came one morning. He usually visited Archippus' house when he was in Colossae. He enquired of Onesimus if he thought Paul would come soon to Colossae.

Onesimus shook his head in disagreement. "I don't really think that Paul meant more than a pleasantry. He is thinking of a quick trip back to the Peloponnese. He wants to see the Corinthians again."

"That was my thinking," sighed Epaphras. "The church at Laodicea is a little miffed because Paul sent you Colossians a letter. Laodicea is the older and larger community, you know. I spoke to Tychicus about it before he left and he said that you might be able to arrange things, that you knew what to do."

Onesimus nodded, "Yes, I think it might be possible to get the Laodiceans a letter."

"Then you must come with it, bearing it in your hands; the church at Laodicea would be happy to hear from you too."

Onesimus acknowledged the invitation with a smile. When they were alone, Epaphras whispered to Onesimus, "There is a young maid servant in the household of Nympha who says she knows you. Her name is Erotion."

Within a fortnight, Onesimus let it be known that he was in possession of a letter from Paul for the Laodiceans. Paul had given him instructions before he had left Ephesus that he should be equipped to produce such letters, for they had constructed many of them—letters of greeting, letters of consolation, letters of advice. Paul was always getting requests for more than he himself could produce. Tertius, Paul's amanuensis, had welcomed the help of Onesimus.

Now Onesimus had a small cell of his own for his writing materials and his books. On the first day of the week, Onesimus found himself in Laodicea with a letter protected by a rough linen cloth. The house church of Epaphras awaited him eagerly.

> *Paul, an apostle not of men and not through man, but through Jesus Christ, to the brethren who are in Laodicea.*

Onesimus pronounced in a loud voice.

> *Grace to you and peace from God the Father and the Lord Jesus Christ.*
>
> *I thank Christ in all my prayers that you are steadfast in him and persevering in his works, in expectation of the day of judgment. May you not be deceived by the vain talk of some people who tell tales that they may lead you away from the truth of the good news which is proclaimed by me. Now may God grant that those who come from me for the furtherance of the truth of the gospel may be able to serve and do good works for the well-being of eternal life.*
>
> *Now are my bonds become manifest, which I suffer in Christ and on account of which I am glad and rejoice.*

They serve me into eternal salvation, which if effected through your prayers and by the help of the Holy Spirit, whether it be through life or through death. My life is in Christ and to die for Him is joy for me.

Let his mercy work in you, that you may have the same love and be of one mind. Therefore, beloved, as you have heard from me, hold fast and do this in the fear of God, so that eternal life will be your portion. For it is God who works in you. And do without hesitation whatever you do. For the rest, beloved, rejoice in Christ and beware of those who are out for sordid gain. May all your requests be manifest before God. Remain steadfast in the mind of Christ. Do whatever is pure, true, proper, just and lovely. What you have heard and received, hold in your hearts, and peace will be with you.

Salute all the brethren with a holy kiss. The saints salute you. The grace of the Lord Jesus Christ be with your spirit. And see that this epistle is read to the Colossians and that of the Colossians to you.

The Laodicean church crowded around Onesimus to see and touch the letter.

"And see, it is written in the blessed Paul's own hand," cried one.

Onesimus struggled to say, "No, no" ... but the crowd drowned out his voice. Epaphras signaled that he should remain quiet.

"After all, you and I know that Paul cannot write all of the letters himself."

Onesimus sighed, "These were the instructions that Paul gave me; that I should answer letters for him as they were needed."

"Of course," returned Epaphras, "Paul is a practical man. Besides, I hear that he has already sailed for Corinth."

Later Epaphras spoke with Onesimus. "I am in need of a helper. The churches in Laodicea, Colossae and Hierapolis are a burden that is more than one man can handle. I have spoken with Archippus about this and he and I agree that you could serve very well as a deacon."

"I, a deacon?" Onesimus was dismayed. "I have not been a follower of Christ for a whole year yet."

"You were trained by the very best leader of all," continued Epaphras. "And you have access to many people. Look at how they loved you here. Philip served us well in Hierapolis, but like so many, he has passed on and there has been none to take his place. I want you to think about this seriously. Archippus approves. Now you must pray for guidance."

Onesimus hardly knew what to say. All he could think was, "And this takes me even farther from Paul."

"But what does a deacon do?" expostulated Onesimus the next time that he saw Epaphras.

"Why, you must know," was the reply. "A deacon sees to it that there is enough bread and wine at the weekly meeting of remembrance."

"That is a fairly simple requirement," returned Onesimus.

"Perhaps for you, sir, but bread and wine are not easily obtained by everyone."

Onesimus still felt shock when he was addressed as "sir," but he jogged his memory and found himself bringing bread and wine to Paul's house in those first days.

Epaphras continued, "Then the deacon sees that the table is properly set and helps to serve those who come to the table. It can be more arduous than you think."

"Somewhat like preparing a banquet for Archippus?" Onesimus smiled at the memory.

"Yes, except this banquet is a symbol, an outward and visible sign."

"I take it that the real banquet is a heavenly one?"

"Yes, a spiritual feeding at the table of Jesus," continued the elder. "However, the deacon has another, much more important role in the physical realm. It is his responsibility to learn which of the brethren do not in fact have enough to eat and see to it that they do not starve."

"Are there many such in Colossae?" asked the would-be deacon. Epaphras was thunderstruck.

"You have lived in Colossae all of your life and you do not know that?" "I have lived my life in Colossae in the house of Archippus. In his house, even the slaves are well fed. However, I lived a short time in Ephesus. I know that food is not so plentiful there."

"Actually, I had thought you had made a good start at being a deacon," mused Epaphras. "I understood that you required that the house of Archippus provide its slaves with shoes and better clothing."

"In Archippus house the slaves are well kept, but this is not so among the field hands. And, of course, our house probably does better than most of the others in the Lycus valley. May I ask you, am I right in bringing the message of Jesus to the slaves? Archippus says that he does not meddle with slave religion."

Epaphras stopped and was silent awhile, "Let Archippus follow his own conscience on that one; but you must follow the words of Christ."

"Which are?"

"I was hungry, and you fed me."

Onesimus rose to his morning prayers, walking slowly up the aerie. The sun had not yet made its way over the eastern hills. Out of his memory he pulled the words of Paul. He had listened to them as Paul said them to Timothy when he went off on a mission.

> *A deacon must be serious, and not double-tongued. Do not overindulge in wine, nor be greedy for money, for you must hold fast to your faith with a clear conscience. You have been tested and not found wanting and therefore you are well trained to be a deacon. And there should be women prepared for this role, and they too should be serious, and in no wise, slanderers. A woman servant should be temperate and faithful in all things. Deacons may be married, but only once. If they are married they should be able to rule their households and their children. A deacon should serve in good standing with the entire community, and they must pursue the faith with boldness to the glory of Jesus Christ.*

Those were Paul's words as he remembered them, and he wondered where Timothy was now and if Paul had indeed arrived in Corinth. When Onesimus met with Epaphras again, he assented to the elder's wishes.

Epaphras was pleased, and then turned serious, "I understand that you have undertaken to study Hebrew with Leah. That is a good thing for you to do. Most of us are unable to read the ancient scriptures."

When the Paschal season returned again, a number of Jewish converts were baptized, and Onesimus read to them in Hebrew the Passover story, translating it into Greek for those who did not understand the ancient language. At the end of that time, he knelt at the table in the House Church of Nympha, and the brothers laid hands upon him and prayed.

Love Never Ends

Whenever he went to the House Church of Nympha, Onesimus would carefully look over the crowd of those who attended as if he were searching for someone. His gaze would end with a small group of veiled women who sat silent, each one alone to herself, even though a member of the group. They were all dressed in similar manner, each wearing a long-sleeved sticharion of a coarse unbleached material and their heads covered with a black maforta, faded from much washing. They covered their heads and hair and reached down to their shoulders. Most of these ladies drew the maforta across their faces during the service and kept their heads bowed. These were the virgins who had given themselves to Christ and had withdrawn from the world. They had been led into this group by one of the daughters of the Evangelist Philip. She had prophesied boldly for the Lord and had led many women to reclaim the right to their own bodies. No other churches with which Onesimus was acquainted had such groups of virgins. The women in the House of Archippus dressed in customary clothing, and rather boldly mingled with their male associates. The women of other house churches in Colossae and Laodicea were wives and daughters and acted in accustomed fashion. There were widows, some of whom had withdrawn into a life of prayer; but this was by no means unusual in any community. Onesimus understood that he had a special duty as a deacon to tend to the needs of widows and virgins who had dedicated themselves, for they often had no one else to depend upon for support. He often brought gifts of food and money, and cast off clothing to be reworked into something wearable or made into patches, sewed together for bedcovering for the poor. For the most part, he had little conversation with these mysterious ladies.

Among the virgins of Nympha, he finally came to believe that he had identified one.

"My Lady," he whispered softly, "are you one that I may have known many years ago?" He had chosen his words carefully, hoping to give no offense.

She replied in a low voice, "Yes, Onesimus, I am Erotion."

"How fares it with thee?" he asked.

"You can see, I have taken a vow to The Lord," she replied. "I have devoted my life to the Lord."

"I understand," confessed Onesimus, "a virgin is concerned about the affairs of The Lord; she has vowed to be holy both in body and in spirit, and I applaud your choice. But, how fares it with thee?"

Erotion looked up at him. "I believed that you were dead; Archippus brought us tokens from Ephesus that seemed to be proof of that. Apphia urged me to attend the needs of Philemon, but as a Christian, she could not ask me to defile myself, even though I was a slave. So she sent me away to Nympha who has treated me well. Nympha herself taught me about Jesus and when I was baptized I took these vows to remain a virgin. I am content with my vows, Onesimus."

Onesimus replied, "Our leader Paul has said, 'Let each one remain as he is.' For Paul believes that the Day of the Lord will not be delayed in the coming and that our lives should be spent in anticipation of that day. There will be time for enjoyment in the courts of the Lord."

"That is a time to which I devote my thoughts, dear Onesimus."

"I too have made a vow to the Lord. I have vowed to serve Paul in this life; to serve Paul as a slave serves his master. This is an earthly service in preparation for the heavenly service. Word comes to me from Paul that I serve him best at the present by being a deacon here; but one day I shall return to Paul as his amanuensis and his servant. This is a vow that I must keep. However, in my heart I am betrothed to you, Erotion. One day, whether in this earthly life or in the time of the Lord, I shall claim you."

Onesimus took the golden chain with the blue bead from around his neck and pressed it into her hand.

"The time is short. We are the more blessed if we remain as we are."

Speaking these words, Onesimus kissed Erotion lightly on the forehead.

She drew her veil across her face and replied, "I believe you, Onesimus, and I will be faithful."

They turned slowly away from each other and walked away. Although they lived in the same house Philemon and Onesimus saw little of each other. Onesimus busied himself constantly with ministering to the troubled ones of Colossae and also travelled much between Hierapolis and Laodicea. Archippus laughingly said that it was worse to keep him in shoes than it had been when he was a child. Philemon acted the gentleman and spent much of his afternoons at the baths and at the gymnasium. He pointed out that he was not neglecting the work of the Lord; it was that he found the Lord's work included the gymnasium and the baths. Onesimus allowed him this right but said that he himself was uncomfortable in the company to be found there.

"Let each one keep to the station wherein he was called," he often quoted. "Philemon was an evergete; I was a slave. Philemon must uphold the honor of our house; I must minister to slaves."

"I had hoped that we could enjoy our common life together," lamented Philemon, "but let it be as it is until the day of His Coming. Nevertheless, I find an hour of boxing followed by a contest of throwing the disc and then relaxing in the afternoon with an hour in the tepid bath followed by time with my masseur, followed by the hot bath, followed by the cold bath, . . . " Onesimus rolled his eyes.

Philemon continued, "I find all of this a colossal bore. Sports and games hold no joys anymore; and an afternoon at the baths is simply a waste of time."

Archippus interceded. "Better to spend your time with the philosophers, as I do."

"You are right, uncle. I am sure that you find Platon better at conversation than I find my masseur. I see your eyes sparkle, Onesimus. I think you have the best of us."

"There is no disagreement from me; what do you propose to do about it?"

"I have a plan," announced Philemon. "If my uncle here will agree to it. I must have his permission, you know; You are freed, Onesimus; but I am not emancipated." Archippus pretended not to hear.

"My plan is to go off and study philosophy for myself."

Archippus looked up in surprise. "Indeed, and where do you propose to go?"

"Well, sir, if it is all right with you, I would like to take up residence at Pergamon. Certainly it is a place of excellent reputation; the library there is unsurpassed. I have investigated and found that there is a church established there; furthermore it is rather nearer to home than some place across the seas."

"Well said!" Archippus agreed enthusiastically. "I suggest that you take Platon with you as your man-servant. He might be a great help in your studies."

"I had hoped that you would give Platon the gift of manumission," interposed Onesimus. "Platon is growing old and has served us faithfully. He deserves his freedom."

"Perhaps Platon should be asked which gift he wants, the life of a freedman or access to the libraries of Pergamon."

They all agreed to this and sent for Platon.

"I must think about this for awhile," said Platon in embarrassment. "These are the two great wishes of my life; now I must choose one over the other."

"It need not be a choice," said Archippus with a kindly voice.

"There is no reason why you may not have both. You shall go with Philemon to Pergamon to help him with his studies as his freedman. We will find another serving man to help you both." And so it was agreed.

Philemon whispered later to Archippus, "You are losing the company of one who was devoted to you."

"I have Onesimus," replied the older man. One morning Onesimus found Stamnion sitting by the fountain. Stamnion struggled to his feet. "Friend," said Onesimus, taking Stamnion by the hand. "Sit you down. You certainly need not rise for me." Stamnion eyed him cagily.

"You are a gentleman now, as anyone can see by your long himation and corded girdle. I wear the short tunic, don't you know."

"We are friends, old Jug-Ears. And you're my elder; I'm just Archipor, a young rapscallion without much sense, who once insisted on his own way."

Stamnion laughed a little and replied, "I know my place. You're educated and you're the master's son. We don't begrudge you that. And you are the Master's son too, you know."

"Oh, now, stop joking. I'm still the son of the Northwind. We are all the sons of the Northwind, and that makes us brothers, you and I. The Northwind is our Master. He is our God. Yes, the God of us all speaks to us whether the wind blows from the North or the South; He is the God of the sunrise and the sunset."

"Are you speaking of God to me?" asked the surprised Stamnion.

"Indeed, I am; for I can tell you a secret. God sent his son to deliver all of us from bondage. I know that because he has delivered me. He has delivered me from a bondage harder than the bondage of chains; he has delivered me from the bondage of sin, and has appointed me to announce this to you. Jesus, the son of God, came to tell all of us that He is our only master." Stamnion looked at his old friend nervously. "You are hard to understand, boy; but tell me more."

And so Onesimus first introduced Stamnion to Jesus, and continued his tale daily until Stamnion brought Asterion with him to listen and see if he had heard aright.

"The business of being an evangelist is not the easy life," confessed Onesimus to Epaphras some weeks later.

As For Knowledge

Preparations were now in order for the new turn in Philemon's life. Not unexpected was Apphia's distress, but after the initial outburst, she became unusually calm and diligently began preparing a wardrobe for her son's new status. Before long Philemon was begging for mercy, for the carriers if not for himself. He confided to Onesimus that he wished that he had the courage to disappear into the night taking nothing with him except what he could carry.

Onesimus replied that he would in that case be taken either for a runaway slave or a missionary, but that he could not testify which would put a traveler in a less dangerous position. It was decided that Philemon should not leave until after the grape harvest when the weather is best for traveling. Archippus pointed out that a journey to Pergamon could be accomplished in a week at the most and that Pergamon was well supplied with all of the necessities of living. Letters were prepared for certain officials and dignitaries there introducing Philemon as the scion of a well established house in Colossae and praising the scholarship and abilities of the Freedman Platon. Two slaves were to attend them and take care of their daily needs. Platon selected two young men from the farm who seemed to show some intelligence. They were brought to the main house and given instructions in behavior and etiquette by Asterion who was considered to be quite superior in household matters. All of these preparations took more than three months, and everyone was quite exhausted when the blessed day came.

Quiet descended; Archippus came out of his library more frequently now, admitting that it was the flurry of household activities and the noise it entailed which had kept him a prisoner in his own domain. Onesimus spent the morning hours checking on the needs of the members of several house churches in the area, purchasing bread and other food stuffs for the housebound widows and old men. Cautiously he would leave choice fruits and vegetables outside the door of the house of the virgins. Late in the morning he would visit the slave quarters bringing gifts of clothing and sandals and playthings for the children who came running at his approach. When he had a crowd gathered he would tell them the story of Jesus and reward those who could answer his questions best with sweets or trinkets.

The laborers soon learned that they would be granted time off from work for listening to Onesimus'sermons; and before long many were demanding to be baptized. The overseer was somewhat less than enchanted by Onesimus' evangelical success, and complained to Archippus that he would have to double his labor force if things continued in that direction. Onesimus would redouble his assurances that the blessed Paul had promised no slave his freedom, in fact, had commended habits of industry and obedience for the enslaved. This was not a tenet that Onesimus found personally acceptable, but the opposite line of thinking was almost too difficult to justify. Onesimus, on the one hand condemned slavery; but on the other could not determine how a world would work without it.

Stamnion, Asterion and the other house slaves along with a number of the weaving women became followers and joined in with the house church as members and worshipers. Indeed there was a congeniality among the free and the enslaved which had not been known before; but the slaves still maintained their places. Stamnion shook his head when manumission was suggested to him.

"What would I do? Where would I go?"

Onesimus, remembering the streets of Ephesus, had no answer, except the answer of Paul. Time in this era was short.

Word came to Epaphras that Paul had returned to Asia and had summoned the elders of Ephesus and the surrounding regions to meet with him at Miletus. Onesimus was overjoyed that he was to join with them there. A collection was made so that Paul could be remembered with a gift to help him on his next venture. Epaphras and Onesimus joined a traveling group to that port city, since it was always wise to travel with a crowd that would be formidable to hill bandits. Most of the travelers walked, but had pack animals to carry their baggage. There were several litters carried by slave bearers. One of the litters bore a high official who had traveled from North Phrygia toward the sea; two other litters were occupied by elderly travelers, unable to stand the walk. Mostly they complained that being carried was more tiresome than going afoot.

About noon of the second day they slowed as they heard moans coming from behind a huge rock. Upon investigation they found a man sorely wounded and bleeding profusely from his wounds. He whispered that he had been attacked by bandits and robbed of all of his belongings. The dismayed group looked among themselves but saw no easy way to carry the poor unfortunate with them. The hilt of a knife protruded from his side making his wound such as to bring about his death if he were moved. They gave the moaning victim water, but did not dare to pull the knife from his side, for that was certain to bring about a death that they wanted no part in.

It was the deacon who stated that it was his Christian duty to stay and tend one who feared to be left to die alone; the rest of travelers moved on, leaving Onesimus with his patient.

"Why would you stay with me?" the wounded fellow panted.

"I have been called to be a minister to all who need me," replied Onesimus. "My mentor commanded me, *"Bear one another's burdens, and so fulfil the law of Christ."* Sitting beside him Onesimus reminded him that in such dire circumstances it would be well for any man to remember his sins and be penitent so that a better life would await him in the next world. So with what little breath remained in him the dying man recalled his life. He had been a hill bandit himself, and indeed his wounds were due to a quarrel over the disposal of the loot that he and his partner had collected. As Onesimus listened to his story and looked into his face, he recognized the thief who had taken his money on that first day of his own escape. The thief began to choke and breathe heavily. Onesimus knelt and prayed for mercy for the man's soul. Finally, he dug a grave.

"Perhaps in his way he saved my life," Onesimus thought. "He left me with nothing worth killing me for.

"Brother, if a man is overtaken in his trespass, you who are spiritual should restore him in a spirit of gentleness. Look to yourself lest you too be tempted."

When finally Onesimus arrived in Miletus, the meeting with Paul was over; Paul had spoken to his faithful followers and had departed on a ship bound for Caesarea. Archippus and Epaphras who were disappointed for Onesimus' sake more than for their own chastened him for lack of understanding that some duties take precedence over others.

Onesimus replied, *"Let each one test his own work; then his reason to boast will be in himself alone and not in his neighbor. Each man must bear his own burden."*

Epaphras commented that the words were Paul's, but the deed belonged to Onesimus. "Love does not insist on its own way, it is not irritable or resentful," he remembered.

Now for Archippus time plodded slowly along. The books of the philosophers which he had collected with such pride no longer appealed to him. With Platon gone, he had no one to test his ideas upon. Apphia was always busy.

As she grew older, she seemed to increase in energy. He had to remind himself that she was fifteen years younger than he, and that she was now living in her most productive age while his years were declining. There was no question that Onesimus was a satisfactory son; in Archippus' eyes he was more satisfactory than necessary. He fulfilled every wish; he anticipated every need.

Tremble, O Earth, at The Presence Of The Lord

At a time when summer was coming on before the days had become too oppressive, Archipppus called Onesimus and suggested that he might enjoy a trip to Pergamon, just to see how Philemon was getting on.

"But we hear from him frequently, almost every other week,"

Onesimus protested.

"I know," replied Archippus, "but sometimes things appear different when you observe them in person; besides, we are approaching his thirtieth birthday, and Apphia and I wish to send him a gift so that he will not feel that he is forgotten."

Onesimus did not require too much persuasion. The thought of the excursion was pleasing to him, and he had missed the company of Philemon. Besides, he wanted to talk to Platon. And so it was arranged. Apphia had packed several bundles of new clothing; Leah and Archippus had gone over the orchard and kitchen garden to find the kind of fruits that could withstand the journey. Baskets of bread were prepared.

"You would think that we were going to the end of the earth," Onesimus protested.

It was decided that Onesimus should ride in a wheeled coach. Walking would not befit a gentleman. When he tired of this mode of travel, he could ride a mule among the baggage handlers. A forerunner would find lodgings for the party each night. Archippus wanted to avoid the dangers that Onesimus might too eagerly get himself into.

The weather had changed from pleasant to hot. Onesimus found the inside of the coach stifling, and the bumping of the iron wheels over the cobbled roads did nothing to increase his comfort. The mule was plodding, and the drovers were not particularly eager for his company. By the third day out, sickness overcame him and he lay stretched out in the airless coach praying only for the end of the trip. On the eve of the fifth day they had reached Pergamon. The runner who had gone ahead had found Philemon's lodging place and Philemon and Platon had come down to the river crossing to meet the party. Before too long they were in cooler air up on a hillside overlooking the town, and Platon was mixing a concoction of wine and juices and pure spring water guaranteed to settle the queezy stomach.

"It is a drink prescribed by the Asclepides, who are prominent in this city," laughed Platon. Onesimus looked slightly askance, but Platon reassured him that the priests of Asclepias were the best physicians in the world, and it was Pergamon where their bodies needed mending. The next few days were happy ones; there was much to talk about; Philemon and Platon were eager to show off the city and introduce new friends. Onesimus began to realize that even the best of deacons requires a vacation. There was a thriving community of the faithful in Pergamon, all of whom were happy to meet new Companions of the Way.

"Tomorrow, we shall go sight-seeing," announced Philemon. We will climb right up to the top of that mountain and there we shall find the very throne of Satan." Others in the congregation smiled, for they were proud of the grandeur of Pergamon's architecture, in spite of the fact that it was dedicated to the old gods.

The climb up the mount was started early, just before sunrise, for the day promised to be very hot before noon. The sun came up over the hilltop just as they were nearing the gates. The marble buildings quickly turned from dawn's rosy color to gold as the sun topped the hill. They stood, quite out of breath, and were delighted as the marble buildings turned from gold to dazzling white before their eyes.

"It is magnificent," Onesimus was awe-struck.

"Just so," replied Philemon. "It is quite the most beautiful work of hands that has ever been created."

"I am forced to weep every time I see it," chimed in Platon.

"Yes, indeed, Artemis of the Ephesians has been bested here," agreed Onesimus.

They walked slowly through the gates and up the steps of the great temple. There were no crowds at dawn; in fact the promised heat of the day had discouraged most of the tourists away from the monument.

It was the sculpture, of course, that drew their attention. The great altar of Zeus is surrounded on its lower level by a frieze which continues all the way around it, depicting the battle between the giants and the gods. Every possible position of limb and torso demonstrates the skill of the artist; every muscle depicts the anatomy of man in rippling movement. Every expression of face from agony to sublimity is there to be wondered at. They had stopped to admire the towering Athena subduing two agonized giants with her outstretched arms. Even the underside of her skirt had been fashioned with the utmost skill; Every hair of the giant's curled hair felt real to the touch.

Was it the rumbling that they heard first? Was it the falling of a single cornice stone from the pedestal above them? Was it the sickening roll of the marble steps beneath their feet? For a moment there was silence and they fell on the step with arms outstretched to catch themselves, just as the gigantic figures above them were bracing their falls. Eternity can be broken into for only a second or two when it is measured against time.

"Earthquake!" they heard themselves shouting.

"Earthquake," the call resounded, as from every cranny people came running out from wherever they had been.

Then it was still. People congregated in silence and looked about themselves in wonder. Very little had changed. A few pieces of marble had fallen; an almost transparent acanthus leaf here; a gigantic finger there; and at the foot of the stair, the fragile leaves of an oak leaf crown had left the head of goddess above them. Up from the valley came a noise like a wail.

Philemon looked up, "The earth has shuddered a bit."

> *The mountains skipped like rams,*
> *and the little hills like young sheep.*

> *Tremble, O Earth, at the presence of the Lord.*

quoted Onesimus quietly.

Far down in the valley where the villagers lived a column of smoke curled up; then another, and another. "The jarring of the earth turns over the cooking braziers in the hovels of the peasants," remarked Platon.

"I think that I should return to Colossae at once," said Onesimus as if he had just been wakened from a dream.

"No need of that," said Philemon, "it was just a small tremor. We have had many jolts of that nature here; they really mean no harm."

"A small jolt in the North may presage a large one in the South," Onesimus continued. "I distinctly feel that I am called home. Get me a horse; this is no time for crawling wagons."

Onesimus could not be dissuaded and before noon he was mounted on a horse and galloped off down the path. By evening the horse was exhausted as Onesimus pulled up before an inn which had a coach house. The innkeeper brought him some boiled meat and sour wine, apologizing,

"We weren't prepared for many guests tonight. It's the quake, you know."

"Has there been much damage?" worried Onesimus.

"Not so much here, but they say it is bad to the South."

Onesimus bargained for a fresh horse, snatched a few hours of sleep and was off again by the fourth watch. By sunset he was riding through the ruins of Laodicea. It was difficult to see through the thick smoke which hung over the town. He could see nothing he recognized; the survivors sat on what might have been their doorsteps, too dazed to tell their story. The horse was exhausted. Onesimus dismounted and ran down to the shallows of the river. It was mid-summer and already the river had sent its waters underground so Onesimus found no impediment there. As he ran he noted trees uprooted and avoided rocks that had rolled into the road. At last he came to a turning where he could look up and see Archippus' aerie high on its rock overlooking the whole valley. His heart almost stopped; there was no rock there.

Panting almost to the point of choking he found the path that went up the backside of the hill. Scaling it he soon reached the top and there was—Nothing. A pile of rubble lay where the house he knew so well had been. He could barely make out the street, for it too was filled with rubble; not a house stood along the entire way.

In the sky, the moon rose, made red by its veil of smoke. Somewhere in the distance was the cry of an owl. Onesimus' legs crumpled under him. Exhausted he sank down on the rubble that had once been his home and fell asleep.

It was already morning when he awakened. It had not been a

dream; what he saw was real? He rubbed his eyes, "Is it the end of time?" he asked himself.

Then he heard someone calling his name. "Onesimus, Onesimus?" a woman's voice called out.

He looked up and saw Apphia struggling across the rubble. He stood up and stretched his hands out to help her. She took the hand and sank down on her knees, weeping.

"You are alive," he said in astonishment. "Where is Archippus?"

She struggled for words, and pointed downward, "Under all this," she said flatly.

Further inquiry brought no more answers. Everyone was gone; only she survived. Suddenly her mind sparked,

"Where is Philemon?" she asked wildly.

Onesimus tried to reassure her; "Philemon is well; he remains in Pergamon."

"Why didn't he come? You are not telling me the truth."

"My lady, I am telling you the truth. I left Philemon, only yesterday, or was it the day before that. The earthquake did not damage Pergamon."

"That cannot be so," Apphia cried. "The whole earth has been destroyed, and you and I are the only ones alive. I know; for I have been wandering for days and I have seen no one."

"No one?" Onesimus was incredulous.

"No one," she replied. "There is no one alive in all of Colossae. It is the Day of the Lord."

Then she screamed, "No, this is the destruction of the Goddess; she is very angry."

And she lay face down on the earth and moaned.

By this time Onesimus, realizing that their situation was desperate, observed that water had seeped through the rubble nearby and was beginning to bubble up through a hole.

"This must be just above the peristyle fountain," he thought and he retrieved water in his cupped hand and drank. He had hardly realized the depth of his thirst; with his bare hands he dug through the dirt and found the source as it came through a broken tile. Taking more water in his hands he poured it over the face of Apphia who revived herself in the coolness. She sat up and played her hands in the water. "You and I alone are here to tell the tale," she kept repeating.

Onesimus began to move more of the crumbled piece of wall and revealed the tile floor below. He found a jar that would still hold water and filled it. Apphia stood up, and realized her own strength. The two of them pushed a path through the rubble. The kitchen at the back of the house lay open to the sky. Rummaging around they found a half prepared meal. A hand stuck straight up. It was Leah. Onesimus uncovered her body;

"She must have died immediately when this wall came down," he said. "Where were you when it happened?" he asked in wonder.

Apphia looked up in surprise, "I can't remember; I think I was out in the street. At least that is where I was when the earth stopped shaking. Oh whatever shall we do?"

She began crying again; her breast heaved with sobs.

"We must pray to the Lord," announced Onesimus. "We must ask for guidance." He stood and looked across the valley. He could see the figure of a horse and rider which came nearer and nearer.

"It is Philemon," he shouted with joy. Now it was Philemon's turn to be in shock. As he was surveying the rubble he looked and saw Onesimus coming toward him. The two embraced and wept; then he saw his mother. Mother and son sat down on the fallen wall and held each other in their arms and cried like abandoned babies. Somehow they survived the day. When the next day dawned, Onesimus announced that he would try to make his way through the town to find whatever he could. Philemon agreed to stay at the house and dig through the earthen walls.

It was not easy to find one's way through the streets. The walls of houses had collapsed outward into the streets; Colossae was a city made of mud; here and there a wooden doorsill might still be standing. The marble fountain of the Nereids seemed in place but the water was fouled. The dead were lying in the streets or in corners where they had fallen. The smell of their decaying flesh was everywhere. Then there were the living. Some were sitting, looking vacantly outward, beside their dead loved ones. Some fled quickly on hearing the approach of anyone. Obviously they were looting the empty dwellings, or if not looting, at least looking for some means to sustain themselves as survivors. There were children; there were old men; there were women; Nature had not been selective in her choices. In the center of the town the civic buildings had fallen together. Onesimus was exhausted and sickened; it was as though an army had struck down the place in a single night and then burned the remains. At last, Onesimus returned home, as empty handed as when he had left.

"We have found the body of Archippus," Philemon announced solemnly. "He was lying in his library. I doubt that he ever knew what had hit him."

"Bless the Lord for that," Onesimus returned in a hushed voice. They had also found the bodies of several slaves. They pointed down the hillside. The weaving room had evidently broken off the rest of the house and had slid down the hillside, taking its toll with it. Nothing remained except a talus slope. The three made their way down the hill into the farm. Quite a number of the farm slaves were standing around vacantly and dully. No one had told them what to do; and they seemed unable to think for themselves. Obviously those who were the most clever had hied themselves elsewhere, seeking their freedom.

"Let them go," ordered Onesimus. "They will find life hard enough without our interference." He rounded up half a dozen children and set some meal to cooking so that they could be fed. The overseer was found in his hovel, still alive but unable to talk or move.

"He has had a stroke," announced Onesimus. The eyes followed Onesimus, and he went over and tried to reassure the old man who closed his eyes. Philemon and Apphia found a hut still standing and determined to make it their home for the time being. Onesimus rounded up some of the slaves and convinced them that with the cooperation of everyone, enough food could be harvested to feed them all. And so new life began to sprout.

Shortly afterward the newly formed community gathered and buried the dead whose bodies had been found.

Do not lose heart, he said to the mourners, *Though our outer nature wastes away, our inner nature is renewed every day. This momentary affliction is preparing us for an eternal glory beyond all comparison to what we have now. Look not to the things that are seen, but to the things that are unseen; for the things that are unseen are eternal."*

Onesimus determined to go back into the city. Alone he found the House of Nympha and entered into the silence there. Toward the back of the house he found that a wall had collapsed into the women's quarters. With mattock and shovel he dug through the wall and found the burial crypt of the virgins. They had evidently died clinging to each other and on their knees. Raising a dusty veil he saw the face for which he was searching.

> The sunken eyes stared back at him.
> O my lovely one,
> By me loved too little,
> The angels have come
> To give you the love,
> So much deserved.
> Would that I had seized the day
> And given myself to you;
> Before you were doomed
> To pass from me forever.
> The earthly tent
> has been destroyed.
> There remains the building
> Not made with hands
> Which we will receive from God.

He covered her with her veil, and then heaped the earth around the women, making a rounded mound which he tamped down solid. Finding two beams of wood he formed them in the shape of a cross and planted it solidly within heaped up stones.

Dreary day followed dreary day. Onesimus and Philemon worked side by side digging into their once beautiful house, weeping over their losses, cherishing any small find that remained unbroken. At last they had restored the small room to which Archippus had first brought Apphia so many years before. When she saw it, Apphia burst into tears, but then refused to leave. It would be her place forever, she lamented as she brought her few belongings to it. The work was hard; few slaves could be coaxed into helping, and the two men had little enthusiasm for enforcing their rights.

Philemon came to Onesimus. "If we could dig up the library, I think I could find the will."

Onesimus shook his head. "There is no need to find a will. I shall gladly relinquish anything that may have been bequeathed to me to your ownership."

Philemon protested, "No, I was only hoping that we could agree upon a settlement. I have no wish to have more than a just share."

"That is not my meaning," said Onesimus. "I intend to quit this place as soon as you and Apphia no longer need me. I am called to do another work in another place."

"There is much work to do here; you must know that you are loved and appreciated. Can we not be equals in this household?"

Onesimus spoke quietly, "I must go and seek my true father, my father-in-God, the Apostle Paul. It was my vow to return to him when I left Ephesus for Colossae. I have put it off too long, and I know that with him is my true calling."

"You cannot go now, You have no clothes, no one to tend you, no money."

"If Paul can rely upon God to provide him with these things, then I can also rely upon the goodness of God to provide for me. I have quite made up my mind."

Within a few days Onesimus had gathered what little he needed together. The little family met together for a prayer and a blessing. Philemon pressed a few gold coins into Onesimus' hand.

"You will have need of these; and if you do not, your gift will make you welcome with others. I found them in your father Archippus' strong box."

Onesimus shed a few tears. "I thank God for you. But as for me, *I have put on the whole armor of God so that I may stand against evil. Let me fasten the belt of truth about my waist, and put on the breast plate of righteousness. The shoes on my feet are ready to carry the gospel of peace. I have the shield of faith to protect me; I wear the helmet of salvation and I am ready with the sword of the spirit, which is the word of God. Pray for me when I speak that the words that I say will make known the mystery of the good news that I bear.*"

Onesimus took the path down the hillside along the river. Philemon and Apphia watched as long as they could keep him in sight, and then turned to each other to weep their loss.

Tongues of Angels

The Search for Paul

It is here that I must begin a new book. I, Eupator, Son of Philemon, have told you the story in the words of my father Philemon, and my grandfather Platon. It was only as a very old man did Onesimus himself struggle to remember his past, for he always lived for the moment with his eye upon the life to come. While in his youth, he struggled with the minds and forces of men, tossed this way and that by what appeared to be blind fate. At one point he gave himself to the power of God, and as he aptly put it, "Wherever I went, I was lifted up and ministered to by angels."

In a short time, as men reckon time, Onesimus reached the hills surrounding Ephesus. For him, it seemed a thousand years. He traveled by day, quite alone, and found no challenges to waylay him. At night he lay down to sleep in grassy places; the few people that he met shared their bread with him; he drank water from the clear stream.

The Lord is my shepherd; I fear no evil,

He said the words slowly, remembering the lilt of Leah's voice as he said them. Once in Ephesus he saw men who seemed like ants at work, shoring up the fallen walls of their houses, struggling to regain the days and the works that they had lost. But the disaster there was nothing compared to the ruin of Colossae. He made his way as best he could to the district which he remembered. The house remained but

179

no one there could remember anyone who resembled a member of the family which it had once contained.

When he spoke the name of Paul, the new owners only shook their heads. While he stood wondering what to do next, a woman came up to him and spoke his name.

"Onesimus?" she asked in disbelief.

He peered into her face and remembered, "Rhoda," he exclaimed with amazement.

She drew her veil over her face, "I was praying, and the Lord told me to come here," she said simply.

"The Lord?"

"Yes, the Lord Jesus, do you know of him."

He took her hand, "He is my master and my saviour. He has sent me an angel who knows him too."

Rhoda said quietly, "Let me bring you to our house. We are followers of The Beloved Disciple."

How quickly he renewed his acquaintance with Ephesus once he had found a house church. But this household did not much resemble the household of Paul; perhaps it was because of the women who lived there. It was true that Paul accepted women as equal members in his community, but none lived in his household, at least none in the time that Onesimus had lived there. This house church did not much resemble the household of Archippus either; for the house church of Archippus was essentially a family affair, of related persons, of both slave and free. Onesimus thought of the household of Nympha; but Nympha's household was essentially a house of women, some old and widowed like Nympha herself, some young virgins like Erotion. In the house where he found Rhoda there were both men and women, but they were not related to each other; in fact, they kept much to themselves, only assembling for a meal once a day, or sometimes two or three in quiet study together.

As Rhoda explained it, "We like to go our own way. Each of us knows the Spirit, and each one follows the direction of the spirit."

In a short time Onesimus had learned the personal stories of several of the members. Like Rhoda, each had been rescued or "saved" from some horrible fate, but now was content in the new life that was shared with each other. Onesimus' own story was quite acceptable and in line with the others; but Onesimus was not satisfied. He missed the companionship of those who surrounded his Apostle. And he missed The Apostle himself. Everyone seemed to know The Beloved Disciple; but that mysterious person rarely presented himself. He was busy; he was traveling; there were other house churches to tend to; he had his own household. Whatever the reason, Onesimus did not feel that he was a part of it.

Onesimus recognized the feeling; he did not belong. He had spent his life analyzing that feeling. He was a slave; yet he never felt at home with the slaves. They regarded him as an outsider, and a dangerous one, at that. He was a blood relative of the household in which he lived; but he never felt that he was one of them. Even when they were kindest to him, even when they showered him with favors, he inwardly felt that he did not belong. In Colossae and in Laodicea where he had labored these past four years as a deacon, there he was welcome in every house, but as a guest; he belonged to no house. And so it was here; he was baptized; he was a believer; but there was a difference; he knew he did not belong. And so it was that after a few weeks he announced to his new friends that he would soon sail to Caesarea, and perhaps from there he would proceed to Jerusalem.

For what little he could learn about Paul's destination after the meeting in Miletus, he knew that it was to a meeting in Jersusalem by way of Caesarea, the nearest Palestinian port city.

He found a ship loading cargo in the harbor. Its destination was Caesarea, but the captain said they would be making short stops along the way. Onesimus signed on as one of the crew; true, he had a little money hidden away; but he deemed it safer to be one of the crew, at least as far as Caesarea. He refused to make any commitments beyond that. The sea voyage was pleasant enough; the work was not difficult; at least it was manual labor and did not tax the brain. Onesimus was still young and muscular, quite used to climbing hills and carrying bundles.

The ship skirted the coast line where rugged cliffs came down to the sea. Little harbors would come in view, where rivers came down from their valleys. At sea mouth a small village, perhaps. The wind would waft in the odor of olive trees. In the little markets there would be figs and apricots, and greenstuffs from the fields mixed with thyme and mint, cassia and rosemary. Onesimus thought of how the Greek poets had praised the scent of the summer fields. It reminded him of home and idle summer days. By night the ship would drop anchor, close to the shore. Onesimus would lie on the deck and look at the stars.

"I am a fortunate fellow," he thought. "I am nearing thirty years in age, and I am strong and still feel young. This is because I was not bent down with hard labor from my youth, like some of these crewmen here whose backs are bent, who have no teeth, and their legs are bowed from heavy work from childhood."

Indeed Onesimus was quite handsome, with sun bronzed skin and dark shining eyes. He still kept his hair cropped short and he had not allowed himself to grow a beard. After a time in the baths or a swim in the sea, he rubbed himself down with oil, and scraped himself with his strigula and thus by his personal habits he betrayed himself to be of aristocratic origin, and a Greek.

Within two weeks the ship arrived at Caesarea, the largest port since Ephesus. Onesimus did his part in the unloading of the cargo; the shipmaster said that they would remain there a few days for buying and selling, and then, depending upon what they found for shipping, the boat would sail again. He hoped that Onesimus would join them then. Onesimus replied that it would depend upon how his affairs in Caesarea turned out.

There was no difficulty finding the followers of Jesus there. In fact, he was astonished to find so many. Philip the Evangelist had lived there with his daughters, before he had gone to Hierapolis; and so there were a few who were eager to hear of how things were in Phrygia. They shook there heads over the news of the earthquake and its destruction.

"Surely the last days are upon us," they said, shaking their heads. There were Christians from Antioch, and from Damascus, and from Jerusalem. Onesimus began to piece together their stories. Paul had indeed gone to Jerusalem; there it had been much the same with Paul; there had been disagreements; Paul had been arrested. Actually he had made a pretty good case for himself and had impressed the authorities, but Paul was always Paul. He had demanded fair trial as a Roman. He had been transported back to Caesarea to await a ship for Rome. In fact he had waited in this very place for months, but only a short time before Onesimus arrived, he had boarded a ship bound for the capital, and that had been the last seen of him.

Onesimus went back to the harbor. The shipmaster was loading a variety of wares; before the summer ended he would be in Corinth and after that, who knows, perhaps Rome itself. Onesimus gladly signed on for another voyage. This time he would keep the ship's lists, for the shipmaster now knew that he could write. The last evening Onesimus met with a community of followers of the way. They sang psalms and celebrated a love feast, as a way of bidding their new friend farewell.

Back on the ship, Onesimus was at peace with himself. He thanked the Lord in his prayers for putting him on the right way, that now he did not insist upon his own way. The shipmaster said that it would be a long voyage. When the weather was good they would sail northward, always staying close to the shore, to Sidon, where they would leave off amphorae of oil and pick up a load of cedar wood. Depending upon the weather they would head straight for Cyprus, on the open sea. There they would unload their cargo and restock with the products of that land. Onesimus took with him writing materials; stylus and wax tablets for the impermanent records, writing implements, bars of ink and papyrus for more serious writing. There would be time, he thought, to begin a project he had long had in mind. There was time for pleasure too. During the summer nights the crew would sit upon the rowing benches or lie on the open decks and sing songs which they had learned in the places where they had traveled, and tell tales of their adventures and of home. Onesimus began to recite to them parts of the story of the Trojan War and of Ulysses voyages, and they congratulated themselves on their good fortune, for having a singer of tales in their midst.

How could he forget the education of his youth, the long days of writing down the lines, of memorizing the verses. Now they came back to him, and he thought of Platon, wondering whether he was still in Pergamon or whether he had gone to the Troad to see it all for himself. The shipmaster came to him and said,

"I marvel how such a learned man would stoop to such a trade as crewman on a ship. For many, it is a life fit only for slaves."

Onesimus smiled and said that the sea air was good for his health, and that whether a man was a slave or free, it was all with one with God. He told him how he had been freed from slavery, and of The Christ for whom all men were alike in value, and all had worth with God. His voyage, he declared, was a search for that father-in-god whom he had lost, a search for The Apostle Paul.

The shipmaster was entranced by the story and pledged himself to join the search. So now Onesimus, when he was free from his duties, would bring out his writing materials; for he had vowed that he would write down every thing that Paul had said, or whatever he could find that Paul had written. There was no doubt that Onesimus had an excellent memory for by the time he was seventeen years of age he had memorized the two great books of Homer, and had already written them down as a school boy's exercise. Not only was he proficient in Greek, but he had memorized the Psalms of David, as they are written by the Hebrews, with only the oral instruction of a housekeeper named Leah. He had listened to the dictations of Paul during that memorable year in Ephesus, and had made copies of several important documents. Not only that, he had listened to Paul's lectures and discussions. So while these things were fresh in his mind, he determined to put them into a more lasting form.

As with any budding author his first problem was: "Where to begin." He thought of Paul among the great philosophers. Of course, he should begin in Athens in the debate with the philosophers there. Paul had delighted in that discourse and had recited it several times in his hearing.

It happened in this way: Those who conducted Paul brought him as far as Athens; and after receiving instructions to have Silas and Timothy join him as soon as possible, they left him. While Paul was waiting for them in Athens, he was deeply distressed to see that the city was full of idols. Then Paul stood in front of the Areopagus and said,

> *Athenians, I see how extremely religious you are in every way.*
>
> *For as I went through the city and looked carefully at the objects of your worship, I found among them an altar with the inscription, 'To an unknown god.' What therefore you worship as unknown, this I proclaim to you.*
>
> *The God who made the world and everything in it, he who is Lord of heaven and earth, does not live in shrines made by human hands, nor is he served by human hands, as though he needed anything, since he himself gives to all mortals life and breath and all things.*

As he spoke, some of his hearers began to pay attention, so Paul continued in an enthusiastic way.

> *From one ancestor he made all nations to inhabit the whole earth, and he allotted the times of their existence and the boundaries of the places where they would live, so that they would search for God and perhaps grope for him and find him—though indeed he is not far from each one of us.*

By this time many were listening, and Paul proclaimed,

> *'In him we live and move and have our being'; as even some of your own poets have said, 'For we too are his offspring.' Since we are God's offspring, we ought not to*

think that the deity is like gold, or silver, or stone, an image formed by the art and imagination of mortals. While God has overlooked the times of human ignorance, now he commands all people everywhere to repent, because he has fixed a day on which he will have the world judged in righteousness by a man whom he has appointed, and of this he has given assurance to all by raising him from the dead.

When they heard of the resurrection of the dead, some scoffed; but others said, "We will hear you again about this." At that point Paul left them.

The captain and the sailors listened quietly to the story. It had been a warm and lazy afternoon. The sea was glassy calm; the morning swell had subsided. The shipmaster strolled about and stopped to watch Onesimus who was hunched over his writing.

"You can read them scraggles?" he asked.

Onesimus laughed and read what he had been writing. "Is that really what your friend Paul said?" asked the sailor, "He's got a lotta nerve, takin' on those shysters from Athens."

"Well, no one has ever accused him of not having nerve," replied Onesimus.

"Can't say I ever thought much about God," the shipmaster went on. "But there's one thing I know; those Athenian thinkers, they don't believe in no God at all—nor the gods neither."

Onesimus chuckled and then looked up and sniffed, "What is that wonderful sweet smell?" "Smell? You can smell something sweet in this stinkin' boat?"

"It's not in the boat; it's like the wind is wafting it in from some-where. Don't you smell it? like lemon blossoms?"

"You can smell lemon blossoms? Oh yes, now you're right. It's the lemony grass you smell; it comes from Cyprus. In a bit we ought to see land."

And sure enough, the dim line of the shore was heaving into sight on the port side.

"Yes indeedy; you'll soon be sucking the sweet cane what grows wild here in the draws that come down to the sea."

"What will we be doing in Cyprus?" Onesimus wrinkled his brow.

"Oh, it should be good business. We have a load of wine jars that we took on in Caesarea, and here we are at the grape stompin' season. We can sell 'em the jars; and then we can take on a load of sweet wine bound for Corinth. They sure like that sweet wine there."

"Don't they have wine in Corinth?" Onesimus asked innocently.

"Of course they have wine. They swill it down faster than water. But sweet wine from Cyprus, that's something else. You never tasted Cyprian wine?"

Onesimus admitted that he had not.

"Well, you've a treat coming. I'll see you tonight at the taverna." The shipmaster ran on shouting orders to the sailors to make for the shoreline. When the sighting was clearer, they found themselves skimming along a palmy shore.

"We be coming in to Paphos town, for sure," called the captain.

Everyone, including Onesimus, took their places on the rowing benches following the orders of the captain who maneuvered for the landing docks. The rest of the day was all work and business, but when evening came, true to the master's word, they found a taverna; and the wine was sweet and heavy. Even though they spent the night on shore, Onesimus felt the swaying of the boat all night.

Bright in the morning they strolled the top of the cliff with the sea on their left and Paphos town on their right. Onesimus was solemn.

"Paul was here once, with Barnabas. It must have been about ten years past. He was arrested here for some sort of local blasphemy, and flogged—probably over there by the pillory."

"I can imagine they didn't like what he had to say," the shipman said, and pointing out to the bay he called, "See that rock in the water over there?"

Onesimus had been admiring the view of the bay all morning; it was one of the most delightful views he had ever seen in his life.

"Well, on that rock, that's where Aphrodite was born." said his friend.

"Aphrodite? the Cyprian, of course. She was born of sea foam."

"That's right," said the old sailor. "She was riding right up to that rock where she stepped off; and the rock, why that's the seashell that she stepped out of."

> *See to it that no one takes you captive through philos-*
> *ophy and empty deceit, according to human tradition,*
> *according to the elemental spirits of the universe, and not*
> *according to Christ.*

"That's the way Paul would put it," quoted Onesimus. "He would see the Cyprian Goddess as an elemental spirit, a demon and not the true God."

"Now that's pretty hard to swallow, lad. Aphrodite, she's Love herself."

"I know," said Onesimus.

"And that's a mighty lovely sight, don't you agree?"

"I agree," commented Onesimus, lost in thought. "Now we know only in part."

The ship was unloaded; the jars were quickly bought up by local tradesmen. The cedar wood from Sidon found an eager builder who was working at constructing a palace for the Roman governor.

"His name is Paulus, just like your'n. Lots of you 'little guys' around," and he laughed as he had another goblet of sweet wine. The brokers found more of the product in the warehouses, and the ship took on a load.

"Well, we're gettin' on toward the equinox and we'd better get our sailing done. So tomorrow we're off for Corinth. But we'll stop at Rhodes on our way," explained the captain.

With a fresh breeze the ship skipped along the waves to Rhodes where they stopped only long enough to take on fresh water and ripe fruit. Onesimus looked long at the harbor where once the colossus stood, before the earthquake—how could he not think of Colossae and the earthquake.

Then on they pressed through the Cyclades, skirting many a little isle which they passed hurrying on in hopes that winter would not delay them there. Not many a shipmaster would take the direct route through the islands without stopping to go to the mainland; for the islands are fraught with danger. The shipmaster showed Onesimus the night sky.

"See, there is the belted Orion; when you see him in the sky you know that the northers will be fast upon us."

"But the weather seems to hold so pleasant," protested Onesimus.

"It can't be trusted, lad," said the seaman. "But I was born in these islands; and since I was a boy I've sailed in and out among them. If we get a bad wind, I'll head right in for the nearest shore, trust me. Then we'll wait the weather out."

"But they say those coves are full of pirates."

"For sure they are," laughed the seaman; "and every one of 'em is a cousin o' mine. Still, I'm betting on the weather this time. See, there's the Bear up there; we steer by Polaris."

In time the shore of the Peloponnese was in view, rocky, dry and mountainous, giving little invitation for the seaman to land there. But on the third nightfall they came to the harbor of Cenchreae, and the shipmaster was pleased and relieved.

"It's a fine place to harbor our boat and make repairs, and from here we can easily go by land to Corinth to trade."

The first night the shipmaster and Onesimus elected to sleep between the benches on the ship; the rest of the crew made a dash for land, the tavernae and the girls who are in every port. In the morning Onesimus went ashore, certain in his mind of the place he was looking for.

The Angel Chloe

On the second road up from the harbor he found it, a tiny shop huddled between other dispensers of seamen's wares. When he opened the door a copper bell tinkled, and quickly an old woman appeared.

"Sister Phoebe?" inquired Onesimus.

The lady at once became animated. "Are you a brother, sir?"

Onesimus identified himself as a servant of Paul, and with that he became her friend forever. He had found someone who was more devoted to the Apostle than he was. She was so eager to talk that there was nothing to be done but sit down on a stool and listen.

"It happened in the 63rd year of my life, five years after the death of my husband Aristo," she began. "A widow my age does not anticipate much excitement, you know; she counts herself fortunate if life does not bring her too much hardship. But I am fortunate. I have my little house here in Cenchreae near to the ship docks, and my girl Cicada to tend me. She's a little sassy nowadays, but I have no one else to spoil. Jason, Aristo's freedman, comes in to help a little.

"We have this one room to keep as a shop, where we sell the remains of wares once shipped from Egypt long ago. Once each week I walk to Corinth where the brothers and sisters meet to share a meal and have some hours of friendship and say our prayers. I am grateful for these few friends to fill my waning days. But, excuse me, I was going to tell you about our Paul.

"It began one summer evening. Cicada burst into my room, 'Lady, the Master is at the door, the Lord Paul.' I got myself right up and ran to the door myself—Brother Paul, is that indeed you?

"Cicada, run quickly, bring some of the amber wine; and there are some honey cakes—and rose water for his hands."

"Lady Phoebe," our Apostle bowed, "I thank you for your hospitality, but I have come to ask a favor of you, as my servant in the Lord."

We were standing in this little shop and there was Paul picking out a sharp shearing blade, imported from the Cypriots.

"I want you to cut my hair, he said solemnly."

"Brother Paul, I protested, I am your slave to do your every bidding, but I am no barber. The City is filled with experts in that trade."

"No, you will do fine; this is no ordinary haircut; for I am about to take a vow in all solemnity and you are to stand as my witness, for you have been set aside in the service of Our Lord Christ. I must within these thirty days find myself in Jerusalem to meet with our brethren there. It is there that my next haircutting shall take place with my vow fulfilled. My ship sails from this very ship yard at dawn tomorrow, and I have errands yet to complete."

I stammered, "My word, a sacred haircut; what will I be doing next?" And so we set about doing it, and I could not help but reminisce about the times that Aristo went out to sea for trading among the isles; and every year when the sea was calm he would go as far as Crete and Rhodes and even Egypt where we laid in supplies of papyrus for writing and black ink and cases for books. In those days I went too, for though I am a woman, Aristo could find no one better than me when it came to totting up the number board."

"You mean you have been to sea? the Apostle asked in amazement."

"Well, not all of us were born fine ladies, you know; with nothing to do but have our slave girls drop jelly candies into our mouths. In my day I could pull the ropes and set the sails with the best of them. At night I slept between the benches with my Aristo; but when we came to port, that is where I shone. I am good at trade."

"Have you ever been to Rome?" Paul mused.

"Once we had a ship bound for Ostia; we skirted round Tarentum and put in at Cortona's harbour before we ran the tides of Charybdis. Yes, we finally got to the City itself. Here let me show you"—And the lady clambered to the top shelf and brought down her treasures, two silver spoons with *ROMA* graven in their bowls.

"Dear Phoebe," said Paul very quietly, "Could you go to Rome for me? I have a letter; our brother Tertius is copying it now. The ship will be ready to sail within the week. I cannot go myself because I am bound for Jerusalem."

Well I was so excited that I nicked the Apostle's chin with the razor. "But what should I tell everyone? I can't just take off for Rome . . ."

"Tell them . . . tell them, that you are going to visit with your sister.

Yes, yes, your sister so many years separated from you. You do have many sisters in Rome, you know—" His eyes twinkled.

Later that day, Paul delivered the letter to me. "—You are perfect for this job, he said. You must give this to a very special lady, a very fine lady indeed, and very highly placed. It will be very easy for you, another lady."

"—I am your diakonos, my Lord."

"That is how it started. I delivered many messages after that. I even went to Jerusalem myself; but that is another story."

Onesimus could scarcely contain himself with delight. "That is the very letter that we were working on when I left Paul in Ephesus. That was just before he made his second trip to Corinth."

"His third," corrected the Lady Phoebe.

Onesimus' eye had spotted some writing materials in a corner of the shop and went over to examine them. He was followed by Phoebe who hovered over him.

"Those papyrus leaves came right from Egypt; the calami are the best you can buy. When they are sharpened they have very strong points; Over there, are some softer ones which you can make into writing brushes, and the inkpots are fine stone brought down from upper Egypt."

"I have to have to assess my needs,"

"Will you be here long?" asked the lady.

"I suspect it will be for the winter; at least that is what the boat captain says."

"And where will you be staying all that time?"

Onesimus was a bit flustered. "I barely come ashore; I have no arrangements yet. I would like to find a room with one of our brothers."

Phoebe examined his face. "You are a follower of the Way, are you not?"

Onesimus lifted his head in agreement. "You must be," she continued, "since you know about Paul. You are a follower of Paul?" Onesimus said enthusiastically, "With all my heart, I follow Paul. He is my father-in-god; and I am on my way to Rome, or Spain to follow him wherever he goes."

Phoebe spoke thoughtfully. "I have room for you here, and I offer you hospitality. But remember, Paul always required that the brothers should work for their living, as he did."

"I am a scrivener" replied Onesimus. "I write letters, or help people make documents and keep records. I simply take my box of writing materials and find a place where people gather for business, and usually the trade comes to me."

"Let me show you the room," said Phoebe.

They went through a back door which opened on a hallway leading to a garden. "Cicada and I live over there," she said with a wave of her hand. "The rooms on the other side are mostly filled with the accumulation of our years, but you will find one or two quite empty and you can take your pick. Sometimes Jason comes and stays a few days, but his room is closed and has some of his belongings in it. We eat in the garden, but there is a small dining room to the back. When the house church meets, we usually put up benches in the peristyle.

"You have meetings here?"

"Oh yes, we're a small church, but we meet every week."

And so it was arranged. Onesimus brought his few belongings from the ship, congratulating himself upon his good fortune. He found a table suitable for writing in a store room, and there were lamps aplenty to furnish light at night. Obviously, Aristo had imported small household stuffs and kept choice items for himself. Within the first few days of his stay Phoebe pried from him the whole story of his life, and began to enter enthusiastically into his project. She, of course, knew where most of the letters that Paul had written to the churches in Corinth were kept, who kept them, and considerable gossip about the conduct of their households.

Within a day or two, Jason paid a visit and he offered to take Onesimus into Corinth to see the sights. Here Onesimus found a bustling commercial center, filled with temples and government buildings and ample space for trade. It would not be difficult to set up his small business here, he thought, whenever it became necessary to earn money for his keep.

Jason was knowledgeable in such matters. He had been a freedman since Aristo's death and had to hustle to support himself, as did everyone else who lives in Corinth, he stoutly assured Onesimus. When he had sailed with Aristo he had learned to buy supplies of small wares that appeal to common people. He carried with him a selection of such trinkets and baubles and with his pack on his back he would visit the villages in the hinterland, supplying their needs. When he exhausted his wares, he would return to Phoebe's house to stay a few days while he found new waresfrom the ships in the harbor.

However, he was eager to show Onesimus what there was to be seen.

"Here" he pointed out, "is a monument dedicated by our own brother Erasto. He has become an important man in our city, an aedile. You see, we Followers of the Way are not just a rag-tag lot. We may not be much on famous ancestors, but we know how to fill our coffers, and how to treat a brother."

But already he was pushing ahead. "Yonder is where we celebrate the Isthmian Games. The Games are getting to be the most famous in all Greece. You know, at some of those other games they give the winner a crown of laurel leaves? Well, our crown is made of celery leaves and stalk." He slapped his knee and laughed. "We are practical people. What good are laurel leaves or oak leaves; our winner can at least make himself a salad when he goes home."

Onesimus joined Jason in his laughter. On another day he took Onesimus on a long trek up a cliff where they could see the blue waters of Ocean on each side of them.

"There on the east is the Saronic Gulf. You can easy get a boat and sail up to Piraeos any day. And there on the other side is the Corinthian Sea."

"Why," remarked Onesimus, "It's almost as though you could take a shovel gang and make the two meet."

"You're right, and that is just what we are going to do," boasted Jason. "At the next games, Nero himself is coming, and he is going to have the honor of digging the first shovelful of dirt. Won't that be something?"

Most of the days, however, were not filled up with sight-seeing. Onesimus unpacked the writing that he had been doing since he left Ephesus. He had determined that something had to be done to keep it safely packed, and yet to be manageable while he traveled. He had been writing on papyrus leaves, which are not as expensive as sheepskin nor so heavy as wooden platelets. Up to now he had rolled the sheets together and tied them, putting a bundle in a leather carrying case. He had noted that Phoebe had a supply of such cases in her shop and consulted her about his problem. They talked about copying the letters on to a scroll which would be rolled up, for she had many scroll cases. However, a long scroll is hard to handle when one is traveling, and blank scrolls waiting for copying would be a nuisance to carry. Phoebe suggested that copying on parchment leaves was certainly less cumbersome and lighter in weight. Then she suggested that they make light wooden covers between which the leaves would lie flat. The covers could be tied together and perhaps be stored in oiled skins during a sea voyage to protect them from the elements.

The time came when Phoebe and Onesimus went into the city and called upon Erasto. The largest group of followers met at Erasto's house, and Phoebe believed that at least some of Paul's letters might be kept there. Erasto lived in a fine establishment which reminded Onesimus of the house of Archippus. He said that he indeed had some parchment leaves of letters that had come from the Apostle. He produced them and allowed Onesimus to examine them. Onesimus recognized the hand of Tertius; and then outlined his project. He wished to copy all of the writings of Paul that he could find, and one day prepare a fine scroll, perhaps of calf skin, which would contain the complete collection. He showed Erasto the writing that he had been doing while on shipboard, recalling Paul's words upon various occasions. He remembered that at his home in Colossae they had unearthed from the earthquake ruins the very letter to the Colossians that he had helped Paul prepare. Erasto was pleased with the idea, and suggested that Onesimus set up a writing space in his library for the copying. In this way the project was begun.

The house of Erasto had only recently been erected in a newer section of the city. Erasto presented himself as designer and contractor.

"When I was young like you," he was fond of starting his conversations with these words. He told Onesimus of his rise to importance. His father had been a freedman and only late in his life had acquired a family. He had seen to it that his two sons received as fine an education as Corinth could provide. In fact, Erasto himself had started his career as a scribe in charge of accounts for the city. Through industry and astute investment, he had come to be recognized, finally becoming an aedile, since he had always been mindful of civic need. From his own pocket he had provided for the paving of a central street which had long been a muddy disgrace.

"The great Augustus once said he had found a city of brick and left a city of marble, and we lesser beings can show our admiration by following his example."

Erasto had in his possession several sheets from a letter written by Paul. Onesimus studied them and decided their order. This was not easy for it was obvious that the sheets did not follow in obvious succession.

Erasto entered the library as Onesimus was rubbing a sheet of papyrus smooth with pumice stone. "You do that like an expert," remarked his host. "Paul stayed here in this house on his last visit, you know. Yes, and he signed that last sheet in his own hand writing; see, here it is."

Erasto found a corner in the margin where Paul had written his signature, but even now the ink was fading. Onesimus said nothing, but he knew that the signed sheet was not the end of the letter. "Yes, he was a talker, that he was. And a finer preacher we just never had; he said we had just about the best house meeting he had ever talked to. For a little fella he certainly had a booming voice."

Onesimus put the work aside. It seemed worthwhile to hear Erasto's assessment of Paul.

"We went to the games together. You know Corinth is known all over the world for its Isthmian games. Well, Paul hadn't ever been to the Greek games before, being a Jew, you know. Sometimes he was downright bewildered by our customs. Corinth is a pretty liberal place. We're a seaport and we get people that come from all over. Why there are almost as many people in Corinth that speak Latin as there are those that speak Greek. That's why those of us that respect the emperor have managed to get ahead.

Well, anyway, I took Paul to the games, and I never saw him more enthusiastic about anything. He liked the foot races and he really liked the wrestling. He said it was really amazing to see what you could do with your body when you disciplined yourself like the wrestlers do. He used to get up in the morning and throw the disc and pummel his body just like a wrestler."

"I have fought the good fight, I have finished the race, I have kept the faith. From now on there is reserved for me the crown of righteousness, which the Lord, the righteous judge, will give me on that day, and not only to me but also to all who have longed for his appearing," quoted Onesimus.

"Yes, exactly, that's how he put it," said Erasto enthusiastically. "Say, you knock it off tomorrow and I'll take you around and show you just where the two of us went."

And so Erasto and Onesimus had a week of good times together, finishing up with the meeting in Erasto's house on the first day of the week.

They were up early singing praises and saying prayers. Newcomers would drop in until there was quite a crowd. After while the wives and children and even slaves began joining them. The women came later because they had spent the morning fixing fancy dishes to eat. There were grape leaves stuffed with ground meats and stews with chunks of lamb and fresh greens, flavored with thyme and mint, and there were sweet cakes filled with ground up nuts. And of course, a different wine for every dish.

"Yes, people get pretty happy around here by afternoon," said

Erasto beaming. "There's always plenty of food. No one goes hungry from Erasto's house."

When they had their fill of singing, and some of them had testified to the goodness of the Lord, they all gathered and Erasto solemnly said a prayer and then repeated the well known story. Taking a fresh loaf he broke the bread, and passed it around so that everyone could share the loaf. Then he poured the wine into a large goblet, and after tasting it himself, the wine made its way around the company so that everyone had a taste. By sunset the party broke up and everyone left promising to return for the next week's festivities. Onesimus admitted that it had been a most satisfying experience.

After all of the pages had been copied and Onesimus felt that he should not use anymore of Erasto's courtesies, he went across town to the house of Stephanas; for Erasto had suggested that Stephanas had been a friend of Paul from the very first. He also thought that there might be some letters there. Stephanas treated Onesimus with no less kindness than had Erasto. He did have a few leaves of letters which Paul had written; in fact, there were two pages on which Onesimus found the work of his own hand. Stephanas was a bit crippled in the joints, but he liked to sit in the sun and reminisce about his early meetings with Paul. He remembered the work of Apollos too, but, he said,

"It was Paul who brought the Lord Jesus to life."

Throughout the winter Onesimus met many admirers of Paul and heard their stories. However, he did spend many of his days at Phoebe's lodgings, and from there he would set up shop writing letters for seamen who were wintering in Cenchreae; for in their days of leisure, the sailors remembered those that they had left at home. One day Phoebe suggested that he really ought to visit Chloe and her people before it was time to leave. She thought that Chloe herself might have a letter, and furthermore with Chloe's people he was likely to have a "different kind of experience."

Onesimus had not heard much praise of Chloe from his other hosts, and he was aware that she had in a letter of her own registered a complaint about their conduct by writing to Paul. He found Chloe hard at work in the weaving room of her house. She was a strong heavy-set woman. Her tanned skin and tousled hair suggested that she put no store in her appearance nor in feminine wiles. Onesimus complimented her shrewdness concerning the knowledge of "things that go on behind closed doors that everyone isn't aware of."

She proceeded to inform Onesimus of a number of the more scandalous doings behind the closed doors.

"But the one that really fried me," she whispered, "was that old goat Cestus. Now Cestus' father was old and doddering; he stumbled around like an old fool, slobber running out of his mouth and down his chin. So Cestus went off and got a young girl from the country—fresh off the farm she was, about thirteen years old. He brought her home and married her off to the old coot."

"Why did she marry him?" asked Onesimus innocently.

"Well, there wasn't anything she could do about it. Her mother got a few drachmas and that was it."

"That's slavery," observed Onesimus.

"No, that's marriage, Corinthian style," replied Chloe. "But let me finish. The old man died shortly after, and then Cestus took the girl for himself. That way he inherited his father's widow, and his wealth, and he didn't even have to cough up dowry money." Chloe spat in disgust.

"Well, I knew that Paul was a Jew and Jews have a law against that sort of thing, so I just wrote Paul about it," Chloe laughed heartily. "Well, it sure hit the spot, and it sure stirred up a fuss."

"You're right about that," agreed Onesimus.

The next day was the first day of the week which began with singing and tambourines, very early. The guests began to gather. Onesimus was surprised to see that they were mostly women and children.

"Most of the girls were married off young," explained Chloe. "Then they were abandoned by their husbands, or they became widowed, or maybe they never really had husbands." Chloe was matter of fact about her statistics. "But they had children, and children have to be cared for, you know. Well, anyway, these are the widows and virgins, and they are consecrated to Christ. Nobody looks after them but the good Lord. Paul said they should 'remain as he was,' and they believe him. They're beholden to no man, Christian or not. They command their own bodies."

Onesimus seemed a little confused. "Come, now, you said you were once a slave. You must know what it's like to have the freedom to command your own body."

Onesimus tossed his head affirmatively. Almost everyone brought food. There was pork and wild rabbit and birds, all fixed in different ways.

"They buy the food at the temples; it's the only place you can get meat at a decent price. Some of our goody-goodies objected you know. 'It's been sacrificed to idols,' they complain. So what's an idol? I tell them. It's food and it will keep your little ones alive. You can't stand on your principles when your kids are hungry."

They gathered together for singing, accompanying themselves with clapping, castanets and tambourines. Then a woman stood up, raising her arms to heaven and praised God and Jesus; all responded "Amen." Soon two women stood together and chanted a duet of praise. The audience responded by clapping their hands and stamping their feet.

> *'I-o 'I-o. pa-lin a'u-d- O*
> *Who walks upon the road?*

sang a woman.

> *Who walks upon the road,*

they all replied.

> *Who comes into this house,*

sang the woman,

> *He comes into this house,"*

they all chanted.

> *E-voe, Io, Ie-sus, Pae-an, Ev-oe,*

they all chanted over and over again. "Hail Jesus, Savior, Hail." A memory stirred in Onesimus' mind.

> *Io, io; sebete nin;*
> *se-bo-men 'o!*
> *'a,'a,'a pyr*
> *a-la-la-lax-e-te ste-gas 'e-so.*
> *Io, Io, dio*

> *They blended the cry of revel with the tone,*
> *the sweet-voiced breath of the Phrygian lute . . .*

But he pushed the thought back where it came from; and refrained from joining in the dance. At last when all were tired, they gathered in meditative thought. Chloe broke the bread with the customary words which Paul had taught them; and each took a sip of bitter wine. Before nightfall they started from their homes. Onesimus retired late that night after writing,

> *As for tongues, they will cease*
> *as for knowledge, it will come to an end.*

The next day Chloe gave Onesimus another sheet of a letter which Paul had written.

> *Hence, as to the eating of food offered to idols, we know that "no idol in the world really exists," and that "there is no God but one." Indeed, even though there may be so-called gods in heaven or on earth—as in fact there are many gods and many lords—yet for us there is one God, the Father, from whom are all things and for whom we exist, and one Lord, Jesus Christ, through whom are all things and through whom we exist. It is not everyone, however, who has this knowledge. Since some have become so accustomed to idols until now, they still think of the food they eat as food offered to an idol; and their conscience, being weak, is defiled. "Food will not*

*bring us close to God." We are no worse off if we do not
eat, and no better off if we do. But take care that this
liberty of yours does not somehow become a stumbling
block to the weak. For if others see you, who possess
knowledge, eating in the temple of an idol, might they not,
since their conscience is weak, be encouraged to the point
of eating food sacrificed to idols?*

In this way, visiting with those who had known Paul, copying the
scattered sheaves of letters, attending the meetings of the First Day,
writing letters for sailors, sleeping in the houses of the hospitable, and
daily watching the sun rise out of the sea and nightly sink back into
the sea, Onesimus spent his winter on the Peloponnese.

Spring comes early in these lands; yet Onesimus had barely noticed
the winter, so pleasant were the days. The penetrating cold that sometimes came to Colossae did not kill the flowers that grew in Corinth.
The rains had come, and the grateful gave thanks for the renewal of the
land. At last the shipmaster called on Onesimus to discover whether he
had an urge to return to Asia. Onesimus bobbed his head negatively;
he still determined to go to Rome.

"The quickest way to Rome," the shipmaster said gravely, "is to
remember that the shortest distance between two points is the hy-
potenuse." He continued, "Go to Patara by road, and there find a ship
bound for Brindisi or some other Adriatic port. Then join a wayfaring
caravan straight along the Via Appennina, the Road to Rome. I've
heard you can do it in eight days."

However the advice went unheeded. Onesimus had enjoyed the last
trip by sea and looked forward to another such adventure. Furthermore,
he had not finished with his business in Corinth although he had by
this time copied all of the written sheets of Paul's composition that he
could find. He was drawn back to the house churches. But he was
anxious to meet all of those of whom Paul had spoken. He wanted
to hear more of the work of Timothy, and so he continued conversing
with them all: Gaius and Erastus, Quartus and Sosthenes, Phoebe and
Chloe, saying that his purpose was that they "examine themselves to

see whether they were living in the faith."

With Onesimus to urge them on, various of the members of the churches came together to discuss the words that Paul had written to them. They found in Onesimus a congenial teacher who could provide them with the words of all the texts. Unlike Paul, he did not complicate matters further, but listened while they provided their own meanings for the words.

> *But we have this treasure in clay jars, so that it may be made clear that this extraordinary power belongs to God and does not come from us. We are afflicted in every way, but not crushed; perplexed, but not driven to despair.*

"Who is more fortunate than we?" counseled Onesimus, who found himself enjoying his new role. He had been promoted from pedagogue to school master to those who were still living on a diet fit for infants as Paul had named it.

> *I fed you with milk, not solid food, for you were not ready for solid food. Even now you are still not ready,*

Onesimus continued to take his case of writing materials down to the docks of Cenchreae, pursuing his trade, but Erastus quoted to from Paul's own writing:

> *Who at any time pays the expenses for doing military service? Who plants a vineyard and does not eat any of its fruit? Or who tends a flock and does not get any of its milk? If we have sown spiritual good among you, is it too much if we reap your material benefits? If others share this rightful claim on you, do not we still more? Nevertheless, we have not made use of this right, but we endure anything rather than put an obstacle in the way of the gospel of Christ.*

Now Onesimus was going about the churches of Corinth, teaching about the Good News and hoping that in his own way he was a faithful follower of his mentor. Erasto was suggesting that he recognize his calling.

The house of Phoebe was always overflowing with guests; some were members of the house church, but there were others—seamen who had returned to this port to recall the days when they had sailed with Aristo, casual patrons of the little shop who quickly became friends. Jason frequently brought hungry villagers in for a meal, and there were children who had been lost or abandoned. Now and then a runaway slave came in for hiding while Phoebe went out to plead his cause with the master. Phoebe bustled about solving everyone's problems, but Onesimus talked quietly and explained carefully about the hope that is contained in earthen jars.

Cicada brought his breakfast. On fine sunny mornings, she unfolded a little table in the garden next to the pool where there was a bench. Then she brought in a tray with fresh baked bread and goat cheese. In season there were figs or blackberries; then there were purple plums and apricots from the tree that was once a seedling brought from Asia by Aristo. At the end of the summer came the grapes and the apples, nestled in a bed of thyme which grows wild all over the Peloponnese. Onesimus was delighted with such attention, and the more he praised her, the more delicacies she found to bring him. Sometimes there was an egg, or a piece of sausage, saved from the evening meal. The day she brought a bowl of currants drizzled over with honey, he grasped her hand and kissed it.

Phoebe began to mention Cicada in her conversations with him. "She was just a toddler when the shepherd brought her," Phoebe remembered. "He said her mother had died and he had no way to care for her. I knew he was lying; he stole her from some herdsman, or found her abandoned on the street. I gave him seven drachmas, not because he owned her, but because she had such winning ways. She's been with me ever since.

"I even stayed home that first sailing season to take care of her. Somehow Aristo and I were never blessed, and she was my baby. I called her Cicada, because she used to hop around like a little grasshopper; and I guess that's the only name she ever had."

Onesimus, long since soured on child slavery, inquired, "Why didn't you free her, or adopt her as your own?"

Phoebe was startled. "Free her? Why, what would she do? There's only one way for a girl to support herself, and I couldn't let her do that."

"Surely you could have found her a husband?"

"A husband? You think a girl with no dowry can get herself a husband? Besides, there's not many Christian gentlemen around. All of the brothers are old and already have wives."

"Hm, well, there is Jason."

"Jason? O la, Jason is an old man already and set in his ways. Besides, he can't support himself, let alone a wife. Besides, I don't think Cicada fancies Jason."

Onesimus was already sensing the turn which the conversation was taking when happily the shop bell rang and took Phoebe away. Onesimus began to notice that Cicada was always in the garden, watering flowers, mending linens, or doing some other small chore whenever he came in to take his ease. She was a comely woman, simply dressed as befits a slave; but in no way were her clothes revealing. Phoebe had been careful about that.

"Did you know the Apostle?" asked Onesimus.

"The Apostle Paul? Yes, I knew them all—Paul and Apollos, and Timothy and Luke. They all came here and stayed. Of course, I was only a child when Paul stayed here."

"How old were you?" Onesimus tested her.

"Oh, that was years ago. Claudius was the emperor then; and Gallio was the ruler of the City. I must have been about twelve. Mother Phoebe was just beginning to teach me how to serve at her table."

A memory stirred Onesimus. "I was ten when Archippus called on me to serve at his banquet."

"Oh, we didn't have banquets," Cicada replied naively, "We always eat simply here."

She smiled so winningly that Onesimus had to restrain himself
from touching her. He was thinking to himself, "If she was twelve
when Paul was here, and the next year I was twenty-two when I first
met Paul in Ephesus—and now I am thirty-three . . . " But he put the
thought from his mind.

A few days later, Phoebe asked him, "Is there someone back at
your home that you are promised to? Or maybe you have a wife and
children, how are we to know?"

With a pang, Onesimus thought of Erotion. "There was someone
once. I wasn't even twenty years old then." He felt the tears welling
up and turned away. Finally he said, "She died in the earthquake,"
and hastily he continued, "But she had taken a vow of virginity before
that."

Phoebe sensed that this was not the moment to reintroduce Cicada.
On another day Phoebe inquired, "You are not getting younger you
know. If you expect to have any heirs you must look about you."

Onesimus tried to pass it off lightly. "I hadn't really thought of a
family seriously. Paul did say that marriage among those of the Way
is allowable. Of course he added, *"This I say by way of concession,
not of command."*

And then he turned quite seriously to Phoebe. "I am not free to
marry at this time. I have taken a vow to find Paul and to stay with
him as his helper. You know what Paul said about that. *"I wish that
all were as I myself am. But each has a particular gift from God, one
having one kind and another a different kind. To the unmarried and
the widows I say that it is well for them to remain unmarried as I am."*

"Well, Paul was much older than you. And Paul was not one to
remain long in one place." Then in a softer tone, "Paul always expected
that the last days would be on us immediately; but obviously that is
not God's plan. I know that you like it here; and surely you must feel
that you have been called to become 'father-in-god' for us."

Onesimus could only reply,
"I must give it more thought."

When Cicada came in to bring his supper, she reddened and cast

her eyes downward, so as not to look him in the face, for that is the
maidenly way for a woman in her position to behave.

The thought came to Onesimus, "It is time for me to leave now,
or I never will." He went to the harbor the next day and found a ship
bound for Crete, and thence to Rome.

The Cretan Angels

They sailed into the westerly breeze and set their sails aslant. Onesimus
was overjoyed to feel the sea-spray against his face. He was back on
deck after seeing to it that his luggage was safely stowed. For this
short voyage, a mere five or six days, he would be a passenger and not
a member of the crew.

Once out upon open water, while the sailors struggled with the
oars, the shipmaster came up to make conversation with his passenger,
for his curiosity overcame him.

"Hae ye been to Kriti afore?" he asked in a strong Cretan accent.

Onesimus' nod was negative.

"An' why be ye cumin' thar naow?"

"I'm on my way to Rome," was the reply.

"Shur, an' thar's faster ways to git a Rome than by Kriti."

"I prefer to sail."

"Naow, Oye suspect yu'r runnin' awaye"

"I'm a free man," protested Onesimus, pained by his thoughts.

"Didna say ye wasn'—Lotsa reasons fer runnin' awaye y'know.
Wimmen, f'rinstance; be ye runnin' awaye a woman?"

With a certain relief Onesimus laughed, "Yes, I'm afraid I am."

"Y're right in bein' afeared o' wimmen, specially a Corinthian
floozy."

Onesimus felt defensive again, "She was not a floozy."

"Oh, she war a good woman. Them's the verra worst kind."

"No, not the worst kind, the best kind. She was chaste and fair to
look at. She was modest and spoke only when she was spoken to."

"So, wat war the problem?"

"They wanted me to marry her."

The shipmaster burst into laughter. "Reason enow, But didn' she hae no dowry?"

Onesimus suddenly realized that he had neglected to look into that matter. "Probably it could have been arranged"; he looked up in amazement, "I probably could have inherited everything." "Then yu're a bit of a fool. Here y'are wi' a gang o' pirates, a-chasin' around the isles, an' ye cudda been a-settin' in yer own house, with a fair wife, a-dandlin' yer own baby on yer knee."

"I told you I am bound for Rome; I have important business there."

"Business in Rome? Yu're a bandit then, or a revolutionary. Thar's no honest man goes a Rome."

Onesimus made no reply.

"Lookee, I'll put ye ashore in Kriti, an' ifn yu've any sense yu'll take the nex' sailin' boat back to Corinth."

The shipman was as good as his word; Onesimus soon found himself on the streets of 'Erkles Town. Even in early morning the town simmered in the summer heat. The little donkeys swished the flies off their hind sides with their tails as they plodded slowly up the cobbled road. Here and there the cobbles had dislodged themselves and swarms of dust and gnats rose up from what in another season have been a puddle, but now was breathed in as dusty air. Street urchins called to each other with insults. But once the harbor area had been left, no other human life was to be seen. Even the dogs had found shaded corners with no curiosity to examine the casual stranger.

For a tourist each new and unknown city calls up a sudden near panic. Onesimus stood with his small bundle of baggage and tried to imagine himself as Odysseus, newly landed on this unfriendly shore. Finally his eye spotted what appeared to be a taverna, shuttered up against the summer sun. It stood across from a sculptured fountain which at the moment was not spouting any water. Apprehensively he made his way toward it as he remembered that Paul had said: *"It was one of them, their very own prophet, who said, Cretans are always liars, vicious brutes, lazy gluttons."*

A slatternly girl motioned him inside to a bench and table already occupied by a dozing old man, who stirred himself enough to acknowledge the newcomer.

"Mornin' to ye," he drawled. Onesimus sat down warily. "And whar be ye from?" asked his grizzled tablemate, his eyes examining Onesimus' baggage.

"I was most recently at Corinth," Onesimus replied with the most casual sophistication he could muster.

"Aye, Corinth. Thar's nae mo' wicked a town."

Onesimus found himself defensive. "I knew some very fine people there." The barmaid came over with some barley beer.

"I wouldna drink that stuff," commented his companion; "The Cretan grapes make very fine wine, but the locals 'druther get drunk on that slop," he pointed to Onesimus' beaker.

He wet his finger in the sweat of the cup and drew a figure on the dusty table.

"What are you drawing there? It looks like a fish."

"Aye, is that what it looks like? Then let it be a fish. Fishin's good in these seas." Onesimus nodded. Wetting his own finger he drew a letter X in the dust, followed by a P.

"Ye be one o' the brothers, then," said the bearded one without changing his facial expression.

Onesimus tossed his head affirmatively. His new friend stretched out his hand in friendship and said, "The name's Nikos. I'm a native of these parts. I have a sma' loft over thar, if'n ye want a place for a siesta," his new friend whispered affably.

The two rose, and Onesimus counted out three leptas which he produced from his sleeve, and put them in the hand of the barmaid.

The two sauntered across the square and went through a gate in the adobe wall. True to his word, his new-named friend took him up a ladder to the loft which was his residence.

"Do you catch many fish this way?" Onesimus asked.

"More than ye might think," Nikos replied. "These days everyone's tryin' to 'scape somewhars. I've lived on the sea the most o' my life, but the old bones git a leetle creaky, and so now I sit and watch the boats that come and go, and greet the people as come from them. No, most of them ain't Christ-followers, but 'most all of 'em 'preciate a friendly word. Father Titus says 'ospitality is a godly gift."

"Titus—Titus is here?" Onesimus grew excited.

"Aye, Th'Apostle sent him to be our 'piscopos, our overseer, y'know. If ye know him, yu'll be glad to see him tomorrow. It's a big holiday for the whole country, with the plays an' the gymnastics and the races. That's why it's so quiet today. They're all getting ready for the morrow. But y'd best git some rest now. We in Kriti rest during the heat o' the day. After sundown, things'll start gittin' lively."

Onesimus didn't need a second invitation. The heat in the loft was stifling, and he drifted off in sleep.

When the pair awoke, there was the sound of noise in the streets. One could hear shouts of men and the laughter of children. There was a skirling of bagpipes, the whine of the flutes and the singing of women.

"Come," called the old Cretan, "You don't want to miss the festivities; and besides there will be plenty of food. Us Cretans be most hospitable with food."

"The poet said Cretans were *gluttons*," replied Onesimus.

"Every country has its soured old men," replied Nikos, "'E called it gluttony; I call it 'ospitality. 'Ere, stow yer belongin's behind that bar; they'll be safe thar. 'Mm, mmm, I kin smell that roastin' pig from here."

The two went down into the street, now filled with dancing and singing people. The sun was low in the sky, about to drop behind a mountain ridge and a fresh breeze came off the water."

It's the Thesmophoria, the time for celebrating the barley queen."

"Ah, that is the reason for the barley beer," interposed Onesimus.

"Ycch," Nikos expressed his distaste. "But tomorrow there will be the plays in the theater."

"Plays?" Onesimus' eyes glowed pleasure. "And what are they

playing?"

"Well, it's real high class, it is. They're a doin' the Agamemnon. I see y're not the kind o' Christian as scorns the plays. There be those as doesn't think they're proper."

"The Apostle said, *'All things are lawful for me, but not all things are beneficial. All things are lawful for me,'* but I will not be dominated by anything, especially by those who think they know what is proper."

While his speech was still on his lips, Onesimus started in amazement, "You mean Aeschylus' *Agamemnon*?"

"That's the one, the whole shebang. It takes all day. Ye better get yourself one of those straw hats; Yep, they'll be carryin' people out feet first afore it's all over. Better wear a long tunic, or some o' those Phrygian pants or you'll fry your laigs on the benches."

"How did you know I am a Phrygian?" shouted Onesimus.

The old one snorted, "'Ow do ye know I'm a Cretan?" and he laughed as he plunged into the crowd. "Come, follow me."

Onesimus followed and called out, "it is written in the law of Moses, 'You shall not muzzle an ox while it is treading out the grain.' Is it for oxen that God is concerned?"

"Nae, He speaks for our sake. An' t'was indeed written for our sake, for whoever plows should plow in hope and whoever threshes should thresh in hope of a share in the crop. Praise be the barley crop. It's like th'Apostle said, *'We have sown our spiritual seed among you, is it too much if we reap some material benefits?'* "

The two entered into the festivities, sampling the sausages here, and the salats there. Of barley bread and sheep's milk cheese there was plenty, and cakes soaked in syrupy cane sugar and sprinkled with currants and pistachio' nuts. And the wine flowed freely enough that later in the evening even the barley beer was palatable. The moon was almost ready to set behind the mountain before the two stumbled into their loft again.

Morning came sooner than needed, and the calls of the hucksters and the clank of metal woke the two before they were ready.

"Where are we?" the roused Onesimus called as he pulled his head up from the hay. And looking down from the loft, he duly noted below him a stable where pack animals were being outfitted and loaded for the day.

"Well, lad, 'tis day; are ye ready fer the Agamemnon?" Nikos called out.

"There's a word of truth in what they say about Kriti," Onesimus said solemnly.

The Play's the Thing

The sun was already burning hot, but the whole town was streaming toward the theater. Nikos had thoughtfully set out a jug of water and some bread and cheese.

"Thar was aplenty last night; no use letting it be thrown out to the dogs," he winked.

"Water?" queried Onesimus.

"Better fer ye than barley beer," Nikos replied. "An' sweet wine wi' the sun like today—lad, y'd be seekin' the underworld."

From a peddler, Onesimus provided himself with a large hat made of straw and some straw mats. "The benches aren't pillows, you know." For an extra obol, they found seats just behind the local magistrates, and on a side not looking into the sun.

"Fine thing, goin' with a man o' money," commented Nikos.

Onesimus smiled his best Archippus smile. "Sh, the play is beginning," he cautioned.

A buskined Clytemnestra spoke slowly through the mask—

> ... *God sent forth light,*
> *And beacon from beacon bright the trail of flame*
> *to me. From Ida first to Hermes' cliff*
> *On Lemnos, and from thence a third great lamp*
> *Was flashed to Athos' lofty mount.*
> *Up, up it soared and lured the dancing shoals*
> *To skim the waves in rapture at the light,*
> *A golden courier like the sun it sped*

Post haste its message to Macistus' rock
Which vigilant and impatient bore it on . . .

"What's she sayin'?" asked the Cretan trying hard to understand the words.

"It's how the word got spread from Asia to Greece," replied Onesimus. "It's like Paul bringing the light of the gospel from the Troad across to Thessalonica and to Philippi . . . "

To the peak of Aegiplanctus it passed the word
To burn and burn, and they unsparing flung
A flaming comet to the cape that looks
Over the gulf Saronean . . .
Such were the stages of this torch relay
One from another snatching up the light.

"Praise God, that's just how it happens," exclaimed Onesimus in joyous discovery. Oh, listen now, here comes the chorus."

By Zeus struck down. 'Tis truly spoken,
With each step clear and plain to track out.
He willed, his will was done.
God regards not the man who hath trod
Beneath his feet the holy sanctities.
Lo, swift ruin worketh sure judgment on hearts
With pride puffed up and high presumption,
On stored-up wealth . . .
          Far best to live
Free of want and griefless, rich in the gift of wisdom.

"There's not many as believe that," Nikos commented solemnly.

Onesimus ventured, "We have been like children, tossed to and fro and blown about by every wind of doctrine, by people's trickery, by their craftiness in deceitful scheming. Now we must grow up in every way into him who is the head, into Christ. You see, Greeks and Jews have been alike in misunderstanding the way that God has commended them to live."

Nikos knit his brows, "You mean that the Gentiles had the law as well as the Jews?"

"Of course the Greeks had laws; that is what this play is about—you will see how they broke God's law and then they suffered for it. That is why my teacher Paul insisted,

> *We must no longer live as the Gentiles live, in the futility of their minds. They are darkened in their understanding, alienated from the life of God because of their ignorance and hardness of heart. They have lost all sensitivity and have abandoned themselves to licentiousness, greedy to practice every kind of impurity. That is not the way we have learned Christ! For surely we have heard about him and were taught in him, as truth is in Jesus. We were taught to put away our former way of life, our old self, corrupt and deluded by its lusts, and to be renewed in the spirit of our minds, and to clothe ourselves with the new self, created according to the likeness of God in true righteousness and holiness.*

"You talk just like the Apostle yerself," admired the old Cretan.

But Onesimus scarcely heard for he was caught up in the action of the play.

By the sixth hour the players went inside their tent for rest; jugglers came out to entertain the crowd. Families broke out their lunches and let their children run free. The audience in the bleachers stood and strolled about, while others gambled at their benches and more than one fight broke out. At last after considerable intermission the third play of the triad began and Onesimus saw that they had chosen their seats well with the sun at their backs rather than in their eyes.

Nikos was weary and dozed off to sleep but Onesimus was riveted to the scene as he identified with Orestes pursued by his furies.

> *I do confess—*
> *An act not wholly mine,*
> *Be thou my judge, whether 'twas just or no,*

I will accept thy ordering of my doom.

"That was the rule of law, the old law," remarked Onesimus to no one in particular. Athena, tall in her cothurnus, and dressed in a golden robe with a golden crown upon her head recited,

> *Too grave a suit is this for mortal minds*
> *to judge, nor is it my right to pass my verdict*
> *on a suit of blood.*
> *Judges I will appoint,*
> *A court set up in perpetuity.*
> *Call your proofs and witnesses.*

Nikos stirred from his nap. "Is it over yet?" he asked anxiously. "They are just winding it up," replied his mentor. "Just listen up."

> *. . . here Reverence*
> *and inbred Fear enthroned among my people*
> *Shall hold their hands from evil night and day.*
> *Let them not tamper with their laws;*
> *For should a stream of mire pollute the pure*
> *Fountain, the lips shall never find it sweet.*
> *If you honour this high ordinance,*
> *Then shall you have for land and commonweal*
> *A stronghold of salvation.*

The golden goddess disappeared and the chorus wound it up with a pious song. The sun hung red above the mountain. The audience rose up, subdued by the long sitting and the marble benches. For most of the audience it had been wearisome; those who understood it walked out in silence.

Out on the street again a friendly voice,
"Ah Nikos, good to see you here; you have a friend with you."

Onesimus looked up with recognition of the sound, "Titus, my old friend Titus."

Titus stared in disbelief, "It is, you are—," and he fumbled for the name.

"I'm from Ephesus and Paul. I'm Onesimus, remember?"

"Onesimus, the Colossian; yes, I remember. But how did you know Nikos here?"

And they fell to laughing and talking all at once, totally forgetful of the crowd of people, of the time of day, and of their weariness.

The Cretans are small of stature, small in height and bone. They carry themselves nimbly over the mountains and rocks of their island as if to compete with the mountain goats and the graceful eagles. Titus stood tall among them, though in another land he would not have been singled out. The sun makes the skin of the Cretans darker than their cousins in more northerly lands. Titus, on the other hand, became more red than swarthy. His skin was more wrinkled than when Onesimus had known him in Ephesus. Now the two together almost appeared to be brothers according to the flesh. More than that, from their mouths came the same speech which did not affect the Cretan drawl. It did not take much explanation for Titus to learn that Nikos had met Onesimus only the day before.

"Surely, he is my best evangelist," remarked Titus. "He has brought more than one lost seaman safe to shore." Nikos glowed with the compliment which Onesimus echoed.

"I was about to bring him to ye anyways," explained Nikos. "But he war prone to see the play. Hey, he understood it all an' could 'splain it good as ary preacher."

Titus agreed that Onesimus was a true scholar and inquired as to where the two were lodging.

"Oh, I took him to m' loft, but 'tis crowded thar for two," explained Nikos.

It was quickly agreed that Onesimus would be welcome at the house of Titus which was up in a village outside of the town. Titus opened his wallet and produced a drachma for Nikos, telling him to keep his eyes sharp for any other wayward Christians who might land on their shores. Two boys appeared for Titus, and they loaded Onesimus belongings on their backs.

"That is all you are travelling with?" Titus was astonished. On their walk they exchanged the news of their lives and their journeys.

"You are a free man now, I take it," Titus began. Onesimus rehearsed the whole story from his return to Colossae at Paul's behest, to the earthquake and finally through his more recent travels.

"And what wind has cast you like a lost Odysseus upon this shore, my friend?" Titus asked almost in disbelief. Onesimus found himself revealing his hopes and dreams of finding Paul and serving him. Titus shook his head.

"You have said you are a deacon; you serve Christ, not Paul; and that is what Paul would expect of you."

Onesimus had to agree, but he kept reminding Titus that once long ago he had made a commitment to return to Paul, and so he was bound for Rome for that purpose. In the meantime, Onesimus continued, he was serving Paul by collecting Paul's letters—making copies, and keeping a journal of his remembered words. Titus was impressed, and added that he had some letters from Paul that perhaps could be added to the collection. Onesimus was excited; this was reason enough for his detour to Crete.

Half a day's journey through the countryside brought them to a collection of houses. There in a cottage tucked in among the trees of an ancient olive orchard was a rambling adobe in which Titus lived.

"It has been here for many years; each owner has added on pieces as his needs demanded. And I, too, have made my little adjustments. Tomorrow when you have rested, you may look around and find a niche to fit your needs."

So it happened. In a set of rooms beyond a blue door lived Titus amid collections of memorabilia from all of his wanderings. Set off to one side of that was an unattached building, almost square.

"We use it as our meeting room," smiled Titus modestly. Onesimus quickly identified it as Titus' personal church. Across a jumbled garden Onesimus found another set of three small rooms, entered through a green door.

"Cretans love their painted doors," commented Titus. Here Onesimus determined to settle himself for a few weeks secretly congratulating himself on his good fortune. He was eager to find out about Titus' life in Crete and how he came by it. He knew that Titus had spent a brief time in Corinth, but had left quickly.

"Corinth was not to my liking," admitted Titus. "There was that constant bickering between one house church and another. Paul finally suggested that I might find my niche in Crete and so here I am."

"Are you then, the apostle to the Cretans?"

But Titus indicated otherwise. "There were many of the faith here already, when I came. One whole community is of Jewish origin. Some of them were born here of Jewish parentage; others came from Alexandria, disaffected by the quality of life there. And then, there were others who were Greek. They too had left Alexandria and Cyrene. Still others have been converted as native Cretans."

"And you are evangelist to them all?" asked Onesimus in surprise.

"Someone has to keep them on track, or they would cease to be a brotherhood and become a debating society. We in Crete are not of the same pattern as those in Corinth. We do not have house churches."

Onesimus was confused. He had not spent much time thinking about Church structure.

In the days that were to follow, Titus and Onesimus had conversations on the subject. They took long walks together.

"Crete is as old as time," announced Titus as they walked up the hill through an ancient cemetery. I think it must have been the original Eden—and Eden it is still, though somewhat rundown and untended," he went on as the branch of a wayward olive tree slapped him in the face. They stopped at the cemetery gate, for it was fenced about like an abandoned city.

"That identifies the world where we came from as 'East of Eden,' to be sure. This is a mysterious place, filled with the ghosts and demons of antiquity."

Onesimus was intrigued, "You have seen these demons?"

"The gods here are very old," remarked Titus as they sat down on a grassy knoll. "Over yon is Mt. Ida,"

"Where Zeus was born?" marvelled Onesimus.

Titus saw the trouble in Onesimus' eyes. "Every race, every country, every island, knows God. The God of Sinai is also the God of Ida. The demons are not God's creatures; they are our creatures."

"Did Paul say that?" asked Onesimus sharply.

"Of course not; at least not in that way. Paul knew the God of Sinai, but he did not grow up with the God of Ida. Paul understood that God is God whatever you name him."

Onesimus nodded.

"You and I, we were taught the God of the Greeks; we did not know the God of Moses."

"Apollo! Apollo!" mimicked Onesimus.

Titus ignored him, *"We all like sheep have gone astray.* Indeed we are like sheep. We need a flock; we need a sheep fold and we need a shepherd. Paul understands that and has written letters instructing us about living the life of the shepherd. The shepherd is necessary to keep the sheep from straying far from the sheepfold.

"Here on this island there was a whole community of Jews, and when they learned about the coming of the Messiah, they all turned to him. It was not as in Corinth or so many other places where the Christ-lovers left the synagogue. Here the Christ lovers owned the synagogue, so it became the meeting place for Christians. A house church doesn't consist of more than a dozen persons, for that is all that can comfortably gather in one room. In a house church the owner of the house becomes the leader. In our situation we choose an elder who is wise."

"You seem to have a whole community of elders," remarked Onesimus.

"Exactly," said Titus. "And so there must be a president of the elders."

"Who is the Overseer," continued Onesimus. "That is much the same as it was in Colossae and Laodicea. Epaphras was the overseer of all of the organizations in the community."

"Yes, Paul has said that is the way we must organize. He has written letters of instruction as to how this is to be done. They are not letters to churches; they are letters to shepherds."

"Do you have such a letter?" asked Onesimus.

"That is what I am trying to tell you. For instance, you are a deacon. Do you have any instructions as to what a deacon does?"

Onesimus admitted that he did not; that he was constantly asking himself what his responsibilities were. Titus took out a page on which he had copied:

> *Deacons likewise must be serious, not double-tongued, not indulging in much wine, not greedy for money; they must hold fast to the mystery of the faith with a clear conscience. And let them first be tested; then, if they prove themselves blameless, let them serve as deacons. Women likewise must be serious, not slanderers, but temperate, faithful in all things. Let deacons be married only once, and let them manage their children and their households well; for those who serve well as deacons gain a good standing for themselves and great boldness in the faith that is in Christ Jesus.*

Onesimus read the page carefully. "So this is why Phoebe called herself a *deacon*, Paul had named her such."

Titus sighed, "Phoebe and I did not always agree with each other; she is a strong willed woman."

"Indeed she is," Onesimus agreed. Then he continued, "But Paul concedes that deacons should be husbands and have households. Had I understood that, I might not be here."

Titus noted that Paul often did not make the same rules for himself that he made for others.

"Why have you not married?" asked Onesimus.

"I suppose because I have spent so many years travelling here and there that I never felt the need for a settled life. At my age I am loath to give up the freedom that I have, however I do recognize, as Paul has recognized, that Christians must set up households in which to practice the faith. Paul has come to this lately because he now understands that the day of the Coming is not immediate, as once he thought."

Onesimus replied pensively, "There are some who believe that we have already passed through that time and that we now are living in the New Age."

"I, too, have heard that theory; and in some respects I believe it. However, I think that right now we are in an age of passage. The old is passing away; and as with the passage of old men it brings pain and sorrow and penitence. The new will come. May we live to see its glorious dawning."

"Is it important that these things should be taught to all of the people?" Onesimus asked Titus.

"I do not believe that we should burden everyone with our speculations. There are many questions for which we have no answers. Paul did write a brief description of what we should teach." Titus produced a sheaf of papers.

> *But as for you, teach what is consistent with sound doctrine. Tell the older men to be temperate, serious, prudent, and sound in faith, in love, and in endurance. Likewise, tell the older women to be reverent in behavior, not to be slanderers or slaves to drink; they are to teach what is good, so that they may encourage the young women to love their husbands, to love their children, to be self-controlled, chaste, good managers of the household, kind, being submissive to their husbands, so that the word of God may not be discredited. Likewise, urge the younger men to be self-controlled. Show yourself in all respects a model of good works, and in your teaching show integrity, gravity, and sound speech that cannot be censured; then any opponent will be put to shame, having nothing evil to say of us. Tell slaves to be submissive to their masters and to give satisfaction in every respect; they are not to talk back, not to pilfer, but to show complete and perfect fidelity, so that in everything they may be an ornament to the doctrine of God our Savior.*
>
> *For the grace of God has appeared, bringing salva-*

tion to all, training us to renounce impiety and worldly passions, and in the present age to live lives that are self-controlled, upright, and godly, while we wait for the blessed hope and the manifestation of the glory of our great God and Savior, Jesus Christ. He it is who gave himself for us that he might redeem us from all iniquity and purify for himself a people of his own who are zealous for good deeds. Declare these things; exhort and reprove with all authority. Let no one look down on you.

Onesimus read the passage. "These are all good admonitions," he agreed, "there is nothing here that could not be presented to people of any background, Jew or Gentile, Greek or Roman, or even Phrygian."

"That is so," replied Titus, "and I would sincerely hope that we can convince enough people of our right thinking so that we may be kept safe from the dangers that seem to attack us."

"Yes," agreed Onesimus, "I do not understand why suddenly we are persecuted on every side by those we would suppose would most agree with us. I vaguely understand why the Jews in Jerusalem would arrest Paul. They consider that he has been a traitor to their cause and has gone over to the Romans. I would think that Rome could easily be convinced that Paul is indeed a supporter of the Roman law."

"Except that," interposed Titus, "Romans are not true to their own ideals; and that is the case with every people that I have met. I have told you that Crete is an old land, a very ancient land. Why on this very piece of ground we walk upon are the remains of civilizations that predate the flood.

"I am telling you this because you must understand that the people who live here cherish every thing that ever happened here, good or evil. And they consider that we are the interlopers. There are those who would say that we have taken over the very land that their ancient King Minos saved for them, and they may be right."

"King Minos is a myth," replied Onesimus.

"Who knows?" asked Titus. "The reality of it is that they see in this ancient king their right to own this land; and they see me, you and me and all of the late-comers here, as usurpers. Envy, my friend, envy and covetousness are the real demons. And I do not believe that Paul may expect any salvation in Rome, for no one welcomes the stranger."

Onesimus could only agree that his experience had not taught him otherwise. "That is why I am a Christ follower. I was a stranger, and they took me in."

With such conversation the days and the weeks passed until one day Titus came to Onesimus' study. "A messenger from a newly arrived ship has brought me a letter from Brother Timothy in Ephesus."

The letter included a parcel of writing that had come from Paul to Timothy, written from Rome. Both of the men were startled to learn that Paul had been in house arrest in Rome for over a year when the letter was written, and no one knew when that was.

> *I have fought the good fight, I have finished the race, I have kept the faith. From now on there is reserved for me the crown of righteousness, which the Lord, the righteous judge, will give me on that day, and not only to me but also to all who have longed for his appearing. Do your best to come to me soon, for Demas, in love with this present world, has deserted me and gone to Thessalonica; Crescens has gone to Galatia, Titus to Dalmatia. Only Luke is with me. Get Mark and bring him with you, for he is useful in my ministry. I have sent Tychicus to Ephesus. When you come, bring the cloak that I left with Carpus at Troas, also the books, and above all the parchments.*

"This letter may have been written as much as three years ago," exclaimed Titus. "As a matter of fact I never went to Dalmatia, and Timothy is in Ephesus now, not Tychicus."

"Paul sounds desperate," Onesimus added. "I have dawdled here too long. I hope that Luke has been able to find solutions. Obviously I have many of the parchments so I must prepare myself to leave."

Titus agreed. Onesimus had already spent precious months in Crete and winter might well set in before he could find a ship to Rome.

The packing took more than a week, for Titus insisted that clothing and foodstuffs from Crete must accompany Onesimus to Rome. At last a sturdy ship bound for Rome on its last journey of the season was found and the passage paid to the shipmaster. The night before the sailing Titus and many of the Cretan friends met in the meeting room and celebrated the solemn meal with prayers for the traveller's safe journey.

At Sea Again

"No sea voyage is ever uneventful," pronounced the master of the merchant ship *Elpis*. The "Hope" was built for carrying merchandise, not for comfort. Its weathered oaken planks betrayed it as a worker. Its wider decks proved to be easier for body movement than the narrow more streamlined versions of other ships that Onesimus had travelled on. Nathan, the owner and captain, was a rugged Jew from Alexandria. He had been sailing and trading for half a century, starting at the age of six, with his ship-master father. He had a wife and grown sons who lived safely in Egypt, but he frankly admitted that he preferred the life at sea.

"We will aim for Brundisium. If the weather holds, we should be there in six days."

"And if not?" Onesimus raised the question.

"If not, we will pull for the nearest shore to wait it out. But it will hold good." It was as if the weather gods had heeded his command.

"What are your plans from here?" he inquired of Onesimus.

"I need to go to Rome as quickly as possible," was the reply. "I have been advised to take to the road across Italy."

"Take the road," roared the captain. "Why, lad, you will be eaten alive. The road goes through forest and mountain, and every inch of it crawling with *ladrones*."

"Ladrones?"

"Bandits," said the captain succinctly. "The fiercest bandits this side of Styx."

"I understand that Nero recently made it across Italy in three days when he returned from the games at Corinth."

"I understand that Nero had the entire Roman army with him for protection, and they were still attacked by ladrones three times."

Onesimus was taken aback. "What happened to them, the bandits, I mean."

"Crucified them," was the retort. "The Roman army ain't gentle. —But you stay with me; we'll be in Rome before you could walk to Zama, that's where the Romans took Hannibal, y'know."

Onesimus had listened to many seamen talk of the dangers of the western sea, wide and wind-swept, with few friendly islands for shipwrecked seafarers to find safe harbor. Still, his experiences with bandits were far from comforting. At last he consented to continue with Shipmaster Nathan, on to Rome.

They coasted close to the shores on the Lavender sea. There were few safe harbors here; the cliffs hung perilously over the waters. Small fishing boats appeared but did not approach the hulking merchant ship too closely, and scurried quickly to their secure shelters in shallow inlets.

The captain called Onesimus to him, "See, yonder, that cloud that hangs straight up in the sky? That's the plume of Etna on Sicily."

Onesimus thought of Odysseus and the one-eyed Polyphemus. "Are we going to land on Sicily?"

"Not if I can help it," replied Nathan. Of course, if we get a Norther by nightfall, we'll have to make for land. It that happens we will probably have to go around Sicily, and that does not make for a speedy trip. We could even get stowed up on Melita for the winter. But that is not going to happen."

"It's not?" laughed Onesimus.

"Of course not," swore the captain. "I have a glass aquarium of tropical fish from Egypt with me. I have to get them to the imperial palace before the week is up. They're a present for Poppaea's birthday."

Nathan took his passenger into his cabin where sure enough there was a glass container of colorful fish swimming among rocks and sea-plants.

"The fish come from the Erythrean Sea; but the water's warm down there. So I have to bring in sea water and warm it up before I put it in the tank. The water has to be changed every couple of days. It's been quite a chore and I'll be glad when it's over."

"Why are you doing it?" exclaimed Onesimus.

"Money, lad, money. Nero may have some wild ideas, but he pays well. But if we go all the way around Sicily, it will be too late for the birthday."

"So what are we going to do?"

"We'll make for the Straits tomorrow."

"Scylla and Charybdis?" Onesimus shuddered torn between fear and delight. Thucydides had described it.

> *The Strait lies between Rhegium and Messana, the place where Sicily is the least distant from the continent. This is the so-called Charybdis through which Odysseus sailed. It is accounted dangerous because of its narrowness and of the currents caused by the inrush of the Tyrrhenian sea.*

"It's the tides that cause the danger," said the captain. "Generally the tides aren't for much in Mare Nostrum, as the Romans name it. But here in the straits the tides are as strong as in the channel that separates Gaul from Britain. Twice a day the water rushes northward and the southern water ebbs; then twice a day the tidal bore is reversed to the south. The force of the stream is greatest where the strait is narrowest. On the Italian side you'll find Scylla, and just north of Messana on Sicily's side is the whirlpool of Charybdis. In between the two the current is the strongest and if the day has a strong north wind, no ship can sail against it."

> *And there is that Scylla, she of the terrible bark.*
> *No one would face her gladly, not even a god if he should*
> *   pass her way.*
> *For she has twelve feet which dangle down,*

> *and six very long necks,*
> > *and on each of them a horrible head*
> *with three rows of close-set teeth,*
> *full of dark death.*

Onesimus chanted his school boy lessons in happy memory.

> *Sunk she is up to her middle in the cave's depths,*
> *but her heads protrude from the dreadful hollow.*
> *There she fishes, searching about the rock for any dolphin*
> *Or other fish which swim in that deep-voiced sea.*
> *No sailors ever boast of passing Scylla*
> *without losing one of their number.*
> *From every passing ship she snatches off a man with each*
> > *of her mouths.*

The captain laughed, "I've never lost a man to the sea-bitch yet."
Onesimus stood facing the wind and sang out the challenge,

> *Charybdis lies lower down, an arrow shot from the Scylla.*
> *On it grows a great fig tree in full leaf,*
> *And below it Charybdis sucks down the black waters.*
> *Three times a day she spouts out the waters;*
> *and three times a day she sucks it down.*

The captain stayed his ship and waited watching the tidal bore through one cycle of its rhythm. Every available seaman had his place upon the benches, ready with the heavy oar in hand once the signal was given. At a moment the Captain hammered down the starting signal and started the rhythm of the oarsmen. Each man in silent concentration pulled with all his strength upon his oar as they began to glide through the sea-river. Well trained they were, so that at a sound of the hammer on one side or the other they would lean hard upon their oars while the other slackened just a bit, thus fending off the dreaded cliffs. The expert helmsman guided them silently as they skirted around the eddies and the whirlpools. Past the sucking Charybdis they flew and then kept a straight course never veering around Scylla's maw. At last they broke into the Tyrrhenian Sea. The wearied sailors rested on their oars and a cheer went up. The captain shouted praises and commanded that they steer for a sandy shore. They dropped their anchor and waded ashore through shallow water to the beach. There they lay down and rested while the captain brought out a jar of wine.

> *He gathers up the waters of the ocean as in a water-skin,*
> *and stores up the depths of the sea.*

Onesimus thought to himself. The man is as disciplined as Paul. He has no thought of self, only to guide others straight through the peril. And though he had only watched, Onesimus discovered that his muscles were as sore as though he had pulled an oar himself.

Back on shipboard the sailors rejoiced as they sailed up the Italian coast in sight of land but far enough at sea to escape the rocks that lurked below the surface of the sea.

They sailed northward and Onesimus sensed a growing excitement among the crew. Another voyage was almost over and they were landing in safety. The captain came to Onesimus who was watching the shore from the deck.

"Over there, that's Latium, the original home of the Latins who built the City. They have a saying: 'Money will buy anything in Rome.' And it's true. It's a wicked city, lad; and if you're not prepared for it, God help you." He paused and then he went on. "If I observe you rightly, you are a Christian."

Onesimus nodded slightly, saying nothing.

"In Rome there's not much difference between Christians and Jews, to the Romans I mean. They haven't bothered to make any distinction."

Onesimus looked dubious. "I'm a Greek, not a Jew; but why should the Romans care?"

"The Romans have their own problems. By and large they're tolerant of other people's religions, so long as they don't challenge Roman authority. Anyway, I'm warning you. It's a bad time for Jews, and therefore Christians, in Rome. Not too many years past they moved all the Jews out of Rome, and they're likely to do it again."

Onesimus remembered Prisca and Aquila who had fled from Rome to Corinth and then again from Corinth to Ephesus. He had never up to this time felt any danger for himself.

"Rome is a dangerous town," the captain continued. "It's no place to be out at night."

Onesimus called up memories of being a fugitive in Ephesus at night.

"Are you trying to recommend some place?" he asked.

"Many Jews have crowded into the section of the city near the Capena Gate. I have a friend who lives there across from the Egeria Gardens. He often has rooms for rent and will offer Kosher meals too. His name is Jacobus Supellex. He is a freedman of a former business associate of mine."

"There is no greater gift when you approach a strange city than to know of a place to stay." said Onesimus with gratitude.

Urbs Roma

They pulled their ship into the harbor of Ostia midmorning. Docking space was not immediately available, so the captain ordered a small boat to take Onesimus and his luggage along with himself to a pier just outside a great warehouse.

"This place is used mostly for grain supplies coming in from Africa," the captain volunteered.

"Rome would starve in a week without Africa. Now you just come with me; we'll hire a cart to get into the city. You can go with me and help me load on these damned fish."

Onesimus saw that the captain had packed the tank in a huge crate and had surrounded it with straw and other padding so that it was quite immovable and unspillable. They tossed Onesimus' luggage on the cart. The two men walked alongside their drayage.

"You'll have your landlegs back before we get to the City," Nathan proclaimed. It proved to be a long walk, and not easy even though the road was paved. Traffic going from the harbor into the Cuty was heavy, but finally they got to the guard station which marked Terminus, the final confine of Ostia. There Nathan palavered with the captain of the guard and finally came back smiling.

"They will give me an escort to the Palace, so you can go find your lodging now. See this road, taking off here. Follow that straight. Eventually it will take you to the Capena Gate. Here's the directions to the pension I told you about."

It was several days before Onesimus saw Nathan again as he entered the house of Jacobus. Together the two of them loudly complained of restless nights and of colds and fevers which had beset them once off their ship.

"One of the chief causes of disease here in Rome," the landlord Jacobus pronounced, "is loss of sleep, caused mostly by the outrageous din in the streets at night. But day or night, Rome is a city for the rich who are carried around in litters while the poor man is jostled all over the pavement. Why there are cases in which a man is crushed to death by the collapse of an overloaded wagon. They just drag away the body leaving his family to wonder what has happened to him."

Nathan agreed, "If you go out at night you are likely to be hit on the head by broken crockery or drenched by the contents of the piss pots that are thrown from the upper windows."

Jacobus continued, "Your friend here has already found out about the drunken roughneck who comes and attacks you merely for the pleasure of having a fight."

Onesimus showed off his bruises.

"The Roman prison isn't big enough to hold 'em all, that's for sure," pronounced the landlord.

Onesimus would rather not have discussed the matter, for he had gone out on the streets looking to see if he could find anyone who looked like a Christian and had ignored his host's advice. His previous experiences in strange harbors had made him overconfident. However, within the week, Onesimus did make contact with a group of Christians who lived in a tenement nearby.

It was very puzzling for Onesimus. Never before was there any difficulty in meeting with the followers of the faith. In fact they had always seemed to spring up out of the ground he walked on, or as if they were angels sent from heaven to guide his steps and make his way easy. In Rome, there were only rude beggars who cursed him when he did not give them alms. The faces which turned away when he approached cursed him. Others fled as though he were a leper. Finally he approached a dishevelled woman sitting amid her spare belongings on the street in front of a tenement. Her vacant eyed children huddled close by. Onesimus stopped thinking to press a coin in her hand, though he was hoarding them carefully in these days.

"May the good Christ be your help," he whispered softly.

At the mention of the sacred name, she grasped his cloak and looked up with pleading eyes. "Help us die," she whispered.

Onesimus sat down on the pavement beside her and heard her story. She and her husband had scraped out a meager living as scavengers of the kind of trash that rich men throw away. They had learned of Jesus from a friend and for some time had attended their simple and quiet meetings. Then came the fire.

"The fire that burned up half of Rome," she said wondering that there could be anyone who had not heard of the fire. "They said that we did it."

"You lit the fire?"

"They said the Christians lit the fire. Everyone knows that it was lit at Nero's bidding. But the informers came around with their lists. Why, they had spied on our meetings and made the lists before the fire was even started. They took my husband away and left us here to starve." By this time a crowd was gathering.

Onesimus was seized with an enormous sense of helplessness. He pressed the coin into her hand and murmured, "Christ be with you; I'll see what I can do."

When he returned to his lodgings he found old Jacobus trembling in fear and anger. "You'll have the precinct guard down on all of us," he shouted. "We Jews have it hard enough making an honest living quietly. Then you Christians come around and stir up all the fuss.

Look at you there, dressed like a gentleman and you haven't even got a patron. What are you here for?"

Onesimus tried to quiet him and told him the widow's tale. "Of course it is a terrible thing, but we all live in terror here. You're a stranger with no one to sponsor you, and here you are out on the street taking on clients for yourself. You're not even a Jew-born Christian. You are a stranger in my house about to ruin us all."

Onesimus feeling a rage rising within himself walked out of the house and across the road to that notorious warren called Egeira's Gardens. Once it had indeed been a park but now it was overrun by beggars and pickpockets drinking and brawling. To walk through the park was like walking through a swarm of hornets. Suddenly Onesimus stopped short. There standing in front of him was a man dressed in a Phrygian cap and wearing Phrygian trousers.

"Good day to you sir," he called out in the Phrygian tongue. The rogue stopped short and replied in the same language. They clapped each other around the shoulders and called each other "Brother."

After a drink of cheap watered wine they conversed about the homeland. Then Onesimus asked the question, "Brother, why do you affect the cap and trousers? They scarcely wear them in Phrgygia nowadays."

"Don't you know," he replied, "here the cap is the cap o'liberty. 'Tis given to a one time slave newly manumitted. It is kind of a rough Roman joke but it identifies you as free to go where you please."

"Then who should have more right to wear it than I?" asked Onesimus. "I was a Phrygian slave and I have been manumitted."

"Then, be my guest," laughed the Phrygian jovially, and he took the cap off his head and crowned Onesimus with it. Onesimus walked back to his lodging thoughtfully. There he washed the cap carefully to rid it of its lice. Going to his sea chest he found an old chiton which he fashioned into trousers.

When Jacobus spotted him at last he stared, "What kind of game are you playing now?"

"Sir, I am playing at being myself. By birth I was a slave of a Phrygian mother. My master freed me and gave me the name Archippides. But my patron is Paulus and my fealty is sworn to him."

Jacobus stared open-mouthed. "At least you're not a Christian," he gasped. Onesimus let it go at that.

Dressed in his ridiculous costume he went again into the street. Seeing the widow still sitting amid her rubble, he raised her up and asked, "Where do you Christians meet?"

"Down in the tombs," she whimpered. "Underground in the catacombs."

They gathered casually near a hillside off the Appian Way, some alone, others in twos. They did not appear to know each other. One or two would wander away hardly noticed, disappearing into a cavelike opening in the shale uplift. From nowhere another visitor would come, hardly recognizable in the pre-dawn half light. These were the tombs. Roman law forbade burial within the city. Outside the city walls along the Via Appia were fine architectural structures, the ossuaries of noble Roman families.

The Romans don't bury their dead, you know. They cremate them, and then gather the bones into boxes and put them in the family vault. The tombs where Onesimus found them have cavelike entrances in the hillside. It is here where the strangers to the city bury their dead. There are tunnels under the hill and people hollow out spaces for their own family members. Some of them are over a hundred years old.

Once inside, Onesimus and his guide lit their candles. The dark corridor widened into a roomy space where maybe a dozen persons gathered in silence. Onesimus identified the widow and her two children. Some of the worshippers were weeping; some were praying. Onesimus noted a simple cross modeled into the tufa. At last, they came together singing quietly.

Rejoice, O childless ones,
  burst into song and shout,
you endure no birthpangs;
the children of the desolate woman
are more blest

than those of the married.

Onesimus recognized the hymn as one he had learned from Paul. Suddenly and in surprise Onesimus answered the call to speak.

> *The child who was born according to the flesh has persecuted the child who was born according to the Spirit.*
> *Friends, we are children, not of the flesh but of the spirit. For freedom Christ has set us free. Stand firm, therefore, and do not submit to a yoke of enslavement to the flesh.*

Onesimus continued in this vein. He looked around himself and saw his listeners in rapt attention. Finally he concluded,

> *We are fools for the sake of Christ, yet we are wise in Christ. We are weak, still we are strong. Others are held in honor, but we spat upon in disrepute. At the present hour we are hungry and thirsty, we are poorly clothed and beaten and homeless, and we grow weary from the work of our own hands. But when reviled, we bless; when persecuted, we endure; when slandered, we speak kindly. We are the rubbish of the world, the dregs of all things, to this very day.*
> *I appeal to you, then, be imitators of Christ.*

"Amen, Amen, brother, Amen."

> *The Lord is my shepherd, I shall not want . . .*

intoned Onesimus and all joined in. They were quiet again and one by one began to depart. A veiled woman came up to the widow and put her hand upon her shoulder. With the other hand she took the hand of one of the children and the group walked out together. At last only Onesimus and his guide were left.

"You speak powerfully, father," remarked the guide. Onesimus ignored the compliment.

"I am looking for Paul, the Apostle. Do you know where he is?"

The man shook his head, "I do not know of such a one. There is no Paul among us."

Onesimus went out into the light alone. "At least I managed one problem," he said to himself as he thought of the widow and her children. "And I have made the acquaintance of Christians. I must be getting closer."

He returned to the house of Jacobus the Jew and made provision for his belongings. He was on his own, a free man beholden to no one.

Daily Onesimus continued to search for Paul but with little success. Early in the morning he would meet worshipers at the catacombs, but even though they were rarely the same group and though he questioned all of the newcomers, none ever seemed to know of Paul. They did come to know of Onesimus, however, "the stranger who was a fool for Christ."

During the day, Onesimus acquainted himself with the city. In fact he became one of the "sights" of the city himself, the Phyrgian Clown. Rome was a cosmopolitan place; strange costumes caused no comment. Turbans from Persia; loin-cloths from Africa; blue tatoos from Britain. The unruffled Romans had seen them all. Onesimus would roll his eyes upward and babble in the Phrygian language. When asked what God he served he would mumble "Baba, Baba," and the street urchins would run away laughing. None in Rome cared what God you served, unless his name were Christus.

Had he been asked, Onesimus would have replied, "God is God, no matter what name you call Him." To himself he argued, "I do not have the gift of martyrdom; my gift is to survive and save others." Before long, he found those who recognized the name of Peter. He learned that Peter was held in chains in the prison called Mamertina, built into a hillside beside the Old Forum. He even went and looked at the prison and inquired of a guard if anyone named Paul might be there. But the guard, talkative enough about his charges, had no knowledge of Paul.

"Paul," thought Onesimus to himself, "would not be one to take another name and go about dressed in outlandish clothing babbling like a fool." He rehearsed the names of the saints in Rome and tried to find them. There was "Julia" whom Phoebe knew. But in Rome there are a thousand Julia's, all of the clan of the great Julius; and all of them have freedwomen, whose names are Julia. Philologus is a title, and Nereus is the name of a sea-god. How many women are named "Olympas?" Even the cats in the alleys bear that name. Once he met a certain Patrobus, but when Onesimus dared to call him "Brother," the man blanched and quickly turned into the crowd. Meanwhile the small amount of money that he had brought with him had been spent, and he too began to scavenge for tatters that could be sold. He tried to set up a writing stand, but he had not mastered the Latin hand; as for the Latin speech, the fact that he could not speak it probably saved his life.

Rome itself was becoming more unfriendly, more raucous, more suspicious. Each day was filled with new rumors. The Emperor's guards were plotting against him; the emperor had arrested his guards. The emperor had poisoned his wife; the emperor had taken a dagger to his brother. The emperor's tutor, the aged Seneca, had been bid to cut his wrists and Seneca had done it. Five persons gathered on a street corner would be pronounced a riot and cut to pieces for treason. Who knows how many Christians were mauled and eaten by wild dogs?

We Will See Face to Face

Wearied by the chaos, Onesimus betook himself one day outside the city gate on the Via Ostiensis, for he heard a rumor that by following that road he would find a marshy place where Christians were known to have been found. The gossip had said it with a leer, but Onesimus would leave no stone unturned. He put on his Phrygian cap and trousers made of a faded woolen stuff which he had cut so that he could tie the two legs around his ankles; this costume he found more suitable for walking. With him he carried a leather bag which had proved useful to hold his collections. Past the gate he went; it was an impoverished territory with rude huts and unproductive fields. Near the Laurentian Way he stopped to get his bearings. Down in a low spot he saw soldiers; then prisoners. He suddenly deduced that he had come upon a place of execution.

The prisoners were led forth, one by one; thrown roughly upon a block, and the grim executioner came down upon their necks with his ax. With a single blow for each, the headsman severed the head from body. Slaves were assigned the chore of picking up the pieces and tossing them on a heap. Onesimus stood at the side with a few other onlookers, his eyes riveted upon the scene. Suddenly a prisoner walked forth on his own two legs with no one dragging or assisting him. Briefly his eyes sought heaven; He was pushed forward to the block and the axeman delivered his blow. "No! No!," was all that the horrified Onesimus could force from his almost paralyzed throat. One of the slaves looked up and with a grimace picked up the head and threw it like a football at the protester. With a reflex action, Onesimus caught it, and held it in his two hands. In his horror, he almost dropped his catch, but suddenly he stuffed the severed head into his leather bag, and fell back into the crowd, almost unnoticed. When at last he reached the road, he began to run.

At last he could run no more. He sat down behind some bushes, panting for breath and tried to remember what he had seen. Then he knew that he could never forget. He cradled the bag in his arms, but could not force himself to open it. He vomited, and blackness came over him. It was evening when Onesimus awoke. He shook himself, trying to rid himself of the nightmare that he had been dreaming. Then he saw the leather bag, and felt its contours and understood that he was not dreaming. He listened for voices, but heard nothing but night noises. Below him a little way he could see the moon lighting the Laurentian Way, but no one walked there. Picking up the bag, he stumbled down to the road and then slowly walked toward the city. If there was something to think about, he did not think it. If there was something to cry about, he did not cry it; if there was something to shout aloud, he was silent.

Onesimus had been living with other beggars under one of the Tiber bridges. It was morning now, and all of his fellows had scattered to their daily pursuits. Onesimus cradled the bag to his breast and fell asleep again. When the others began to return to share a meager meal or to show off a particular treasure, he hid the bag amid some trash next to a piling.

Pounding in his brain was the question, "What am I going to do with it?"

He went down to the river foul smelling as it was to wash himself. Not far away the Great Cloaca emptied itself and from thereon the river became a sewer.

"I could just bring it, bag and all, to the river bank and let old Tiber wash it away," was his first thought. It certainly would not have been the first such carrion to be thrown into that sewer. But what would happen to it then? It could be eaten by fish; and if the fish were caught and eaten by a man? No, the thought was inadmissible.

Onesimus lay awake long into the night. For Onesimus a light seemed to shine on the very spot where the bag was hid. Why did everyone not awake and see it there? What if someone did awake and investigate the mysterious glow? No, the head must be treated with the respect that is due such a treasure. This is the very head of Paul, Apostle to the Gentiles.

> *We look not at what can be seen but at what cannot be seen; for what can be seen is temporary, but what cannot be seen is eternal. For we know that if the earthly tent we live in is destroyed, we have a building from God, a house not made with hands, eternal in the heavens. For in this tent we groan, longing to be clothed with our heavenly dwelling—if indeed, when we have taken it off we will not be found naked. For while we are still in this tent, we groan under our burden, because we wish not to be unclothed but to be further clothed, so that what is mortal may be swallowed up by life.*

The next morning as the beggars broke up camp, Onesimus arose and took his terrible burden with him, thinking that perhaps he could find a proper place to put the mortal remains of one so loved and so distinguished. He came in his quest to the Celian Hill, that pleasant place where once poets composed their melodious lyrics. It overlooked a spacious view. Looking outward he mused, "One day, men may build a monument in precious memory of so great a soul. One day when the world has changed and respects its prophets."

He found the very spot, between some rocks, sheltered by sweeping pines. But the ground was hard and the earth too shallow to be dug out with a mere stick to make a proper grave. Finally he gave it up and at evening returned, still carrying his fearful burden.

It was a night when there was no moon. In the glowering dark a demon came to him and embraced his dream.

"Such a treasure you have there!" it cooed with a seductive voice. "Think what power there is in that head. With that head you and I can conjure up such wealth as not even Rome has seen. We can solve such mysteries as the magicians of the East have never imagined. Keep the head in your possession, and guard it well," the demon whispered. "You shall never want for wealth and power."

Onesimus awoke with a start, "Get thee behind me Satan," he called out loud. The other beggars thrashed around in their sleep, disturbed but not awakened.

> *Creation was subjected to futility, not of its own will but by the will of the one who subjected it, in hope that the creation itself will be set free from its bondage to decay and will obtain the freedom of the glory of the children of God. We know that the whole creation has been groaning in labor pains until now.*

Before dawn, Onesimus rose and once more took his burden with him. No one had assembled at the tombs yet. In the darkness Onesimus and Paul scrambled into the catacomb. Although there was no light, light seemed to come from the leather bag. Onesimus with bare hands scratched a hole deep into the tufa, and when it was large enough he placed the bag inside, and covered up the space so that it might go unnoticed.

The morning worshippers began to assemble, not thinking it in any way odd that their self-appointed leader should have preceded them. With unusual intensity, Onesimus began to prophesy:

> *Jews demand signs and Greeks desire wisdom, but I proclaim Christ crucified, a stumbling block to Jews and foolishness to Gentiles. But to those who are the called, both Jews and Greeks, Christ is the power of God and the wisdom of God.*

In great earnestness he continued,

> *Someone will ask, "How are the dead raised? With what kind of body do they come?" Fool! What you sow does not come to life unless it dies. And as for what you sow, you do not sow the body that is to be, but a bare seed, perhaps of wheat or of some other grain. But God gives it a body as he has chosen, and to each kind of seed its own body. Not all flesh is alike, but there is one flesh for human beings, another for animals, another for birds, and another for fish. There are both heavenly bodies and earthly bodies, but the glory of the heavenly is one thing, and that of the earthly is another. There is one glory of the sun, and another glory of the moon, and another glory of the stars; indeed, star differs from star in glory. So it is with the resurrection of the dead. What is sown is perishable, what is raised is imperishable. It is sown in dishonor, it is raised in glory. It is sown in weakness, it is raised in power. It is sown a physical body, it is raised a spiritual body. If there is a physical body, there is also a spiritual body. Thus it is written, "The first man, Adam, became a living being"; the last Adam became a life-giving spirit. But it is not the spiritual that is first, but the physical, and then the spiritual.*

When he finished some were weeping and some were praying. Onesimus turned to his newly dug grave and whispered, "My father Paul, so well you have delivered your own funeral eulogy."

The Roman Angel

Thus Onesimus returned to the world of the living, reconciled in his spirit. Within the next few days, from diverse sources he received a variety of reports about Paul. Those who had been too frightened to speak up before, now came forward and admitted that an undisputed source had told them that Paul had been beheaded at the special request of the emperor at a place in the Laurentian Marshes. Onesimus walked down the road again and found the low and marshy place, still stinking with fouled water, but no sign there of what had happened on that terrible day.

A Lethargy overcame him. No more was there any cause to tread the streets of the city looking for some clue that would lead him to the end of his search. By day the cold and stench of the river would send him out to seek the warmth of the sunlight where he sat on the steps of some public building. Mornings he would appear for the daily service at the tombs; usually only two or three persons would be there; occasionally he would find himself alone, but he continued to come. Soon he realized that there was no reason for sleeping under the bridge. He had chosen that place because it was centrally located with easy access to any part of the city. Now he had no reason to go out into the city. He found a little cave near the entrance to the tombs and dug it out so there was room enough for him to sleep and keep his small belongings. During the day he would sit in the sunshine, scarce paying attention to any visitors who might arrive.

"I am wasting away," he thought to himself. "The purpose for my living is gone, and there is no further need for me." He would mumble prayers and remember bits of psalms that he had learned long before. He lived on scraps and crusts that visitors would leave for him, the clown of the tombs.

One morning on the first day of the week, the veiled lady came up to him and touched him.

"Father, you are ill," she said. He could not even mumble assent.

She took him by the hand and said, "Come."

Without resistance he followed. They walked along a pathway through the fields and came at last to a country house, a small villa surrounded by trees and covered with vines. A slave brought in some bread and a cup of a warmed sweetened drink. The two shared the meager meal wordlessly.

A boy came in and led Onesimus to a simple room where he lay down on a mat to rest. When he woke, the boy helped him wash. A simple white tunic had been laid out for him to wear.

The veiled lady greeted him and said, "Jonah here will take you to the baths; you would enjoy that, I think."

Onesimus thanked her with his eyes. He spent his time in the *tepidum*, soaking in its soothing warmth. The boy rubbed his fragile skin with oil and began to comb his beard. He showed Onesimus a hand mirror in which he saw a face he did not recognize, gaunt and scraggled. Onesimus put his hand to his beard. He had not really realized that it was there, for he had never kept a beard before. The boy continued to comb and trim.

It occurred to Onesimus that he was becoming a new man. He sought his memory and said,

> No longer present shall I present my members to sin as instruments of wickedness, but I shall present myself to God as one who has been brought from death to life, and present my members to God as instruments of righteousness. For sin no longer has dominion over me, since I am not under law but under grace.

He had the freedom of the house, but rarely saw anyone except the boy who had been assigned to him. From time the lady appeared, but she was always veiled, and spoke but little.

One day she walked into the garden unexpectedly, "Nero is dead, and by his own hand," she announced with agitation in her voice. "In life he brought great evil to the city, but now the streets will run red with blood."

Onesimus looked up, "Perhaps this portends the predicted end."

The lady shook her head, "There will be wars and rumors of wars, but the end is not yet," she quoted.

"That is what the Lord Jesus said," replied Onesimus. "Do you know more of his sayings."

"I learned more of his word from Luke," she replied.

Life stirred in Onesimus, "Luke? You know Luke? Is he here in Rome?"

The lady shook her head; "He has gone, long ago. I do not know where he went, but he is no longer with us. When you came, I recognized that you and he were of the same spirit. Did you know him too?"

Onesimus recalled his memory of Luke when they all lived together in Ephesus under the tutelage of Paul. The lady replied that Luke had spoken of Paul but that she had never seen him.

"Since Luke has gone, I have been alone," she said simply. "Luke ordained me as a widow, and I live here helping the helpless as best I can."

"That is your gift," replied Onesimus.

"Yes, father, that is what Luke said. Luke was our elder; when he left we had no elder, and then you came. I recognized that the Lord had sent you, but for a time you faltered and I was fearful. But then I came to understand your sickness, and you have been brought back again. I rejoice for I know that our little community has a new presbyter."

Onesimus was silent; he did not understand his role as presbyter.

Word came that there was a new emperor. "He is Galba," said the lady. "I know the family; but I do not know how he can rule this unruly city. He has no army. The time when one could rule the city by making speeches is over."

"Will his policy toward Christians be as hard as Nero's?"

"Bah, he knows no more of Christians than he does of anything else," replied the lady with some acerbity.

A new word came saying that Marcus Salvius Otho had come at night with the Praetorian guard and murdered the unfortunate Galba.

"He was Poppaea's first husband," the lady whispered. "He has an army. Now the streets will indeed run with blood."

Onesimus began to understand that his veiled lady was very knowledgeable of Roman society, though she showed no enthusiasm for it. True to her word, the streets did become very dangerous. One could in no way anticipate what lieutenant's cadre was going to declare their man princeps on the morrow.

"It's the war in the East that is behind all of this," and the lady outlined troop movements from the Danube on the north to the Nile on the South.

"And now the army is moving on Jerusalem," she announced.

A zest for life began to return to Onesimus and he began to listen as eagerly as did his lady at the latest political and military movements. They began to meet more regularly. The slave would bring lunch out into the garden—bread and cheese, a salad of greens, a piece of fish. They talked of religious matters.

Sometimes the lady wanted to know of the ancient scriptures. Onesimus told her of Sarah and Hagar.

> *It is written that Abraham had two sons, one by a slave woman and the other by a free woman. One, the child of the slave, was born according to the flesh; the other, the child of the free woman, was born through the promise. Now this is an allegory: these women are two covenants. One woman, in fact, is Hagar, from Mount Sinai, bearing children for slavery. Now Hagar is Mount Sinai in Arabia and corresponds to the present Jerusalem, for she is in slavery with her children. But the other woman corresponds to the Jerusalem above; she is free, and she is our mother. Now we are children of the promise, like Isaac. But just as at that time the child who was born according to the flesh persecuted the child who was born according to the Spirit, so it is now also. But what does the scripture say? "Drive out the slave and her child; for the child of the slave will not share the inheritance with the child of*

*the free woman." So then, friends, we are children, not of
the slave but of the free woman.*

"I see," replied his friend. "All that is happening has been foretold to
us in these ancient writings. We must learn more of them."

She queried Onesimus of his past. "Do I guess aright, that in
dressing in your Phrygian costume you attempted to draw attention to
yourself and thus become a martyr?" she accused.

"My lady, had I desired to become a martyr, I should have gone
out preaching Christ crucified on the very steps of the Senate. I wore
the Phrygian cap to denote that I am free; I wore the Phrygian trousers
to throw the cat off the track, so to speak. They all deemed that I was
insane, and I said—so be it. I have no gift for martyrdom."

"And what is your gift? Tell me about gifts."

*The gifts God gives are that some should be apostles, some
prophets, some evangelists, some pastors and teachers, to
equip the saints for the work of ministry, for building up
the body of Christ, until all of us come to the unity of the
faith and of the knowledge of the Son of God, to maturity,
to the measure of the full stature of Christ. We must no
longer be children, tossed to and fro and blown about
by every wind of doctrine, by people's trickery, by their
craftiness in deceitful scheming. But speaking the truth in
love, we must grow up in every way into him who is the
head, into Christ, . . .*

"It is easy to ascertain your gift, father. You are a teacher and a
pastor. When you brought me that poor woman with her children, you
gave me the opportunity for ministry which I had been seeking."

"How well you do it, my lady, how well you have ministered to
me," replied Onesimus with a bow.

Shortly afterward, the lady came much perturbed.

"Vitellus and his legions have come into northern Italy. Otho went
to check him with his army and was defeated, and Otho has committed
suicide."

"What will happen now?" asked Onesimus.

"The brother of General Vespasianus has demanded that Vitellus resign and has stirred an uprising in the City. Everyone is in hiding and the soldiers are rampaging in the city to the very steps of the Curia."

"Who is this general?"

"My own brother, Titus Flavius Vespasianus. He is legate to Jerusalem and has been besieging that city. Oh we are in great danger. Vitellus has Primus cornered in Northern Italy, and if Vitellus is successful I do not know what will become of us." The next day calm was destroyed.

"The troops of Primus have stormed Rome and Vitellus is slain. The Senate has declared Flavius as *princeps*, and he will return to Rome." Everyone in the house breathed quietly, and Onesimus realized that he was closer to the center of power than he desired to be.

In the days that followed Vespasian returned to Rome from Judaea. The new emperor was popular with the military for he had successfully defended the empire on several of its frontiers. Onesimus reasoned that if the new emperor's sister was a Christian, surely Christians would be benefitted by an alliance with him. The lady cautioned him to silence.

"Flavius does not know everything," she said. However, activity against the Christians seemed to cease. Imperial attention was turned elsewhere.

Vespasian returned to Rome, but he had not acquitted himself of the Jewish affair and shortly after he appointed his own son, named Titus after his father, as the *dux* to finish off the siege of Jerusalem. By now Onesimus had regained his health and had developed a considerable antipathy for Rome and its politics. Not wanting to offend the lady, he expressed as carefully as he could his desire to return to Asia. He reminded her that Jerusalem was as foreign to him as was Rome, but that Jerusalem was closer to home than Italy.

He also pointed out that while it was true that she and a few of her friends were happy to accept him as their presbyter, he himself would feel much freer to act in that role, had he been ordained in a more normal fashion. He felt that once in Ephesus that end could be achieved. Though the lady was loath to lose him and his company, she was also eager to have a minister ordained in good order and so she approached a member of her family with her request. In no time at all he came back with orders naming Onesimus as a special secretary to the legate.

> To: PAULUS ARCHIPPIDES FLAVIANUS, fil Archippus, civ Romae, nat. Phrygiae,

read the document.

"Is it proper?" asked the lady nervously. Onesimus read the document.

"Yes, yes. It is proper and true; I am the son of Archippus. But what is this 'Flavianus?' "

"I have adopted you," the lady replied.

There seemed no reason to press the point further. His protectress provided him with a fine white chiton and a purple cloak, sturdy sandals with fine leather lacings.

"The army will provide you with whatever armor and equipment you will need" she added.

> *I shall be strong in the Lord and in the strength of his power. For I shall put on the whole armor of God, to stand against the wiles of the devil. Our struggle is not against enemies of blood and flesh, but against the rulers, against the authorities, against the cosmic powers of this present darkness, against the spiritual forces of evil in the heavenly places. Therefore I take up the whole armor of God, so that I may be able to withstand on that evil day, and having done everything, to stand firm. I stand therefore, and fasten the belt of truth around your waist, and put on the breastplate of righteousness. As shoes for my feet put on whatever will make me ready to proclaim the gospel of peace. With all of these, take I the shield of faith, with which I shall be able to quench all the flaming arrows of the evil one. And now I take the helmet of*

salvation, and the sword of the Spirit, which is the word
of God.

In this way Onesimus took his oath into the service of the Lord. But before he reported for duty he went secretly on an errand. Without difficulty he found the Capena Gate where the house of Jacobus the Jew was still standing. The old man was stunned to see Onesimus standing before him; in fact he scarcely recognized him.

"Do you still have the casket of my belongings which I left with you?" asked Onesimus.

"In the Lord's name, it is safe," replied the Jew.

"Good, I shall retrieve it now." He pressed a leather wallet into the old man's hand. Jacobus looked inside and saw the gleam of sesterces within.

"I have saved it carefully," he called as he went for the casket. "See, the locks have not been tampered with."

"I thank you with all my heart," said Onesimus. He almost added, "I'll see you in Jerusalem," but then he thought better of it.

"How fortunate I am," he thought as he examined the contents later. My treasures, my work. They are all still here."

He Bears All Things

A subaltern arrived with slaves to carry Onesimus' belongings. Dubiously Onesimus mounted his horse; he had not mounted a horse since his ride from Pergamon to Colossae.

"I was thirty years old then, and now I am forty. Lord Jesus, I bear all things in your service for your glory."

The detachment of soldiers rode grandly out of Rome, south the Appian Way. Through villages, through forests and across mountains they rode. Never was there a sight of a *ladron*. The duties assigned to Onesimus were light. He composed letters for the mayors of villages complimenting them on having the good fortune of providing for the needs of the Imperial Army as it came through. Never a complaint was heard. The mayors provided well for the army's entertainment.

At Brundisium they boarded waiting ships, sturdy quinqueremes with galley slaves, five to an oar, who kept to a relentless pace.

Sooner than Onesimus could have imagined they landed at Caesarea and marched both day and night to Jerusalem. Onesimus kept a log for his commander.

"Can you write in Hebrew?" asked the officer.

"Yes sir, I can," was the reply. Onesimus wrote a demand to the fathers of the city to surrender. Titus was unperturbed.

"They will ignore our demand, of course; but we have time."

The days dragged on. The soldiers gambled and swore. The heat in their tents was oppressive; the inactivity was monotonous. The officers paced about and complained. But the siege continued. Onesimus pursued his assignments with diligence. At last he knew that there would be an attack. He climbed the hill looking westward toward the city and had one last view of its shining towers and sheltering walls. He observed the prepared catapults and the soldiers armed for attack. At nightfall he went into his tent. Quietly he changed his clothes into those of a rough peasant. His military clothes and writing equipment he strewed carelessly around as through there had been a fight.

He put his pack upon his back and disappeared into the darkness. At the beginning of the third watch the sound of battle was heard. Unnoticed in the melee, he went through the lines of the rear guard away from the fighting.

Before dawn he had walked to Bethany where he hid himself behind a tomb. When the townsmen settled down for the afternoon siesta, he started out along the high road, the path that skirts the tops of mountains. He could hear the din of battle and see the smoke from the burning city. Briskly he walked like a nomadic shepherd along the road to Jericho.

"This is the road that Jesus walked," he thought; and he prayed that he be kept in safety. Nothing occured to trouble him. Mingling with nomad herders he learned of the Roman attack. The news of it was widespread. Few travellers were abroad, for everone was in hiding seeking places of safety. By nightfall he could see the Jordan

river and the gates of Jericho. All was peaceful there. The next day
he followed Jordan's stream northward, rejoicing in its waters, making
his way through small pools and the reedy marshes. When he reached
the Lake of Galilee he stopped to rest in a nearby village. In all of this
time no one challenged him. He paused to wonder if his commander
had missed him. Did they think that he had been attacked that night?
Perhaps they assumed that he was a victim of the battle. Northward
he continued, and finally he found the road to Damascus.

He may have wondered at what turning that Paul had seen the Lord;
but no stone marked it. In Damascus he found food and lodging, but
the town was in no mood to question poor herdsmen. Their thoughts
were on the fury in Jerusalem. Straight he took his road to Antioch
and at last he found a community. He had not expected to be known
there, but he was taken in by friendly brothers and he stayed and rested
in the home of a youth named Ignazio. For the first time since leaving
Rome, he talked of Paul who was known there. When the brothers
wondered where the Apostle might now be, Onesimus shook his head
and replied that no one had seen him.

He continued his way northward as Paul had once walked, to Lystra
and to Derbe and Iconium. At each town he stopped, sometimes for
many days. He found those who remembered his apostle; and he copied
down what it was that they remembered. At last in the mountains the
road branched; one road led straight down to the sea. From there
northward, the road continues along the great highway to Ephesus.
The other road leads through the valleys and hills—to Colossae and
Laodicea and thence to Sardis and Smyrna and up to Pergamon. His
heart strings pulled him into the mountain road.

In a few more days he could see the Lycus threading through the
valley. Slowly he walked an abandoned road that led into the town,
but in Colossae the desolation remained, much as when he had left
it. He sought out the hillside where once he had played as a boy; the
house was gone; only a few low adobe partitions remained, overrun by
weeds. He took the path down to the river. The olive trees were still
there; the figs bore fruit. A low ramshackle farm house stood where

once the slaves had lived. As he stood there looking at its door, the door opened and there he was, looking in Philemon's face.

Philemon stared at the bearded traveller. For both men the years faded away and they became two young brothers greeting each other for the first time.

A child peeked around a corner and was observed by Onesimus.

"You are married," he exclaimed.

"Oh yes," Philemon admitted and motioned the child to come to him. As she scrambled up on her daddy's knee, another child came running behind crying for the attention that the first had succeeded in obtaining. Onesimus scooped up the second child who seemed to be satisfied with the substitute knee.

"I will find my wife to greet you. She is quite shy, for she was not brought up to greet company." And then he caught himself, and in a subdued whisper he added, "She is Platon's daughter."

Onesimus could only register astonishment. Platon, the impenetrable, the unperturbable martinet of the book; he had a family?"

The answer was yes, though it was a slave family. When his previous master offered him his freedom, he chose to give it to his wife and infant daughter while he was sold to another master.

Onesimus knit his brows and wondered whether Archippus had known of it.

"I doubt it," replied Philemon. "But do you remember, that Platon did not return with me from Pergamon. It was there in Pergamon that he retrieved his family."

Philemon put his child on Onesimus' other knee and went out of the room, soon to return with a small woman who drew her veil across her face. Onesimus removed the children from his knees and rose. "Madame, I am much beholden to your father; and for him I hold you in great respect." He spoke with the grace of a nobleman. The lady smiled and allowed him to see her face.

How could I forget that day, even though I had scarcely three years to practice the art of living? At the knee of Onesimus I took my first lessons.

In the days that passed there was forgiveness and renewal. Philemon lived modestly.

There was no way to restore the old days, he remarked. No one was willing to live up there, and he motioned toward the ruined city.

What can one say? To this very day the earth still rumbles, and after each quake more walls fall down. We stay away from that haunted place; its desolation still unnerves us. My father maintained a Christian household, and worked the farms. He kept no slaves; he said it was a debt paid to his dearest brother. Some of the older slaves remained with us on the land, and farmed their little plots. They were free to go, but only the younger ones left to seek their fortunes in Smyrna and in Ephesus.

Onesimus inquired about Epaphras. My father Philemon could only reply with tears that Epaphras had gone into the greater life.

"He is missed for now we have no elder," and suddenly he added, "Perhaps you will stay here and be our elder."

Onesimus refused in quiet sadness, remembering in remorse that he still had not completed his other commitment. There remained something yet that he had to do in Ephesus.

On that last day with his family, Philemon took him aside into his private room. "I found among Archippus' effects a treasure of gold nuggets. I have set it aside and kept it because I knew that it was meant for you."

Onesimus pushed it aside, "I have no need for this kind of treasure; I have always been able to take care of myself. Platon, Archippus, and yes, Epaphras gave me treasure that cannot be taken from me. You must provide for the family that takes our places." They walked along the river and watched where the water swirled around a rock. "There is where King Midas took his bath," remarked Onesimus.

"There is where my father was drowned one evil day before my birth," remembered Philemon. The wind ruffled through the reeds and whispered their age old song, "Midas has asses' ears."

"And he covered them with a Phrygian cap," Onesimus stood laughing, but Philemon did not quite understand. For both of the men there was much to be said, much to be remembered. There were deeds to weep over; there were words to remember and words to forget.

He Believes All Things

After the peaceful quiet of the country, Onesimus tried to accustom himself again to the din of Ephesus.

"It's almost as wild as Rome," he said to an acquaintance. There is unceasing noise, beggars everywhere, and the waste and filth clog up even the main streets."

"The city is filling up with Jews who have fled from Jerusalem. They have lost their wealth; there is no place to keep them; and they cannot return even though the war is over. Even here there is a price upon their heads. We have a great opportunity, brother, to turn their hearts to Christ."

Onesimus lingered, distancing himself a bit from the community of the faith. He walked the streets of Ephesus, remembering former days. The house of his first captivity had vanished, though he noted that the quality of the neighborhood had not much changed. He walked more boldly in the civic center, investigating the public buildings. By now he dared to enter the great library, and found himself on a par with the scholars there. On a day he found himself in the great temple of Artemis. Little had changed, except the presence of Demetrius was not to be found. Other entrepreneurs had taken his place. He entered the temple and felt a wave of civic pride.

"Surely, not even in Rome can one find such magnificence. One day, all of this shall serve Our Lord," he predicted. At last he sought out the pool behind the Odeon where he had first met Paul, where his life had been forever changed.

The fountain had not changed; by moonlight it was a calm and peaceful as that first night. Onesimus filled his cupped hands with the cool water and offered it in a prayer for the soul of Paul. He climbed the hill behind the theater and looking down on the sleeping city, he called out,

Sleepers, awake!
Rise from the dead, and Christ will shine on you.
Everything exposed by the light becomes visible,
Everything that becomes visible is light.

Now this city had become his city, and he was prepared to continue the work of the Apostles.

In time he found old friends, and now he sought out the bishop. Timothy had died. The new bishop was one unknown to Onesimus but his enthusiasm was overwhelming.

"My prayers have been answered," he exclaimed. "There is one yet here among us who knew the Apostle. And there is such a need. There are a dozen places at once to fill with new elders."

Onesimus demurred, "I have much work to do. I have made a commitment to gather together all of the writings and history and sayings of the Great Apostle."

"Oh, that too must be done," replied the bishop, "but you are also called to serve the living. You will come before the council tomorrow and participate in our worship and our decisions."

At the meeting on the next day Onesimus knelt with the council. They prayed and laid their hands upon his head.

Let this elder rule well and be considered worthy of double honor, especially when he labors in preaching and teaching; If anyone persists in sin, let him rebuke that one in the presence of all, so that the rest also may stand in fear. In the presence of God and of Christ Jesus and of the elect angels. Be instructed: do nothing on the basis of partiality. Do not ordain anyone hastily, and do not participate in the sins of others; keep yourself pure. Good works are conspicuous; and even when they are not, they cannot remain hidden. Teach and urge these duties. Seek godliness as a means of gain. There is great gain in godliness combined with contentment; for we brought nothing into the world, so that we can take nothing out of it; but be ye content with the blessings that are given.

From then on Onesimus served the followers of The Way in charity and with meekness. There were those who claimed that he never sent anyone away dissatisfied.

Daily he made his visitations. He prayed for the sick; he put a few coins in the hand of a widow; he comforted a child. One morning a woman confronted him, "Do you remember me?" He strained his mind for the recognition.

"You are Rhoda, you are my conscience" he exclaimed.

"Come with me once again to the Temple of Artemis," she beckoned him.

The two walked briskly through the crowds that still surrounded the place, and entered by the gate that first they had entered. Rhoda led him to a great pillar which he recognized as the place where he had left her once so many years ago. Rhoda started to walk around it and suddenly stooped to pick up a bundle of rags. Onesimus peered over her shoulder and saw a swaddled child. Rhoda was cradling it in her arms; she motioned with her eyes,

"There is the child's mother." A woman in dark clothing was turning away and quickly disappeared.

"They know that I will be along and take up the infant."

Onesimus looked at her with some amazement.

"The Lord did not abandon me in my distress. I must not allow others to be abandonned."

"How did you know that this infant would be here this day?" he questioned.

"There is always someone here," she replied simply. In the distance was the sound of a brassy gong. While the throngs stopped in awe; the two Christ followers slipped away.

Hopes All Things

Luke returned to Ephesus and none was more eager to greet him than Onesimus. They remembered the old days and recalled old friends.

"And what do you plan to do now?" Onesimus asked his old friend.

"Intend? I am doing it. I am writing a book."

"Of course," acknowledged Onesimus. "I too am writing a book."

"Of the making of books there is no end," they both laughed in unison.

"My writing is about the life and teachings of our Lord Jesus," Luke stated simply.

"Oh wonderful," replied Onesimus. "There has been a surge of writings about that recently, but none really seem to lay the subject out authentically. There is something so elusive about His life. Do you approach that question?"

"You are right," replied Luke. "It is one thing to say flatly that Jesus did such and such a miracle; or that Jesus made such and such a statement; or to repeat a parable. But when you have spoken of the substance of his life, you know that you have left out most of the essence. That is my problem, how to catch the spirit and bind Him with one's words."

"Oh tell me about that," Onesimus glowed with enthusiasm. "How can you put a net of words around the spirit so that He can be captured on paper?"

"You know, I am a bit of an artist; I mean, I have dabbled with paint and the art of putting it on a wooden tablet."

"You have found the secret of doing that?"

"The secret is creating an illusion. You cannot get on paper the thing as it really exists. There is too much detail which distracts the eye from the object that the painter wishes you to see. But by focusing on the subject with line and with color, you may cause the beholder to see what you have seen and to ignore any distraction. While in Rome I turned myself to the reading of some of their authors. In Rome there was much need to turn your mind from the terrors of what was going on there."

Onesimus was in agreement. "I noted that in order to create a situation of truth," Luke continued, "it is necessary to turn your subject into an icon, and disregard the distractions that surround you. If, for instance, it is necessary to have a great prince speak, then the author must create a speech that displays the prince's worthiness and gives proof of his leadership. It may well be that the prince himself was incompetent to do this, but the author improves his competence, so to speak—no, no, do not interrupt my thought,"

Luke waved his hand, "And so the author writes a speech. The prince himself may never have said any thing which resembles the author's speech; he may have said it in a different language; he may have drawn out a quite different response. But these are things we have no way of knowing. It is in this way that the writer creates his drama. Seneca was able to create this magic in his tragedies. I saw one such on the stage."

"Seneca came to an ignoble end," commented Onesimus wryly.

"So be it; we are not judging Seneca the man; we are we are admiring the work of the playwright. In his art he punctuated the drama with choruses, and rolled down the curtains of the stage to reveal the lives of those that most of us can never know. I read portions of a play in which he brought speech to Nero's lips which made a hero from that base man. And thus he instructed us in higher things."

"And that is how you wish to tell the life of Jesus?" inquired Onesimus.

Luke ignored the question.

"If I had the pen of the old writers, if I could write like Aeschylus, I could not make it glorious enough. My attempt is to dream the story as it was played on the stage of the world, with the angels of heaven and the demons of the earth participating. Even the virgin Mother must sing a psalm worthy of her calling."

"Is it coming along well?" asked Onesimus. "I mean how far along are you?"

"Actually," admitted Luke, "I have found it difficult. And so to clarify my thinking I have begun to write a second book. This book is more earthbound. I am reviewing what we did; what we few did in those first days after Our Lord arose."

"Some one ought to document those days," agreed Onesimus.

"Yes, it is about us. How we lived and thought and walked about.

I have to train my mind backward, and there are so many things to remember. Sometimes it is so difficult to recall them." Luke stooped to bring out of his satchel a sheaf of papers.

"When I knew I was to visit you, I snatched these up. I wish you would take time to read them, and make corrections. I am getting old, and I need a critic. You are my Friend in God. Would you read this for me?"

Onesimus rose, "I am honored by your thought, and I shall read this history in great eagerness."

A few days later the two met again. "I was so eager to read your story," admitted Onesimus, "that I stopped everything and have neglected my other work. Never have I been more entranced."

"You liked it then?" pleasure danced from Luke's eyes. "Have I remembered aright?"

"What you remembered, you remembered," continued Onesimus. "And sometimes I remembered differently; but mostly you have clarified things I had not known. But I have one disappointment."

"And what is that, friend?"

"I too was in Rome in those last days. And I could find no trace of Paul or of yourself there. You end your story abruptly. What happened to the two of you? I know you were there for I have a letter from the hand of Paul himself saying that you were with him. I must know what those days were like. Tell me, Luke, how did he die?" Onesimus pleaded with sincerity.

"I cannot write it, Onesimus. Because I do not know. When first we got to Rome, Paul was in house arrest. Oh, actually we were quite free. Free, as we were here in Ephesus when Paul was in house arrest. Surely you remember that."

Onesimus remembered with pleasure.

"Then one day the word came down that we were free to go; that is, Paul and I were free because all of the others had gone about their business by that time. Paul went about preaching; and I gathered together a small group of followers. Persons with connections, I might add."

"Flavia?" interposed Onesimus.

"Yes, Flavia. She was recently widowed and was being drawn against her will into the maw of Roman politics. It was then that Flavia veiled herself and retired to a villa which her husband had left her. How do you know Flavia?"

"She was my angel," replied Onesimus. "But what of Paul?"

"Of Paul I cannot say. After the fire Nero became more contemptuous, more blasphemous, and Christians began to disappear."

"You heard no stories about his disappearance?" asked Onesimus anxiously. "Something ought to be said. Your story has no ending."

"Yes," replied Luke thoughtfully. "I have heard many stories. But, I tell you this in all truth. I have never met a single person who actually saw Paul after that. I have never spoken to anyone who could in truth say that he had witnessed Paul die, or meet any other end. For ought I know, Paul may have escaped and gone to Spain. At least, I pray that is so."

Onesimus was silent. "I will be satisfied with your answer," he said at last.

Love Never Ends

In all of his spare moments Onesimus continued with his writing. What he had copied on his travels was fading. The pages were torn and sea-stained; and on a few there remained the flakes of Paul's very blood. Onesmus rewrote, and revised. He tried to put the pages together in some kind of order. He tried to remember how he came upon them. Meanwhile, new sources kept pouring in. Hardly a week went by, but what some enthusiast came in with his latest find. Onesimus accepted everything with thanks and later attempted to evaluate what he had. Several times he started a roll of parchment, and then gave it up as he revised his material or changed his mind.

He had found a small house up on a hillside, beyond the main part of Ephesus. There he kept his books and there he took such rest as he could find time for. The bishop who had ordained him breathed his last, and when the proper rites were finished Onesimus received a commission who came to tell him that he had been chosen by them to be their Overseer.

"Who am I to be a bishop?" asked Onesimus; but they were not dissuaded. Again he was tossed into the furnace of political terror. The Flavians Vespasian and Titus had ruled sternly, but not maliciously. With Domitian as emperor, all was changed; Christianity was again openly challenged.

One day an aged man came to the door of Onesimus' house. He pointed to a small house just down the hillside.

"I live there."

For years Onesimus had gazed upon its rooftop, but rarely seen anything to reveal its occupants.

"My name is Joannes. I have known of you for a long time, but I had other business on my mind."

Onesimus jumped up, "You are Joannes? The Beloved Disciple of our Lord?"

"I am he," the old one replied. "I have kept a little group of followers, those who seriously desired to live the kind of life Our Lord wanted us to live."

"I know of them," replied the Bishop thinking of Rhoda.

"I want to leave them in your care," continued the Disciple. "I have learned there is a warrant out for me. I am too old to resist it now. I do not know whether they desire to put me to death or to exile me. I am ready to go when they find me."

"I am certain that I can find a place to hide you," said Onesimus in agitation.

"No, No, I do not wish to be hidden away. I only ask for someone to minister to my little ones."

"It shall be done," pronounced the bishop. "But why have I not known that you were so close.?"

"It was better that way," replied John. "For years I sheltered Our Lord's Mother in that house and I preserved it as my shrine for her. Let the house fall to the elements. I would not have it trampled over by wonder workers."

The old man fumbled, "I have here some papers; I have written a book of Our Lord's Life. Perhaps they would be of some use to you." Onesimus took them; his eyes glazed over.

The old one turned to go. Then he stopped, looked back and said, "Whatever has happened to Love?"

Slowly Onesimus came to life,

> *For now we see in a mirror, dimly,*
> > *but then we will see face to face.*
> *Now I know only in part;*
> > *then I will know fully, even as I have been fully known.*
> *And now faith, hope, and love abide, these three;*
> *and the greatest of these is love.*

John listened attentively, then spoke.

> *Beloved, let us love one another, because love is from God; everyone who loves is born of God and knows God. Whoever does not love does not know God, for God is love. We have known and believe the love that God has for us. God is love, and those who abide in love abide in God, and God abides in them.*

With this, the old man turned and shuffled off in the way that old men do, not waiting for response or asking for assistance. Two days later the constabulary picked him up and hustled him off to Patmos.

All Will Come To An End

Onesimus continued his work of editing, commenting upon, and re-editing the writings and thoughts of Paul. Domitian had been princeps for almost two years before the bishop felt that there was no more that he was likely to collect or learn on the subject. Up to now he had done the work himself, writing, rewriting, adding, deleting, endlessly. At last he noted that his eyesight was failing him. Only in the brightest sunlight could he make out the script; sunlight which sent his attendants fleeing into the shade to shelter their eyes. At last he brought out a long scroll.

"This is as nearly perfect as I am able to make it," he announced to his little staff of cronies. But I am not sure how we will get more copies. The price of parchment of any kind is more than we have money for, especially in these times. "And," he added with a wry smile, "I do not think that the great Library of Ephesus is likely to underwrite the project."

The group sadly took the matter under advisement. They were six of the best amanuenses that Onesimus had been able to draw to him in the Church. A few days later Onesimus came to them,

"I have a proposal. We will write these chapters on papyrus." The professional scribes looked on dubiously. Onesimus continued.

"I have obtained a shipment of papyrus folios, shipped to me by a friend in Alexandria. The parchment needs to be sized and scraped down, but it is good material. We will prepare carefully good black inks. We will write on only one side of the leaf. This will be done in the way perfected in the scriptoria."

The scribes listened carefully and understood. Each of the six had his own desk and papers, and his own materials for making inks. At a time in the morning when all were ready, the reader began his reading of a line of the script. The writers then wrote down the line, each in his own hand. When all were finished, the reader counted the number of letters on the line. Each writer counted his letters to see if his copy agreed. If not, all waited until everyone had produced the same count. Then they proceed to the next line. It is tedious work. When the day's assignment is over, they exchange writings, so that each page can be rechecked for correctness.

This work went very slowly, for these writers were at best amateurs, not used to a daily task of writing. Most of them had other duties within the community. As they were nearing the end of the commitment, Onesimus greeted them one morning.

"I have good news; I have one more book." The weary team tried to show enthusiasm. Onesimus had taken upon himself to write a summary outlining what he considered to be the heart of the thinking of Paul.

"We have labeled the other writings with titles, as though they were epistles, such as "To the Corinthians," or "To the Colossians." This letter I shall label "To the Ephesians," for it is to them that I am most constrained to speak."

When all was finished and all of the sheaves had been collated in proper order, two deacons brought in stacks of thin wooden blocks, the kind that are frequently coated with wax, ready for writing with a stylus.

"In Rome, when a leader wishes to commend someone, he may have the commendation written in inks upon such a block, and the resulting plaque is presented to the one to be honored. This plaque is called a *codex*. We shall bind all our papyrus sheaves together between the two wooden blocks and strap them with leather bindings. And I must thank the Lady Phoebe who first taught me this skill, may her soul rejoice in glory."

And so it came to be that the Letters of Paul have taken this form. Because of this good bishop they will remain as a heritage for the ages to come. It was on the following Lord's Day, in all of the Churches of Ephesus, even those which had been the care of John, that a new scripture was read.

> *For this reason I bow my knees before the Father, from whom every family in heaven and on earth takes its name. Pray that, according to the riches of his glory, he may grant that you may be strengthened in your inner being with power through his Spirit, and that Christ may dwell in your hearts through faith, as you are being rooted and grounded in love. I pray that you may have the power to comprehend, with all the saints, what is the breadth and length and height and depth, and to know the love of Christ that surpasses knowledge, so that you may be filled with all the fullness of God. Now to him who by the power*

at work within us is able to accomplish abundantly far
more than all we can ask or imagine, to him be glory in
the church and in Christ Jesus to all generations, forever
and ever. Amen.

The troubled reign of Domitian drew to its whimpering end. Onesimus grew somewhat corpulent and with the extra weight he tired easily. Although terrifying tales of persecution in various parts of the empire frequently came to his knowledge, the Bishop of Ephesus sometimes joked that that city had been spared because he was, after all, one of the Flavians. It was an inside joke which few were able to appreciate. Bishops have been known to outlive princes. In Rome Domitian died. On Patmos John died; The last disciple of the Lord's reign on earth survived his persecutor by a few days. Now a Spaniard reigned. Word came to the Bishop of Ephesus, that a linked chain of prisoners were being brought to the harbor, to be trans-shipped to Rome. Their fate? The pleasure of the citizens of Rome who would see them torn to pieces by wild beasts in their newly built Coliseum. The charge?

"Atheism. They believe in no Gods," claimed the centurion. "They pose an incipient danger to the altars and homes of the honest citizens of Rome."

Onesimus was distraught, but could find no way to countermand the order. Finally he determined,

"We cannot let them go unblest, unloved, as though none would have the slightest care or pay the least attention."

He himself faced the lieutenant in charge, who could see no good reason why visitors and friends could not come to bid the unfortunates farewell, and serve them with a simple meal.

"But, mind you, keep it simple. Their digestive processes are not working well, and we have to keep things clean, you know."

Onesimus wrote letters to his fellow bishops, who held their offices in neighboring jurisdictions and begged them to come with other Christian supporters who would dare such a mission to meet with him in Smyrna where the prisoners were being held.

So they came on one sad day. For the day, the lieutenant loosed their chains, for there seemed little chance that any of them should escape. The delegation arrived and greeted their Antiochan brothers with the kiss.

After talk and singing and prayers, the bishops brought out the simple meal of fresh baked loaves and good quality wine. Presiding at the table spread with white linen cloth, the three bishops intoned together,

> *For we received from the Lord what we also hand on to you, that the Lord Jesus on the night when he was betrayed took a loaf of bread, and when he had given thanks, he broke it and said, "This is my body that is for you. Do this in remembrance of me." In the same way he took the cup also, after supper, saying, "This cup is the new covenant in my blood. Do this, as often as you drink it, in remembrance of me." For as often as you eat this bread and drink the cup, you proclaim the Lord's death until he comes.*
>
> *And the Word became flesh and lived among us,*
> *and we have seen his glory,*
> *the glory as of a father's only son,*
> *full of grace and truth.*

Epilogue

To The Deservedly happy church in Asia: ... I was on my way from Syria as a prisoner of the Name and the Hope we all share ... and thus I was able to play the host, in God's name, to your whole community in the person of your bishop Onesimus. His endearing kindliness is beyond all words. I pray you to cherish him in the true spirit of Jesus Christ, and everyone of you may be the sort of man that he is. Blessings on Him who gave you the privilege of having such a bishop!

The more reserved a bishop seems to be, the more he ought to be respected. When someone is sent by the master of the house to manage his household for him, it is our duty to give him the same kind of reception as we should give to the sender; and therefore it is clear that we must regard a bishop as the Lord Himself. Onesimus spoke personally in the highest terms of your own correct and godly attitude, that truth is the guiding principle of your lives ...

Farewell to you in God the Father,
and in Jesus Christ who is our Common Hope.
Ignatius of Antioch

Finis: Trinity Sunday, 1994

Appendices

Chronology

Date AD/CE = 753 + date AUC (Ab Urbe Condite, from the founding of the city).

A.U.C.	739:	Reign of Augustus Caesar begins.
B.C.E.	4:	Birth of Jesus
A.D.	1:	Birth of Archippus
A.U.C.	767:	Reign of Tiberias begins
	768:	Birth of Apphia
	770:	Birth of Sambatis
A.D.	30:	Birth of Philemon
	32:	Birth of Onesimus
A.U.C.	790:	Reign of Caligula begins
A.D.	37:	Paul on the road to Damascus
A.U.C.	794:	Reign of Claudius begins.
	795:	Archippus entertains the Roman Legate at Colossae.
	800:	The Octo-centennary of the City of Rome.
A.D.	47:	The visit to Hierapolis.
	50:	Onesimus becomes a fugitive.
	53:	Demetrius the Silversmith causes a riot in Ephesus.
A.U.C.	807:	Reign of Nero begins
	813:	Earthquake destroys Colossae.

A.D.	66:	Paul martyred in Rome.
A.U.C.	821:	Nero, a suicide.
	822:	Vespasian becomes Emperor.
A.D.	70:	Titus conquers Jerusalem.
	79:	Titus becomes emperor.
	81:	Domitian becomes emperor.
	91:	Onesimus, Bishop of Ephesus
	96:	Nerva becomes emperor.
	98:	Onesimus publishes the letters.
	98:	Trajan becomes emperor.
	107:	Meeting with Ignatius

Bibliography

Aeschylus. *The Oresteia,* Translated by George Thompson. Portable Greek Reader, 1964.

The Anchor Bible dictionary. David Noel Freedman, editor-in-chief. New York : Doubleday, c1992. Articles: Archippus, Laodicea, Apphia, Onesimus, Colossae, The Epistle to the Colossians, Names, Ephesus, The Epistle to the Ephesians, The Epistle to Philemon, Hierapolis, Laodicea, Slavery, Phrygia.

Aries, Philippe & Georges Duby, Eds. *A History of Private Life.,* Vol I. "From Rome to Byzantium." Cambridge MA: The Belknap Press of Harvard University Press, 1987.

Barth, Markus. *Ephesians 1-3 .* Anchor Bible, 1974.

Barth, Markus. *Ephesians 4-6.* Anchor Bible, 1974.

Barr, Stringfellow. *The Mask of Jove.* Lippincott, 1966.

Barrett, C. K. *The New Testament Background: Selected Documents. Rev.* Harper Row, 1989.

Beker, J. Christiaan. *Paul the Apostle.* Fortress, 1984.

Berry, George Ricker ed. *The Interlinear Literal Translation of The Greek New Testament.* Zondervan, 1958.

Bradford, Ernie. *Ulysses Found.* Harcourt Brace, 1963.

Brown, Raymond E. *The Community of the Beloved Disciple.* Paulist Press, 1979.

Chrysostom, St. John. *In Praise of St. Paul.* Thomas Halton, trans. St. Paul Editions, 1963.

Clark, Gillian. *Women in Late Antiquity*. Oxford: Clarendon Press, 1993.

Cumont, Franz. *Oriental Religions in Roman Paganism*. Dover, 1956 (Orig. 1911).

Epictetus. *The Enchiridion*. Translated by Thomas W. Higginson. Library of Liberal Arts. Indianapolis: Bobbs-Merrill, 1948.

Erim, Kenan T. "Ancient Aphrodisias and its Marble Treasures." *National Geographic*, August, 1967.

Euripides. *Bacchai*.

Finley, M. L. "The Old World's Peculiar Institution." In *The Light of the Past; A Treasury of Horizon*. The American Heritage Publishing Co., 1965.

Fitzmeyer, Joseph A. *Romans*. Anchor Bible, 1993.

Francis, Fred O. and J. Paul Sampley. *Pauline Parallels*. Fortress, 1975.

Furnish, Victor Paul. *II Corinthians*. Anchor Bible, 1984.

Gokovalt, Sadan. *Ephesus*. Izmir: Ticaret Matbaacilik T.A.S.

Goodspeed, Edgar J. *The Key to Ephesians*. University of Chicago Press, 1956.

Grant, Michael. *The World of Rome*. Cleveland: World, 1960.

Harrison, Jane. *Prolegomena to the study of Greek Religion*. Meridian, 1957.

Harvey, A. E. *Companion to the New Testament: The New English Bible*. Oxford, 1970.

Hennecke, Edgar, and Wilhelm Schneemelcher, Eds. *New Testament Apocrypha*. Fortress Press, 1963.

Kazantzakis, Nikos. *Report to Greco*. Simon & Schuster, 1965.

Kelly, J. N. D. *Early Christian Doctrines*. Revised edition. Harper Row, 1958.

Knox, Bernard. *Classical Literature*. Norton, 1993.

Knox, John. *Philemon among the Letters of Paul*. University of Chicago Press, 1935.

Kraemer, Ross S., ed. *Maenads, Martyrs, Matrons, Monastics*. Fortress, 1988.

Lanciani, Rodolpho. *Ancient Rome*. New York: Benjamin Blom, 1888.

Marrou, H. E. *A History of Education in Antiquity*. Mentor, 1956.

Meeks, Wayne A. *The Origins of Christian Morality*. Yale University Press, 1993.

Morgan, Douglas N. *Love: Plato, the Bible & Freud*. Prentice Hall, 1964.

Munck, Johannes. *The Acts of the Apostles*. Anchor Bible, 1967.

The New Testament: RSVR. Colossians, Philemon, Ephesians.

Neyrey, Jerome H. *2 Peter, Jude*. Anchor Bible, 1993.

Orr, William E. and James Arthur Walther. *I Corinthians*. Anchor Bible, 1976.

Paton, W. R. *The Greek Anthology*. Loeb Classical Library. Harvard University Press.

Plato. "Meno" *Great Dialogues sof Plato*. Translated by W. H. D. Rouse.

Quinn, Jerome D. *The Letter to Titus*. Anchor Bible, 1988.

Quintilian. *On the Early Education of the Citizen-Orator*. Translated by John Selby Watson. Library of Liberal Arts. Indianapolis: Bobbs-Merrill, 1965.

Reader's Digest. *Atlas of the Bible*. 1971.

Rider, Bertha Carr. *Ancient Greek Houses; their history and development from the Neolithic period to the Hellenistic age*. Chicago: Argonaut, 1964. Argonaut, 1964.

Rieu, E. V., ed. *Early Christian Writings*. Penguin.

Robinson, James M., ed. *The Nag Hammadi Library*. Harper and Row, 1977.

Schmidt, Evamaria. *Le Grand Autel de Pergame*. VEB Edition. Leipzig, 1962.

Seneque, *Tragedies,* Pseudo-Seneque, *Octavie*. Translated by Leon Herrmann. Societe D'Edition Les Belles Lettres. Paris, 1961.

Staniforth, Maxwell, translator. "Ignatius of Antioch," *Early Christian Writings*. Penguin Classics, 1968.

Staniforth, Maxwel, translator. *The Apostolic Fathers*. Penguin, 1968.

Stendahl, Krister. *Paul Among the Jews and Gentiles*. Fortress, 1976.

Wilson, Harry Langford, Ed. *D. Iuni Iuvenalis Saturarum. (Libri V)*. D. C. Heath, 1903.

Wire, Antoinette Clark. *The Corinthian Women Prophets*. Fortress, 1990

Young, Rodney S. *Gordion*. Turk Tarih Kurumu Basimevi. Ankara, 1963.

Ziesler, John. *Pauline Christianity*. (Rev. Ed.) Oxford Bible Series, 1990.

An Imagined Biography

Onesimus is the story of an actual person who really lived. At first glance, there doesn't seem to be much substance for a biography, but a little digging reveals many treasures.

The most obvious reference to Onesimus is in the New Testament *Epistle to Philemon*, an undisputed writing of the Apostle Paul. Onesimus is referred to as a fugitive slave, converted to Christianity by Paul, who has been of service to the Apostle. Paul intimates that Onesimus is legally the property of Philemon, and begs Philemon to pardon the slave and perhaps send him back to Paul. Paul does not openly state the nature of the offense that Onesimus may have committed against his master. Paul again refers to Onesimus at the end of his *Epistle to the Colossians,* suggesting that at this time Onesimus is a Christian worker traveling with other followers of Paul. The only other reference to "Onesimus" is found in a letter of Ignatius of Antioch, written at the beginning of the second century. Ignatius names Onesimus as the Bishop of Ephesus. From these few references, I have attempted to construct a biography. One would think that there is ample leeway to imagine any kind of life falling in between the facts as they are known. But these facts set their own parameters.

Place: The place is Colossae, a small provincial town in Southern Phrygia, situated in the Lycus River Valley between two towns of greater importance, Laodicea and Hierapolis. Here live the characters named in Paul's epistles: Archippius, Apphia, Philemon and perhaps Nympha. Epaphras is mentioned as the Christian leader of this place. He seems to have a wide circuit including Laodicea, Colossae, Hierapolis and Ephesus.

The second important location is Ephesus, perhaps at the time the second largest city in the world, or at least competing with Alexandria for that title. Rome, of course, is the largest. Ephesus is an important seaport city. Religiously, it is known as the center of the worship of the Goddess Artemis, who is variously identified in the religions of the varied cultures of the Middle East. In Ephesus stands the Temple of Artemis, one of the seven wonders of the world. (In another century its columns would be floated to Constantinople where they still stand in *Santa Sophia.*) Ephesus was for a short time a sort of headquarters for the Missionary efforts of Paul to the Gentiles. It was also known as the home of the Church founded by John, the Beloved Disciple. It was to this city that according to tradition, John brought Mary the Mother of Jesus.

Time: The time is the First Century. Scholars seem to be chary of putting dates on St. Paul's travels, but the most likely date for his residence in Ephesus seems to be 53-55 A.D. This then, must be the time limits for Onesimus' conversion, and the circumstances surrounding it.

The town of Colossae was destroyed by an earthquake in 60 A.D. and never rebuilt. Except for Onesimus, the other characters in our story are mentioned no more. But Onesimus did not die in an earthquake. If he was in his early 20's when he met St. Paul, it is believable that he could be a bishop in 105-107. His biography begins to take substance.

The Roman Empire: The Empire is certainly well documented in our time line. We see Onesimus born during the reign of Tiberius. Caligula and Claudius follow. Claudius is especially important because he became a follower of the religion of the Phrygian *galli* whose chief shrine was at Hierapolis. During the reign of Claudius the 800th Anniversary of the Founding of the City was celebrated. Rome was certainly in charge of the Province of Asia. Nero followed Claudius, and during his reign St. Paul was martyred in Rome. The Flavians followed the Caesars, and it was the Flavian Titus who conquered Jerusalem in 70 A.D. Vespasian, Titus, Domitian and Trajan– the century is over and Onesimus has lived through it all.

In the twentieth century, some scholars have looked at Onesimus again, and marked him as the most likely candidate for compiling the *Pauline Corpus.* Was it our Onesimus who assembled the Letters of Paul as we know them? Was it Bishop Onesimus who wrote the *Epistle to the Ephesians* as his lasting tribute to the man he most admired? How did an unknown slave happen to have the kind of learning and training to make this possible? This is the subject of our story.

The purpose of this story is to make the life of Onesimus credible. It is an attempt to show how Onesimus developed from a man on "the most wanted" list to become a man on "the most admired list." He does not fill his life with deeds of derring-do; he lives a life possible to someone living in his century. He changes from a frightened, unwanted slave boy to an admirable, faithful and devout follower of The New Way.

The story is put into the words of his last living relative, who in his old age remembers the uncle who lived more than half a century before. It was to Eupator that Onesimus told his secrets.